Complete
Write
a Novel
Course

Will Buckingham

First published in Great Britain in 2014 by John Murray Learning An Hachette UK company.

First published in US in 2014 by The McGraw-Hill Companies, Inc.

This edition published in 2014 by John Murray Learning

British Library Cataloguing in Publication Data: a catalogue record for this title is available from the British Library.

Library of Congress Catalog Card Number: on file.

Paperback ISBN 978 1 473 60048 5

eBook ISBN 978 1 473 60050 8

1

The publisher has used its best endeavours to ensure that any website addresses referred to in this book are correct and active at the time of going to press. However, the publisher and the author have no responsibility for the websites and can make no guarantee that a site will remain live or that the content will remain relevant, decent or appropriate.

The publisher has made every effort to mark as such all words which it believes to be trademarks. The publisher should also like to make it clear that the presence of a word in the book, whether marked or unmarked, in no way affects its legal status as a trademark.

Every reasonable effort has been made by the publisher to trace the copyright holders of material in this book. Any errors or omissions should be notified in writing to the publisher, who will endeavour to rectify the situation for any reprints and future editions.

Typeset by Cenveo® Publisher Services.

Printed and bound in Great Britain by CPI Group (UK) Ltd., Croydon, CR0 4YY.

John Murray Learning policy is to use papers that are natural, renewable and recyclable products and made from wood grown in sustainable forests. The logging and manufacturing processes are expected to conform to the environmental regulations of the country of origin.

John Murray Learning

338 Euston Road

London NW1 3BH

www.hodder.co.uk

For my students

Acknowledgements

Most, if not all, of what I know about writing novels comes from other people. It comes from friends and fellow novelists with whom I have discussed the intricacies of the craft in which we are engaged. It comes from the students I have taught over the years. And it comes from reading the novels over which other writers have laboured. The list of those I have learned from could go on almost for ever, so here I will restrict myself to a few people with whom I have had the good fortune to work closely. I am grateful, firstly, to Jonathan Taylor, Simon Perril, Maria Taylor, Kate Pullinger and Kathleen Bell, my fellow writers and colleagues while at De Montfort University. I am also very grateful to my agent, Marilyn Malin, who has been tireless both as a supporter and as an astute critic of my work.

When I first decided to become a writer, my parents were anxious that I was embarking upon such a precarious course. They have eventually come to terms with my wilful commitment to a life of financial insecurity, and I am grateful for their support over the years. Elee Kirk has been a consistently steady, kind and reliable companion every step of the way. There is not a page of this book that is not in some way influenced by our endless rambling conversations about life and literature.

I would not have got mixed up in writing this book were it not for my friend, the children's writer and scholar Clémentine Beauvais. I would also like to thank everyone at Hodder & Stoughton for their enthusiasm for the project. Finally, I cannot say how much I have appreciated Yesim, a Turkish café in Leicester – a haven for thought, friendship and excellent coffee.

Contents

About the author

Will Buckingham is a writer of fiction, philosophy and children's books. He lives and works in Leicester in the UK. His first novel, Cargo Fever, *was published by Tindal Street Press in 2007. Since then he has written three further novels, as well as a number of non-fiction books, and for children. His writing has appeared in a wide range of print and online journals, and for the past 15 years he has taught creative writing in universities, schools, and with community groups. He holds a PhD in the philosophy of storytelling and is currently Reader in Writing and Creativity at De Montfort University, Leicester.*

How to use this book

This book is designed to be a comprehensive course to get you up and running with your first novel. It aims to take you from the first thoughts and ideas, to the time when you eventually have your published novel in your hands. Writing a novel is a complicated task, something that takes a good deal of time to accomplish; and along the way you will find yourself drawing upon all kinds of different advice. So this book is not designed to be the *only* source of help and advice to which you turn. However, it is designed to work as a kind of guidebook to the journey that you may find yourself taking. It is designed to warn you of some of the pitfalls, to give some practical advice that will be useful as you travel along the road to publication, and to provide hints and tips that may make the journey easier.

Who is this book for?

If you are thinking about writing a novel, if you are setting out on writing your first full-length work of fiction, or if you are in the middle of a big novel-writing project, this book is for you. Whatever stage you are at, the aim of this book is to help guide you from initial aspirations, early ideas and rough drafts to your final, published novel.

Much of the advice here, however, may be of use to writers more broadly; and if you are already established as a novelist, with one, two or even more books out, I hope that you might still find plenty of practical information here that can be of use to you. While this book is designed as a complete course, it can also be used as a companion book for those on creative writing courses.

How to use this book

Novels are remarkably varied beasts. This book is designed for *all kinds* of novelists and aspiring novelists. This means that it is written for those who want to write genre blockbusters as well as for those who want to write literary fiction, or novels for more obscure, niche markets. Whatever kind of novelist you are, I hope that the advice here is both flexible enough to apply to you, and also precise enough to be useful for you to get to where you want to go.

There is no one way to read this book. It is entirely up to you. Novelists are different, and they work in different ways. Some readers will want to start from scratch and work their way through the book systematically, while others will want to read particular chapters at particular times. Writing is never a straightforward linear process: often writers continually spiral between drafting, redrafting, editing and research, so you may find that moving through the book less systematically is more useful. This book is designed to be read in both ways. Each chapter is relatively self-contained, but the course as a whole can be followed from the first chapter, before you even put pen to paper, to the last, when your novel is eventually out there in the world. Along the way, there are various practical exercises that may be useful to you. Do not feel under any compulsion to complete every exercise. If anything strikes you as not appropriate to your own situation, then skip it. There is no exam to sit when you come to the end of the book. Ultimately, what matters is the novel itself.

A big job

One of the things I say again and again in this book is that writing a novel is a big job. You cannot write a novel in a day. It is a task that requires a wide range of different ways of working, and a variety of often complex skills. This book aims to break down the process into smaller, more manageable chunks. However, this book is not just focused on the question of getting the job done. It is not just about the *writing*, but it is also about you, the *writer*. So a fair amount of the book explores not only how you can make your book as good as it can possibly be, but how you can navigate all kinds of practical issues, from finding time to write, to managing money, to dealing with contracts and agents, to keeping more or less sane (if that is what you want) while you get your novel written and launched into the world.

A writer's workshop in a book?

The book is divided into six parts. The first part, 'Getting started', sets out what you need to know before you embark upon your novel. Part two, 'Writing', then dives in to look at the process of drafting your novel, going from the blank page to a finished – albeit rough – manuscript. The third part of the book, 'Redrafting', looks at the often extensive work of refashioning your rough early draft until it is something that is convincing and powerful. Part four, 'Keeping sane', provides practical advice on how to go about working as a writer, and how to keep both body and soul together. Part five, 'Publishing', looks at how you can move from a final draft to a published book – whether it is in digital format or on paper, and whether it is self-published or published by a third-party publishing house. Finally, Part six is about what to do once your novel has emerged into the world – not only how to let the world know about it, but also how to deal with questions about finance, money and how to continue your writing into your second novel and beyond.

Each part of the book has an introductory chapter, followed by a series of chapters exploring these issues in more depth. Each of these in-depth explorations concludes with a practical workshop that offers a sustained way of looking at some of the questions, issues and technical challenges that have been raised in that chapter. Some of these workshops may be focused on the act of *writing*. Some may be about editing and redrafting. Some may involve other practical tasks. But all of them aim to *get you somewhere* when it comes to writing your novel.

The idea of a writer's workshop often brings to mind the image of a *group* of writers industriously working away together. This book can be used as a course book and, if you have friends who write as well, you can team up and work through the book together. But this book can equally well be used by individuals.

In addition to the workshop tasks, smaller tasks are scattered throughout the book. These are divided into three loose categories:

 Write: practical writing exercises

 Edit: editing tasks, many of which may involve your work-in-progress

 Snapshot: other tasks that involve reading, thinking, research and investigation.

What this book can and can't do

Unfortunately, this book cannot actually *write* your novel for you. Nor can it give you a *recipe* for how to write a bestselling novel. One reason for this is that not all novels can be bestsellers (and, besides, bestsellers are not necessarily the best novels). But another reason is that there *is* no single recipe for a bestselling novel – as the philosopher Immanuel Kant argued in the eighteenth century, there is no recipe or rule for producing a work of art. A book such as this cannot give you a sure-fire way to write a masterpiece. That's up to you. However, it can do some of these things:

- provide down-to-earth and practical advice at every stage, from generating ideas to promoting your work post-publication
- set out some of the common issues and pitfalls you may face
- offer help and encouragement
- provide suggestions for how to solve problems in your work
- demystify the process of writing
- demonstrate that – given the right approach and commitment – writing a novel is a perfectly attainable goal.

Advice on advice

There is a lot of advice in this book, and I have done my best to make it as practical and useful as possible. However, I don't expect you to agree with all the suggestions I make here. No two novelists will agree on everything, and all will have different ways of working, opinions and ideas; so working out your own approach is crucial to becoming a novelist in your own right. But I do hope that you have fun disagreeing with those things that don't strike you as right, and that in thinking through these issues – whether you agree or disagree – you come to more deeply understand the process of writing, and to develop your skills further.

Where to next?

Part one of this book, 'Getting started', looks at what novels are, and asks whether you have what it takes to write one. The first part also explores the relationship between reading and writing. The next chapter begins with the question 'Why write a novel?'

PART ONE
Getting started

1

Introduction: why write a novel?

One day, the idea occurs to you that you should or could write a novel. You may not be clear where the idea has come from, but after the idea has gone round and round your mind for a while, at last you decide that you have to *do something* about it. Perhaps you already have a story that you simply *have* to tell; or perhaps you want to write a novel, but are casting around for some subject-matter. Either way, eventually you get hold of a book such as this one, in the hope that it might help you bring this curious idea to fruition.

This book aims to help you on the long journey that is ahead. Think of it as something like a travel guide, a companion that does not tell you exactly which paths to take, but which offers pointers, advice and assistance along the way, whatever kind of novel it is that you want to write.

Before setting out on a journey, it can pay to have some sense of the territory that you are going to cross, and also of the destination in which you are heading. This first chapter aims to do just this, by asking what a novel actually is, and why you might want to write one at all.

Write: why write a novel?

For this first exercise, spend ten to fifteen minutes writing freely in response to this question:

Why do I want to write a novel?

Use the writing exercise as a way of exploring your motivations and your aspirations. You can write in any style you like. Feel free to go off on a tangent if you wish.

What is a novel?

Bruce Chatwin

'Everyone says: "Are you writing a novel?" No, I'm writing a story and I do rather insist that things must be called stories. That seems to me to be what they are. I don't quite know the meaning of the word novel.'

Human beings are storytelling animals. Almost as long as people have been able to write, they have harnessed the power of writing to communicate stories to others. Throughout prehistory, before the arrival of writing on the scene, our ancestors told stories face to face; but the invention of writing allowed stories to be carried to distant times and distant places. Written stories can travel a long way: almost four thousand years after it was first written, we can still read *The Epic of Gilgamesh*, an ancient Sumerian tale of the unlikely friendship between King Gilgamesh and the wild man Enkidu.

Scholars often debate the questions of how we might define what novels are, and where they come from. Some claim that the first real novel is Samuel Richardson's *Pamela: or, Virtue Rewarded*, published in England back in 1740. Others trace the history of novels back to Miguel de Cervantes's great Spanish book, *Don Quixote*, the first volume of which was published in 1605. Still others say that the first novel was Murasaki Shikibu's *The Tale of Genji*, which dates to eleventh-century Japan. Literary scholars like debating definitions; but, as novelists, we don't have to worry too much about these debates. The following simple definition will be good enough for our purposes.

Key idea

A novel is an *extended, fictional* story that is *written down* so that it can be communicated to people the author might never meet.

And so, if human beings are storytelling animals, and novels are simply ways of harnessing this obsession with storytelling in written form, then – given that you too are a storytelling animal – it is not at all surprising if you want to sit down one day and weave tales of your own.

Steven Moore, *The Novel: An Alternative History*

'Any book-length fictional narrative can be called a novel.'

The variety of genres

One of the reasons why novels are so fascinating is that they are so very varied. They can be short or long. They can have an almost documentary attention to the everyday, or they can be works of wild inventiveness. They can be simple or complex. They can be told in single voices or in a riot of multiple voices. They can have pictures. They can tell their stories forwards, backwards or sideways. They can consist of chapters that are bound separately, to be reshuffled into any order. They can come in bite-sized instalments or in large, hard-to-digest chunks. They can be profoundly serious or deeply silly – or both at once.

Among this huge, seething variety of novels, there are some recognized species and subspecies. These are referred to as 'genres' and 'subgenres'.

Key idea

'Genre' is a way of categorizing books in terms of their content, style, form and anticipated audience. 'Subgenre' is a way of further subdividing genres.

Genres are broad categories that *readers understand*. In this sense, the division of books by genre can be seen as a marketing tool that aims to place the right stories in the hands of the right readers. But, from another point of view, genres are broad *traditions* of storytelling, each with their own conventions.

Focus point

The following are some common genres in contemporary fiction:

- Historical fiction
- Science fiction
- Fantasy
- Erotica
- Horror
- Thriller
- Literary fiction
- Crime fiction
- Romantic fiction.

Sometimes people distinguish between literary fiction and genre fiction, but I find it more useful to think of literary fiction as itself a particular set of genres. 'Genre' is not a term of abuse: it is just a recognition that within the ecosystem of literature there are different kinds of stories that people tell, and that certain groups of stories have stronger family resemblances than others.

Ursula K. Le Guin

'Genres exist, forms and types and kinds of fiction exist and need to be understood: but no genre is inherently, categorically superior or inferior.'

Snapshot: thinking about genre

To get started, have a look at your bookshelves (when I refer to 'bookshelves' in these exercises, these can be either *actual* shelves or *virtual* shelves). Write down a list of the major genres that are on your shelves, in roughly descending order from the most to the least common.

If you already have an idea for your novel, or if your novel is under way, can you identify its genre? Can you identify any subgenre to which it belongs?

If you find that your novel is in a genre that is under-represented on your shelves, you may want to read more deeply in that genre before you proceed.

If you find it hard to place your novel in any known genre, then don't worry too much about this for the time being: you may not know what you have on your hands until you are further into the project (or even until the novel is finished); but be aware that third-party publishers will be a little more wary of accepting a novel if they do not know where it is going to sit on the shelves.

'Getting away with it'

This talk of genre shouldn't feel restrictive or claustrophobic. The idea of genre divisions and conventions is just a useful shorthand. As a writer, you are free to cross between genres. It is perfectly possible to write literary science-fiction erotica, or historical crime fantasy. In reality, genres are always slightly vague and fuzzy at the edges. So you can define your own terms of operation. If you write a strange, genre-busting thing that doesn't look like any other novels in existence (think of Mark Z. Danielewski's *House of Leaves*), then the onus is on you to persuade potential publishers or readers that the thing that you have written is a novel and that it is worth publishing.

Key idea

A novel is what you can get away with calling a novel.

'Getting away with it' may be relatively easy if your book fits in a very established genre. If your novel is strangely shaped, if it straddles genres or confounds expectations, then you may have a bigger job on your hands when it comes to persuading people that this *is* a novel. But it can be done, if the book is good enough, and if you are persuasive enough.

Commercial fiction and niche fiction

While it is hard to second-guess the market, there are some projects that are going to look more propitious when it comes to gaining a wide readership, and there are some projects that are going to be more restricted in their circulation. It is not true that the best books have the most readers. Neither is it true that the worst books have the most readers. Some very good books are not particularly commercial and some commercial books are not very good; but, conversely, some very good books are also commercially quite an easy sell, and some books that don't do well commercially don't do well because they are not up to much.

> ## Focus point
>
> There is no direct correlation between the commercial potential of a novel and its quality.

When you are starting out on your project, alongside having a sense of the genre in which you are working, it can be useful to have a realistic sense of the possible commercial scope of your novel. Think of the world of fiction as being like an ecosystem, and think of bestsellers (or bestselling novelists) as the big beasts who stalk through the jungle: the charismatic megafauna of the literary world. No ecosystem is made up only of charismatic megafauna. Nestling under leaves, in the holes of trees, or hidden high in the canopy, are all kinds of strange and wonderful creatures less flashy than the pumas and boa constrictors, less ostentatious, but equally well suited to their particular ecological niches. When I read, I sometimes like to admire the big beasts, the Margaret Atwoods and Ursula Le Guins. But sometimes I like to crawl through the undergrowth and find equally fascinating, but more overlooked, niches of the literary ecosystem. As a writer, you may find yourself becoming a big beast, or you may find a smaller niche to occupy. Neither is nobler than the other. The world of books *needs* this varied and rich ecosystem; and it needs you to add to this richness.

Demystifying novels

The most important thing when starting out is to strip away some of mystique surrounding novels, novel-writing and novelists. Writing novels is an extension of the storytelling in which we all engage as human beings. A novel is a more sustained act of storytelling than the day-to-day stories that we tell, but it is rooted in this human fascination for telling stories. To write a novel and get it published requires that you work on developing a range of more-or-less ordinary skills, including:

- an understanding of how various kinds of novels work from the point of view of their *craft*
- an appreciation of genre
- skill and finesse in storytelling
- an understanding of the publishing world and how it works
- a good sense of the ever-changing ecosystem of literary world.

In the next chapter, we will look at all of this more closely to ask the question: *Have I got what it takes?*

Where to next?

Having explored the question of what novels are, we can move on to ask about the things that you need to write your novel. Chapter 2 is about novel writing as a learned skill. It is also about knotty questions such as luck, talent and money.

2

Have I got what it takes?

This chapter explores the question: *Have I got what it takes?* At the beginning of any journey, it is natural to be beset by doubts and apprehensions. If you are in the early stages of writing your first novel, you may not have told anybody about your literary ambitions. When I started writing my first novel, I didn't know any novelists, nor did I have much idea of what writing a novel entailed. And because I didn't really have a clear idea of what it takes to write a novel, I felt uneasy about broadcasting what I was up to.

This chapter aims to put some of these doubts to rest, and to explore what is necessary, and what is unnecessary, for you to be a novelist.

Learning to write novels

There is one criterion that is essential for the writing of a novel, and it is this: *you need to want to write a novel.* You need to want to write one enough to actually write one. Beyond this, everything is up for grabs. There may, of course, be further criteria when it comes to writing a *publishable* novel, but we'll come back to those later.

The strange mystique around novel-writing is, in part, down to the self-mythologizing mumbo-jumbo put about by novelists themselves. In public at least, many novelists like to pretend that somehow their skill was a gift from the gods, that they were divinely blessed, that they didn't really have to *learn* their craft. According to this quaint little mythology, one day the writer in question just sat down and wrote, and the words simply scattered like magic dust.

Those who like to hold on to the idea that the ability to write novels is a mystical gift are fond of claiming that books such as this one are entirely without value. What is the point of trying to teach what cannot be taught? After all, if being a novelist is akin to a genetic disorder in that you either have it by birthright or you don't, then all attempts to teach the craft of novel-writing are an elaborate fraud.

This, however, is nonsense. It is nonsense because it makes no sense at all to talk about an *unlearned skill.* All skills are learned. Nobody bursts from the womb, picks up a pen, and starts work on *War and Peace.*

Key idea

The ability to write novels draws upon a range of learned (and learnable) skills.

Snapshot: learning to write novels

Here are some of the ways novelists learn to write novels:

- Reading novels by other writers
- Taking advice from other readers and writers
- Apprenticeship in different forms
- Trial and error
- Study
- Self-tutoring books like this one.

For this exercise, write down the names of three novelists that you admire. Now do some research either in books or online (try, for example, interviews on blogs and media sites) to see whether you can find out how *they* learned to write novels. Having a sense of the different ways in which writers learned their craft can help give you a sense of how you yourself might better learn the skills required.

Of course, people are different. There are many reasons why I write the kind of novels that I write, why you write the kinds of novels that you write, and why these are not the same kinds of novels. To say that the skills needed to write novels are learned is not to say that there is only one way of learning them: books such as this are not essential (even if I hope that this one is useful); but *all* writers learn their craft in one way or another, however they learn.

READING

It is fairly obvious that reading is the one thing that you cannot skimp on if you care about writing well. You may choose to read alongside others, through book groups or literature study courses, or under your own steam, but reading is essential. The next chapter on reading explores this in more depth.

Stephen King, *On Writing*

'*Reading is the creative centre of a writer's life.*'

ADVICE FROM OTHERS

Sometimes you read in the press about some novelist who pops up as if from nowhere, having produced a work of genius, and everybody marvels at this prodigy. The writer never went on a single writing course, never bought a single creative writing textbook, never sat at the feet of another writer... But often, when you look beneath the surface, you find that the novelist in question had a huge amount of help in fashioning this apparently miraculous novel. Friends, mentors, family members, editors and agents – all of these people may have contributed to the novelist developing their craft, even if these contributions are invisible in the final work.

Robert Gottlieb

'*The editor's relationship to a book should be an invisible one... Nobody should know what I told Joe Heller and how grateful he is, if he is. It's unkind to the reader and just out of place.*'

Even if writing can be a solitary activity, publishing isn't: it often involves a large number of people who have input into the book, all of whom are sticking their oar in and giving advice. If you are a writer, you can learn a lot from all this advice.

APPRENTICESHIP IN OTHER FORMS

Some novelists manage to write terrifically good first novels because they have apprenticed themselves in other forms. There is a tradition of journalists who have honed their craft in the newsroom turning to writing novels. Journalists-turned-novelists know how to work with editors and subeditors. They know what language can do, how to grab and keep the attention of their readers. And if they move in the small, incestuous world of journalism, they probably also have an inside route towards reviewers (who may be former friends and colleagues), which means that, when they are published, they get nice write-ups in the press.

Similarly, there are many poets, short-story writers, TV and radio scriptwriters, stand-up comedians and so on who turn their hand to novel-writing. There is a big difference between writing a script or a collection of poetry and writing a novel; but skills from one domain can be carried over into the other. In fact, any job where you are working with words and with the power of words can be a good training-ground for writing novels. Salman Rushdie was an advertising copywriter when he wrote his Booker-winning *Midnight's Children*: he cut his teeth on writing jingles and slogans.

TRIAL AND ERROR

Other writers manage to learn how to write novels through the long, hard slog of trial and error. This is, more or less, how I learned myself. I wrote, and rewrote, and rewrote again. As I wrote and rewrote, I continued reading and asking advice from people who knew what they were doing better than I did; and gradually my writing improved.

Trial and error is perhaps not the quickest route: there are many novelists (like me) who have drafts tucked away of novels that *didn't quite work*, early projects that, even if they are not without virtue, never quite turned into fully fledged, publishable novels. This may be dispiriting news, and this present book aims to help you give the novel you are writing its best possible shot. But not all novels make it off the runway – and you don't really know whether something is going to work as a novel until you try it.

STUDY

Finally, you can learn how to write novels through creative writing courses, or self-study books such as this one. These cannot give you a *formula* for writing a novel, but they can help you avoid some of the pitfalls, give you a leg-up, encourage you to try things you would not otherwise think of trying, and save you quite a lot of time. Ignore the people who say you can't learn to write better. The evidence is against them. Just like any other art or craft – painting, design, architecture, dance, computer programming or music – there is much that can be learned through serious study.

 Key idea

All novelists learn their craft. They do it through a combination of study, trial and error, reading and advice from others, or by taking insights and skills developed elsewhere and applying these to the writing of novels.

But, you may say, what about natural talent? Aren't there people who have some kind of inborn talent? Well, perhaps. And doesn't luck also play a part? Again, perhaps.

Broadly speaking, I would agree that to write a good novel, alongside the willingness to put in the hours, days, months and years that it takes to hone your craft, you also need a range of talents and a smidgeon of good luck. But too much fretting over natural endowment and luck is not really going to get you anywhere.

What does a novelist look like?

You will be familiar with the famous 'duck test', which says that if something looks like a duck, walks like a duck and quacks like a duck, then it probably *is* a duck. This works well enough for ducks, but it does not work nearly so well for novelists. The terrifying thing is this: as we are walking down the street, or riding on the bus, or standing in line for a sandwich, there are novelists moving among us, like spies and terrorists, entirely invisible to the untrained eye. Nothing singles them out as unique or different.

Snapshot: a rogues' gallery

Go to a bookshop and select a single letter of the alphabet at random.

Now browse through the novels filed under the names beginning with that letter. Don't bother looking at the novels themselves. Just look at the author photographs. Examine this rogues' gallery closely:

- You will notice that some novelists are drop-dead-gorgeous and some less so.
- You will notice that novelists come in all shapes and sizes.
- You will notice that a novelist, when it comes down to it, can look like anyone at all.

Now go and have a long, hard look at yourself in the mirror until you can see that you, too, look like a novelist.

It can be easy to think that *people like me* don't become novelists, to imagine that novelists are a particular breed. But a novelist can look like *anyone at all*. Even, strange as it may seem, *you…*

Talent, luck and money

If you can learn to write novels, then what about those other things that may be *unlearned*, things such as talent, luck and money? Let's look at these in turn.

TALENT

Writing novels involves a wide range of skills; and given that novels are often very different from one another, writing different *kinds* of novels requires different *kinds* of skills. There is no single talent that can be summed up as a talent for novel-writing. Novel-writing is not a hardwired biological ability.

It makes much more sense to forget about this mystical idea of a single novel-writing 'talent' and to think instead about *talents* in the plural, about your own dispositions and singular interests, and how they can be channelled into writing the best book possible.

Beryl Bainbridge

'I am of the firm belief that everybody could write books and I never understand why they don't. After all, everyone speaks.'

The reason why not everybody writes books, of course, is that they don't want to. *Wanting to* is half the battle. It's hard work writing a novel; but many of the skills and talents that are put to work in carrying out this hard work are ordinary and everyday.

Focus point

Worrying about talent gets things back to front: we find out what our skills, abilities and talents are by committing ourselves to doing things, by seeing what we do well, and by developing the various capacities that we have in the directions that seem most fruitful.

It is not your job as a writer to worry about some abstract notion of 'talent'. Your job is to write, and through the effort that you put into your writing, to write better.

LUCK

Emily Dickinson

'Luck is not chance
It's Toil –
Fortune's expensive smile
Is earned.'

Any honest novelist will tell you that luck plays a big part in writing, as in everything else. But, as Emily Dickinson points out, luck is also something *earned*. In his wonderful book, *Chase, Chance and Creativity: The Lucky Art of Novelty*, the neurologist and author James H. Austin divides 'luck' or 'chance' into four categories. The categories go like this:

1 blind luck – things just happen
2 the luck that comes from being *in motion* (as Austin writes, 'the posture of creativity is forward-leaning')
3 the luck that comes from having a prepared mind
4 the luck that comes from your own distinctive personal 'flavour', from the fact that you are an idiosyncratic individual, engaged with the world.

The first of these is out of your hands. There *is* such a thing as blind luck. But the other kinds of luck are things you *can* do something about. If you keep moving – exploring new things, making new connections – then opportunities will arise, sometimes when you least expect them. If you make sure that you have a prepared mind – by accumulating a rich store of reading and experience upon which to draw – then you are more able to make the most of unexpected events. And if you cultivate your own idiosyncratic interests, then you will find that you also develop your own unique voice and your own sets of concerns, obsessions and themes that will distinguish you as a writer.

So don't wait for good luck to fall from the skies. There are things you can do to encourage good fortune. Firstly, keep your eyes open for blind luck, in case it passes you by. Secondly, keep moving, keep investigating the world, keep your work changing and alive. Thirdly, accumulate experience, read as much as you can, and reflect on your experience and your reading. And finally, follow those things that matter to you; cherish your idiosyncratic interests. If you do all this, you will get lucky.

MONEY

Edith Wharton, *The House of Mirth*

'*The only way not to think about money is to have a great deal of it.*'

If luck and talent play a part in success, so too does money. This is not something that we talk about very often, in part because money is linked to class, and nothing makes people more uncomfortable than talking about class. The novelist Ann Bauer, in a terrific article written for the *Beyond the Margins* blog in 2013, calls the topic of money and privilege 'the conversation we never have'. In her article (www.beyondthemargins. com/2013/12/the-conversation-we-never-have), Bauer talks about attending two talks by different American writers. The first was very wealthy, the second very well connected. But when these writers were asked about their own successes, they did not say, 'Oh, you know… wealth and privilege.' Instead, they put it down to talent, or to hard work, or to the decisions they had made in their lives.

Bauer's point is not that the writers didn't work hard; it is only that connections and money *can make a difference*. If you have the good fortune to have money and connections, it will almost certainly smooth your passage from unpublished to published novelist. But if you don't have money and connections, then you will have to think about how to keep food on the table, and how to cultivate connections yourself. Life will be *harder*. If you lack these shortcuts to success, then you will need – as Edith Wharton so acutely points out – to think *more* about money, not less.

The truth is that most novelists I know are *not* in the privileged position of having access to great piles of wealth, or being fabulously well connected. So take heart: you can do it without all of this stuff. But it would be dishonest not to mention the role that money and privilege can play in helping some novelists on with their careers. For those who don't enjoy the luxury of not having to think about money, later on in this book we'll return to practical questions about finding time to write, budgeting and managing finances.

Qualifications

Another thing that might bother you as a would-be novelist is the question: *Am I qualified enough?*

The simple answer is *yes, you are.* There is no required qualification for writing a novel. You do not need to have passed a single exam in your life. You do not need certificates. You do not need accolades, badges pinned to your lapel, or letters after your name. There is – thank goodness – no such thing as an 'accredited novelist'. You do not need a literature degree, or any other kind of degree. You do not need to have completed a course in creative writing. All you need is to write a novel that is good enough to publish.

Of course, qualifications may help. If, in gaining those qualifications, you have also managed to hone your craft as a novelist, then they may be useful. A qualification as a barrister might be quite useful if you want to write courtroom dramas; a qualification as a welder might be useful if you want to write a novel about shipbuilding. If accumulating qualifications has also helped you to accumulate experience, then this experience may help you with writing your novel. But the qualifications themselves do not matter. You may be proud of them, and perhaps justifiably so; but in deciding to write a novel, you are entering a world where they are entirely beside the point.

Conversely, if you don't have any qualifications, remember that your *lack* of qualifications doesn't matter. Do not hold back because you feel unqualified. It might well be that, while other people were sitting in drab grey rooms, getting qualifications, you were out there in the world, enriching your stores of experience, gathering up stories and ideas and dreams.

 Key idea

What matters most, when coming to writing novels, is not the accumulation of qualifications, but the accumulation of experience.

What really matters

When it comes down to it, it seems to me that there are four things that make a novelist:

1 **You must be a reader.** Wanting to write novels but not being interested in reading is like wanting to play the violin but not wanting to listen to music, or wanting to be a lion tamer but not wanting to have anything to do with lions.

2 **You must have determination.** You need to apply yourself not just for an hour or two, or for an afternoon, but for days and weeks and months and perhaps years. Novelists and novels, like elephants, have a long gestation period.

3 **You must be able to respond to criticism of your work.** Criticism is *essential* to the process of writing. Do not expect first drafts to be right. Make the most of all the feedback you can get.

4 **You must derive some satisfaction from writing.** You need to take some pleasure in not just the goal (having your book published) but also the means you use to get there (the writing of the thing).

Snapshot: the essentials

Rate yourself on a scale of 1–5 for each of the four 'essentials' listed above, where 5 is high. If there is any area where you don't score so highly, remember that these things can be worked on: you can spend more time reading, you can develop determination, you can get better at responding to criticism, and you can cultivate greater satisfaction in writing.

In it for the long haul

As I suggested in the introduction to this book, a novel is a big job. It is not something that can be accomplished in a short while. You will need to have a degree of patience if you are going to get to the end of your novel.

Key idea

Writing a novel will take a big investment of your time. You will need to think in terms of being in it for the long haul.

How long does it take to write a novel? The novelist John Boyne wrote the first draft of his bestselling *The Boy in the Striped Pyjamas* in two and a half days. This is probably about the minimum time it might take to get a draft of a (slim!) novel written. And of course, you may have heard of, or participated in, National Novel Writing Month, more popularly known as NaNoWriMo, for which participants write an entire novel draft (or 50,000 words of a novel draft) within a single month.

Focus point

NaNoWriMo (National Novel Writing Month) was started in 1999 by writer Chris Baty. It takes place every November, and it is free to take part (see www.nanowrimo.org).

Some complain that this is an unpromising way to go about writing a novel, but it has had some notable successes. Erin Morgenstern's bestselling *The Night Circus* started life as a NaNoWriMo novel. One of the virtues of NaNoWriMo is that it helps writers break with the fear of writing all those words. Before I started my first novel, writing a book of 70,000 words or more seemed like a huge mountain to scale. NaNoWriMo can help people get over this fear of the mountain slopes.

There are earlier examples of novels drafted in a very short time. Famously, Jack Kerouac wrote his *On the Road* in three weeks in 1951, while fuelled up on coffee and Benzedrine. I don't recommend this as a combination, although it seems to have worked for Kerouac in the short term, if not in the long term.

In all these stories of novels drafted in breathtakingly short amounts of time, what is often omitted is the fact that both *before* this intensive drafting and *after* this drafting there has usually been a huge amount of work. Kerouac had the initial idea for *On the Road* in late 1947, and in writing the book he drew upon extensive archives of notes, drafts and chapter outlines he had written over the previous few years. Again, after his three weeks of intensive writing, the manuscript went through several years of intensive revision until it was eventually published in 1957. Did *On the Road* take three weeks to write? Or did it take ten years? The answer is, both.

So even if you do write your novel in a single month (or, like John Boyne, in two and a half days), I would recommend thinking in terms of at least a year to edit and refashion it before sending it out.

On the other hand, you may write slowly. You may write five hundred words a day, every day. Don't be cowed by people who churn out thousands and thousands of words. You may feel like a tortoise in a world of hares. But your tortoise-like sense of methodical direction may mean that you spend far less time haring off down blind alleys and going in wrong directions. Whichever way you look at it, the creation of a final novel is going to take a matter of months or years, not days or weeks. And the more quickly you can get used to this idea, the more you can settle into the process.

Workshop: thinking like a writer

One thing that you will need to do to be able to write a novel is to take yourself seriously as a writer. This workshop is designed to ease you in to this way of thinking. The workshop is in two stages, and involves two different writing exercises. If you want to work with another writer on this workshop, this might help you think around the issues that the workshop raises.

1 The creative CV

The first task is to write what I am going to call a 'creative CV'. This is a version of an exercise we use with students at the university where I work, and it often gives rise to some interesting results.

'Curriculum Vitae' roughly means 'the course of one's life'; so a CV is a document that gives an account of your life to date. Usually CVs are boring documents that list qualifications, achievements and jobs you have had. This CV is not going to do this. Instead, it is going to be creative in two senses:

1 It is going to be about your life as a *creative writer*

2 It is going to be written not as a formal document, but instead in a creative form.

To write your creative CV, first of all choose *three* incidents from your past that you feel are important to you in leading you to the decision to write a novel. These could be dramatic (that occasion when you were stuck in a lift with Margaret Atwood) or they could be much quieter and more everyday. Now write down a title for each of the incidents, along with a rough date (something like 'Summer 2014' will do the trick).

When you have done this, spend 20 minutes writing an account of each incident, exploring how and why it is of significance to you. You can do this however you like. You can write the incidents as stories, poems or essays. Don't feel that you need to write each piece in the same way. See this as play, not work.

When you are done, if you are working with another writer, take turns reading out the passages one by one and discussing the incidents. If you are working alone, after you have finished, take a short break and read through them. Then reflect upon how these incidents have led you to the point you are now at.

2 The author bio

The first part of this workshop should have helped you think *as a writer* about your past, allowing you to see how often everyday events have led to your decision here and now to write a novel. The next task is to write what is usually known as an 'author bio', short for 'author biography'. This is the short biography that appears on books and in marketing materials. An author bio produced for publicity purposes will be in the *third* person, while, if you are sending out query letters to publishers, you will usually write a bio in the *first* person. We'll be looking at third-person author bios here.

First, take ten or twelve contemporary novels from the shelves, and read *out loud* the biographies of the authors. You will find these at the very beginning, or at the very end, of the books (also, occasionally, on the back cover). Get a feel for the different styles of author bios. Some will be more extensive while some will be relatively brief. Don't be intimidated by biographies that list great successes and arrays of literary prizes: all these writers started out somewhere. If you can, it might be good to try this exercise with *first novels* (which might necessitate a trip to the library).

When you have got a feel for the genre of author bio, ask yourself the following questions.

- Typically, how long are author bios?
- What three factors make an author bio most convincing?
- What kind of author bio do you want? What do you want to convey?

Now write your own author bio in the light of your answers to these questions. If you are working with another writer, compare your work with theirs.

Where to next?

This chapter has been about your own unique set of skills, quirks and interests, the raw material out of which your novel will be fashioned. But as a novelist you are not working in a vacuum. When it is published, your book will be part of a broader world of books. The next chapter is about this world, and about the art of reading as a writer.

3

Reading

There are many reasons why people read novels: they believe, rightly or wrongly, that novels might offer them a deeper insight into life; they want to relax and take time out; they want to be transported to another world; they love the feeling of being swept away by a story; they are studying a course in literature and have been told that they need to read novels for their examinations; they have the curious conviction that reading novels is somehow morally improving; they find that only in novels can they indulge in their most deliciously degenerate fantasies; they believe that reading novels in public makes them sexually irresistible; or they may have one hundred and one other reasons.

As a novelist, you may read for all of these reasons. But there will be one more reason why you read as well, and that is that you read to better understand the craft of writing. You will be reading, in other words, to *see how other writers have done it.*

This reading for the sake of the improvement of your own work is often referred to as 'reading as a writer'. This phrase comes from Dorothea Brande's famous book *Becoming a Writer*, which was first published in 1934. In this section, we will be following some of Brande's recommendations, and looking at what it means to read as a writer.

Dorothea Brande, *Becoming a Writer*

'To read effectively it is necessary to learn to consider a book in the light of what it can teach you about the improvement of your own work.'

What does it mean to read as a writer?

Francine Prose, *Reading Like a Writer*

'If we want to write, it makes sense to read – and to read like a writer.'

Writing is a kind of craft. It involves taking raw materials – words, ideas and thoughts – and fashioning them into stories, just as a chair-maker uses raw materials such as wood, metal, plastic and fabric to fashion chairs.

Write: thinking like a craftsperson

Find yourself a chair and sit on it. Are you sitting comfortably? Good. Now relax. What is the chair like? Is it comfortable or uncomfortable? Is it soft or hard? Is it a good reading chair? What purposes might suit the chair best?

Now imagine that you make chairs for a living (which, for all I know, you may do). What other things would you want to know about the chair? You'd probably want to know:

- what it is made of
- how it is engineered
- what the designer was trying to do.

So now take a good, long look at the chair as a craftsperson might look at it. Turn it over, look underneath it, look at it from all angles. Try to understand how the chair holds together, or how it works, as a chair.

Now write for ten minutes about the chair, from the perspective of the chair-maker or designer, as if they are reflecting upon their work. Use the first person.

Is there a difference between a *craftsperson*'s approach to the chair and a *user*'s approach to the chair? Does thinking about the craft of the chair differ from thinking about it as something to be used and enjoyed?

This exercise aims to show that there is a big difference between thinking about *use* and thinking about *craft*. As a novelist, you need to think about both the *use* of novels (the reader's experience of reading) and the *craft* (how you manage to construct or make possible this experience).

Killing the magic

At this point, you might sigh and protest that reading in this way is going to somehow kill the magic of reading, that somehow it will turn your love of literature into something cold, dead and analytic. But just as a chair-maker can still take pleasure in sitting, so a writer can still take pleasure in reading. Not only this but, as a craftsperson, you have all kinds of pleasures open to you that ordinary readers do not: there is a particular delight – and, indeed, magic – in understanding, from the point of view of craft, what a novelist is up to, in reading a book and seeing quite how *elegantly* a novelist has pulled off certain tricks, and in thinking how you might learn from these.

As a writer, you may want not just to read novels, but to *re*read them. Sometimes I see the first reading as something like flying over the territory of a book and getting an aerial photograph, a sense of where the major landmarks are. On the second, third and fourth readings, you can go through on the ground, hacking your way through the jungle of the book with a machete, taking now this route and now that, exploring the book much more closely.

The workshop at the end of this chapter explores rereading in more depth.

What should I read?

There are some writers who think that, if you want to write novels, you should first carry out a long apprenticeship by studying every single big fat doorstop 'classic' text out there. In this view, before even having the temerity to put pen to paper, you should read *Tristram Shandy* and *Jane Eyre* and *Oliver Twist* and *War and Peace* and *Ulysses* and *To the Lighthouse*… In short, you should get out your library card and go to the 'classics' section and work through from Jane Austen to Stefan Zweig: you should read what is sometimes called the 'canon', and *only then* will you be able to write a novel.

This is nonsense. There is no core curriculum for novelists. Take any great novelist, and it can be *guaranteed* that they have not read all of their predecessors. This is not to say that they haven't read huge amounts of stuff, but what they have read will typically be idiosyncratic, curious and multifarious.

 ## Haruki Murakami, *Norwegian Wood*

'If you only read the books that everyone else is reading, you can only think what everyone else is thinking.'

This is not to say that there is no benefit to reading the classics. As a novelist you *should* have an interest in diving into the great classic works within the genre, because it makes sense to learn from those who are considered to have developed the art or the craft of novel-writing to a high degree. But being a novelist is not the same thing as being a professor of English Literature. So, in answer to the question 'What should you read?', the best answer perhaps is this: *read anything, but make sure that you read*. However, for practical reasons, it might be useful to break this down into a few different categories.

READING THE 'CLASSICS'

As a writer, you are part of a tradition of writing. You may think that your decision to write a novel is wholly free and spontaneous, but the fact that you have the idea in your head of a 'novel', and that you think that it might be worth your time to sit down and write such a thing, is the result of being a part of a tradition.

Reading is not some kind of terrible moral duty that will somehow 'improve' you as a writer. Whether reading classic books is genuinely morally improving or not is an empirical question, and goes beyond the scope of this book; but what *is* clear is that approaching classics like this is enough to kill them off. In fact, one of the pleasures of reading the classics is the delight of finding out that they are stranger, more singular, and infinitely richer than the popular image of them might suggest. To read a classic book is to enter a richly seething jungle of possibilities of thought, language, meaning and image.

Focus point

When you come to reading the 'classics', try to shake off the sense of moral obligation, the feeling that you *ought to* read them. Read them instead for pleasure, for craft, or as a way of exploring new worlds.

READING IN YOUR GENRE

In other words, read books that are *somewhat like* the book that you are writing or that you want to write. If you are writing science fiction, read contemporary and classic science fiction. No book is a one-off. Books do not exist in a vacuum; instead, they exist as a part of a teeming society of other books. Get to know this society.

READING OUTSIDE YOUR GENRE

If it can help to read *within* your genre, it can also be useful to read *outside* your genre. If you read intelligently and with an eye for craft, you can learn a lot from books to which you would normally not be drawn. Avoid genre snobbery. You can learn a lot about pacing from reading detective fiction, a lot about how to build a convincing world from reading science fiction, a lot about how to play with the complexities of human desire from reading romance.

Key idea

Reading outside the genre in which you write will extend your range as a writer, will open you up to other possibilities and will teach you things that you could not have learned otherwise.

READING WHAT IS POPULAR

Popularity is no sure sign of quality. Nevertheless, reading what is popular can be a good way of gauging trends in the book world, seeing what people are writing about and how they are writing about it, and seeing how the critics respond. Writers who refuse to read anything that is popular miss out on understanding these broader trends. However, don't try to chase these trends to write the next 'big thing'. If you are writing a novel based on what is popular *now*, by the time your book is out, the market may have changed. The vagaries of literary fashion are hard to predict.

READING WHAT IS UNPOPULAR

There's something enjoyable about reading books that are *unpopular*, books that have slipped under the radar of the mass media. There are many good books out there that, for one reason or another, have never made much of a splash in the media circus that is the literary world. Some of the greatest finds among novels I have read over the years have been published by curious, niche publishers, books that may never reach the *New York Times* bestseller list, but that are nevertheless wonderful, compelling and enriching.

READING POETRY

As a novelist, you may spend much of your time reading other novels, but don't neglect other forms. Poetry can be particularly interesting to a writer of fiction, because it can force you to *slow down*, to play closer attention to the possibilities of language. Poetry is language with added space: look at a page of poetry compared to a page of a novel, and you will see that – in most cases – there is simply much more white space on the page, much more breathing-room. Reading poetry allows you to stop, to take a bit of time to breathe, to see how language goes about its strange work, how it affects us as living, breathing human beings. Reading poetry can strengthen your feel for language, can give you a sense for rhythm, cadence, precision of word choice and sensitivity to how words look on the page.

Nicholson Baker, *The Anthologist*

'There's no either/or division with poems. What's made up and what's not made up? What's the varnished truth, what's the unvarnished truth? We don't care. With prose you first want to know: Is it fiction, is it non-fiction? Everything follows from that.'

The following exercise is an exercise in reading. It will take a few days or a few weeks, depending on how fast you read.

Snapshot: serendipitous reading

For this exercise, dust off your library card (or apply for one if you haven't already got one) and go to your local library. The purpose of this exercise is not to go and find the *exact thing* that you are looking for, but to open yourself up to chance encounters. Even a small library may contain more books than you can read in a lifetime, so there is plenty of scope.

Once you have got to the library, wander among the shelves. You are on a hunt for four different books:

1   a fiction book in the genre that you are writing in
2   a non-fiction book on a totally different subject
3   a fiction book in a genre you would normally never read
4   a book of poetry.

Take yourself to the relevant parts of the library, and see what grabs you as you pass. Don't think too hard about making the 'right' choice; just select four books, take them to the counter and check them out. Now take them away and read them.

This exercise may seem very simple; but it is really worth doing, and worth repeating. If you get into the habit of going to the library to cultivate chance encounters, you will find that over a very short time your literary horizons will broaden, and you will be significantly enriched as a writer and as a reader.

READING NON-FICTION

As a writer of fictional prose, don't ignore non-fiction. You may read non-fiction for research purposes: if you are writing a book about horse breeders in Kazakhstan, for example, you may want to read anthropology, history and travel books. Similarly, if you are writing about your home town, you may want to read local history or memoirs. But don't neglect the pleasures of non-fiction simply in terms of the quality of the writing. Reading non-fiction can extend your knowledge of the world, can expose you to some superb writers, and can open you up to the serendipitous pleasure of stumbling across something new.

Reading books and knowledge of books

All writers are familiar with far more books than they have actually read. Some books they know by reputation. Some they have read and reread carefully. Some they have only skimmed. In his book *How to Talk about Books You Haven't Read*, Pierre Bayard points out that we read different books in different ways. Some books are unknown to us, some we have skimmed or *sort of* read, some we have heard of, and some we have once read but now forgotten… Being familiar with the world of books is useful to you as a writer. But you cannot read *everything*. It can help to think of books as being arranged in concentric circles: the books most familiar to you – books you return to again and again – are close to the centre; further out are books with which you have some familiarity; and over the horizon, there are the many, many books that are unknown to you.

Key idea

As a writer, it is useful to develop a broad knowledge of books; but this does not mean that you have to read *everything*.

This broad knowledge of books can alert you to books that *may* be related to the book you are writing, to books that *may* be worth reading, or to books that seem to be doing well in the market at the moment. Cultivate a broad knowledge of books; but don't feel under an obligation to read everything.

Thinking about the book world

See if you can get hold of a recent copy of one of the big book-trade journals. In the UK the best-known one is *The Bookseller* (www.thebookseller.com), while in the US it is *Publisher's Weekly* (www.publishersweekly.com). You may find the print versions in your local library but, if not, visit their websites.

Read through the recent content, and ask yourself the following questions:

- What are the recent trends for the genre in which you are writing?
- Which books are people talking about? Which books are generating 'buzz'? Why are people excited about these books?

Literary contagion

Some months into writing my first novel, *Cargo Fever*, I stumbled across a bargain six-volume boxed-set translation of Marcel Proust's *In Search of Lost Time*. It was so cheap that I could not resist buying it. Over the next year and a half, on and off, I read through the six volumes (it took a while, because I found that I could only manage Proust in small doses). But the more Proust I read, the more I noticed something odd happening to my writing. When I went back to edit my novel, I noticed that halfway through my first draft my sentences were getting longer and longer and longer. And I realized that I was suffering from Proust Poisoning. Having become accustomed to Proust's long, rolling sentences, I found myself unconsciously stretching out my own sentences.

Some writers have overwhelmingly strong literary personalities: it is hard to read them without them leaving a stamp on your work. Writers often worry about this influence. How can you keep your prose distinctive if you are going to be always falling under the spell of the great literary heavyweights? Isn't it better not to read at all?

The answer to this is *no*! Literary contagion is a fact, and there is no escaping it. But, firstly, it is not a wholly bad thing: who would not want to be influenced by the world's greatest writers? And, secondly, it cannot be cured by reading *less*. It can be cured only by reading *more*. If you have Proust Poisoning, read some Emily Dickinson poems instead, or read some Raymond Chandler. Both are known antidotes. If your influences are mixed, eventually the urge to write just like somebody else will settle down. Your influences will become more organic, less pronounced; they will become woven into the fabric of your own unique, developing style.

Focus point

Don't be afraid of the influence of other writers. Influence is something to be embraced, not something to be resisted.

Workshop: rereading as a writer

This workshop task was inspired by Dorothea Brande's *Becoming a Writer.* It is a workshop that involves rereading a novel that you have read, and enjoyed, in the past year. You can do this workshop alone, or meet up with a fellow writer and work together.

Stage one: selecting a novel

Choose a novel that you have already read within the previous year (if it has been a particularly demanding year, and you haven't read any novels, then read one first and then take a couple of months' break before you come back to this exercise).

Put the novel on the table in front of you without opening it, and make some notes about the book. What did you enjoy about it? What did you not enjoy? What was it *about*? (If you want to cheat a little and flip through, or read the blurb, that's fine; but don't start rereading it quite yet.) What are the images or phrases or incidents or characters that you remember? Do you remember any things that you didn't like, that you didn't think worked, or that you were unconvinced by? Note down any questions that you have about the book.

Don't worry if you can't remember very much about the book. This is not a memory test; it is simply a way of exploring how the book has lingered, or failed to linger, in your mind since you last read it.

Stage two: rereading

Now reread the novel chapter by chapter. Make a few notes as you go, either in the margins in pencil, or in a notebook. If there are any passages that you particularly enjoy, or that impress, intrigue or baffle you, go over them again, and make notes on what it is that has caught your attention. Similarly, if there are passages where your attention wanes, go back and ask why it was *there*, and not *somewhere else*, that your attention began to give out.

Stage three: thinking about craft

Having read the book a second time, try answering these questions. If you are doing this with a friend, get together with them and discuss these points at leisure. If you are doing this on your own, make notes.

- What were the particular craft challenges that the author faced?
- Was the author successful in responding to these challenges? If so, why? If not, why not?
- Were there any points where you thought that the book didn't work? If so, try to identify what went wrong (at least, as far as you are concerned).
- For each problem you identified, think about what changes you would make to resolve these problems. Would these changes have improved the book? If so, how?
- Finally, ask how the book *you remembered* differed from the book you *reread*. What does this say about the most and least memorable aspects of the book?

Where to next?

In this part of the book we have covered most of the groundwork that you need to set out on writing your novel. The next part of this book explores the writing process, from the very earliest sketches and notes, all the way to the end of the first draft. Because your book has to be about something, we are going to start the next section by looking at ideas.

PART TWO
Writing

4

Introduction: ideas

In this part of this book, we will be looking at how to take your novel from its very earliest beginnings to the completed first draft. This chapter looks at ideas. Then, in the chapters that follow, we will move on to explore how to build convincing fictional worlds, the role research plays in writing fiction, and the finer mechanics of plot, character and storytelling.

Every novel has to start somewhere, with an image, an impulse or an idea. The first chapter in this part of the book is about how you can develop these initial impulses, images and ideas into something that will sustain you for a complete novel. This chapter will help you winnow your ideas, think through what will work well and what will work less well, and give you ways of nudging these ideas towards something more sustained and worked out.

There is, I think, no such thing as a bad idea for a novel. There are, however, more or less *promising* ideas, and there are ideas that are *well developed* and *poorly developed.* This chapter should help not just with generating ideas, but also with exploring how ideas can be developed and nurtured. Sometimes exceptional novels come out of what may seem to be unpromising ideas; similarly, and for all kinds of reasons, astonishing and fascinating ideas can fail to turn into novels that work.

A seething cauldron

The world is a seething cauldron of possibilities. If you feel that you are short of ideas, then all you need to do is to go out and explore the world and see what sparks you off. Ideas often fall into your lap when you are least expecting it: you might not seek them out, but you end up finding them, or they end up finding you. Newspapers, books (both fiction and non-fiction), encounters with strangers, stories told by friends, memories, dreams, journeys and travels – all of these things can be the starting point for a novel.

Kate Pullinger

'The truth is that ideas are all around us, in the people you meet, in the things you read and see and hear and experience, in your own childhood and family, in the wilder reaches of your imagination.'

These initial impulses or ideas are *only* starting points. They get you up and running. But the ideas that make up any single novel are often complex and multi-layered. The idea or impulse that gets you started *as a writer* may not be the same as the central idea of the finished novel. The important thing about this initial impulse is that it should engage you; it should provoke you into further thought, reflection and investigation. The best ideas are the ones that interest *you* as a novelist, the ones that preoccupy you, the ones that keep you awake at night.

Snapshot: kick-starting ideas

Ask yourself the following questions as a way of kick-starting some ideas:

- What are the things that preoccupy you, the images, stories, memories and thoughts that rattle around your mind, that come back to you again and again?
- What are the stories that you find yourself telling people over and over? What are the incidents in your life and your past to which you find yourself returning?
- What stories have other people told you that have struck or moved you?
- What are the things that matter to you most?

Think about these questions, and write a list. Then put it to one side and come back to it a day later. Are there any seeds here that could lead to interesting possibilities for a novel?

But what if you are not being kept awake at night by anything at all? What if you want to write a novel, but nothing at all grabs you? The following writing exercise might help.

Write: 'I want to write…'

This is a quick and very simple writing exercise to free up your ideas. The aim is not to produce beautiful writing, but to begin to glimpse possibilities that could turn into the seeds of new stories and novels. This is a timed writing exercise, and it can help if you follow these rules:

1　Don't go back or cross out.
2　Don't stop – keep writing, and keep your hand moving.
3　Don't worry about quality.
4　Feel free to go off on a tangent.
5　Don't think too hard.

The exercise is this. Begin your first sentence, 'I want to write…', then write down the first thing that comes into your head. Follow the thought until it runs out. Now start a new sentence with 'I want to write…' and follow *that* thought. If nothing comes to mind, then just write, 'I want to write, I want to write, I want to write…' until something eventually appears. Write for 10–15 minutes.

When you are done, put what you have written to one side, and return to it a day later. Mark down any ideas or thoughts that are interesting, intriguing or promising.

If you still feel that you need something more to work on, then it is time to get out there into the world, and to get exploring. Through *taking an interest* in the world around you, you will almost inevitably find yourself turning up interesting things.

Hunting and gathering

Before the invention of things like cities and writing and novels, our ancestors were hunters and gatherers, making use opportunistically of the resources of the world in which they found themselves. As a novelist, you too are an opportunist, a hunter-gatherer of ideas, stories and images. It can be good to find ways of accumulating stores of ideas, thoughts and insights so that you can use them to sustain you through lean periods. There are all kinds of ways you can do this.

Snapshot: accumulating resources

Think about how to accumulate a store of resources to draw upon. This might involve:
- keeping a notebook or diary for jotting down ideas, thoughts and snippets
- accumulating clippings from newspapers, web pages, journals and magazines
- collecting old photographs and postcards
- making sketches, drawings and maps.

Try setting aside a couple of hours and going on the hunt for stories. Read newspapers, surf the Internet, go to the park to watch people and take notes in your notebook on anything that takes your interest, anything that seems intriguing or that stimulates your imagination.

Remember to find ways of working that suit you. For years I felt guilty that I wasn't carrying a notebook around with me at all times, because I had been told repeatedly that this is what *proper* novelists do. But I'm just not a notebook kind of person. I'm terrible with notebooks. I scribble for a few pages, then temporarily lose the notebook and buy another one, and eventually I end up with an accumulation of half-filled notebooks that are so jumbled that I never bother to look through them.

Finding through doing

Another way to accumulate material is through writing exercises. I know novelists who keep journals in which they write for a set amount of time, say 20 minutes every morning. These journals are strictly separate from any novels-in-progress that they are writing. They are spaces for experiment, freed from the constraints of being a part of a big project. They are ways of trying out all kinds of things and of accumulating material that can be pillaged for new ideas.

There are plenty of exercises that you can do with writing 'prompts' to encourage new conjunctions of ideas (like the snapshot above). Writing exercises of this kind are sometimes a good way to break through when you are stuck.

 Key idea

You don't necessarily need to wait for an idea before you can start writing. Instead, it may be that, once you start writing, ideas begin to emerge.

Incubation

Once you have an idea that you think you might like to pursue, it can take a while before it takes shape into something like a novel. Ideas are like eggs: they take time to hatch out. Some hatch quickly; others have a longer gestation period – you have to sit on them for a long time, brooding, clucking and worrying, making sure that they are kept warm, until one day you hear a tap-tap-tap on the inside of the shell, and something begins to emerge. This can take time and patience.

 Walter Benjamin, *The Storyteller*

'Boredom is the dream bird that hatches the egg of experience. A rustling in the leaves drives him away.'

Don't be afraid of this *waiting* for an idea to take shape, even if the process of waiting is full of frustrations and difficulties. The more time you spend working on your writing, the more you will get a feel for this strange gestation process.

Ideas in dialogue

Ideas do not exist in isolation. The richest, most interesting novels are not just based around a single idea, but instead draw upon multiple ideas. If you are finding it difficult to come up with a starting point for your novel, it may be because you are trying to base it around a single idea, when you would be better off with multiple ideas that can interact in interesting ways.

> ## John Steinbeck, *Conversations with John Steinbeck*
>
> *'Ideas are like rabbits. You get a couple and learn how to handle them, and pretty soon you have a dozen.'*

Having multiple ideas, and drawing connections between disparate things, can spark off new creative possibilities.

Write: ideas multiplying like rabbits

The following exercise will help you explore how different sets of often unconnected ideas can bounce off one another, leading you in new and interesting directions:

1. Take a newspaper, and cut out 10–15 headlines (or short articles) that catch your eye.
2. Turn the headlines upside down and shuffle them.
3. Pick two headlines at random, and lay them on the table in front of you. Your challenge is to write a short story that uses themes and ideas from *both* sets of headlines. Write for 20 minutes.
4. If the two headlines are not intriguing or challenging enough, then choose a third, and write a story that uses themes and ideas from *all* of them.

What is my novel about?

Once your ideas for your novel have begun to hatch out, it can be useful to examine them a little bit more closely to see what you have on your hands. At this stage, think of asking the question: *What is my novel about?* All novels are about something. At the surface level, they always have *subject-matter*: they involve particular worlds, characters and events. But, on a more fundamental level, novels may be exploring deeper philosophical themes and preoccupations. You can think of these themes and preoccupations as *guiding ideas*.

Focus point

There are two kinds of answer to the question *What is my novel about?* – firstly, the story's *subject-matter*, and secondly the *guiding ideas* you are exploring through writing about this subject-matter.

There are some people who suggest that, as well as guiding ideas and subject-matter, your book should have a clear thesis: in other words, that you as an author should be trying to say *something specific* about your subject-matter and about these guiding ideas. However, while some finished novels have a very strong thesis (it is absolutely clear what point they are making), this is by no means always the case, and nor should it be. There is a risk that, if you are too focused on thinking about what your thesis is, your novel will become didactic. Conversely, if you don't have *any* sense of what you want to say about your subject-matter and your guiding ideas, your novel may lack focus.

A good way of getting an overall sense of what your novel is about is by drafting a blurb for your work-in-progress.

Write: blurbing your ideas

The text on the back of a novel that tells you about the story and provokes the reader's interest is sometimes called a 'blurb'. If you are finding it hard to focus your ideas, it can be useful to write a blurb for your future book.

Read a few blurbs of books on your bookshelves; and then write 150 words that sum up what your book is about and that draw the reader in, without giving away too much of the story.

Ideas and audiences

Another issue to think about early on is that of audience. This is not to say that you should tailor your writing precisely to a market; but it would be foolish to embark upon a novel with *no* sense of who you want to communicate with.

Key idea

Because novels are a way of *communicating* ideas, images and stories, it is useful to have a sense of *who* you want to communicate with.

As your ideas are taking shape, think about the other books out there that explore similar territory. See what you can find out about the readership of these novels. Look at blogs and websites that discuss these novels. Read reviews. Get a sense of the particular niche of the publishing ecosystem your novel might occupy. This can help you get an idea of who your readers might be. No novel is entirely original or wholly novel; no novel is exactly the same as any other. Between these two poles, there are degrees of sameness and difference.

Snapshot: 'If you enjoyed this book…'

Sometimes book reviews have sections at the end saying, 'If you enjoyed this book, you can also try reading…'

Think about the books out there that you might recommend readers of your own book to read. Make a list of at least five. Why have you chosen these books? What do your choices say about your potential audience?

If you discover that somebody else has written what seems like *exactly the same book* as the book you are planning to write, don't panic. It is early days for your own book, and no two books are exactly the same. If you take it seriously enough, your book will almost inevitably end up with its own distinctive voice and feel. But, if at the early stage your book feels *too* close to another book on the market, think about how to give it a different angle or slant, or introduce some new elements that will take it in new directions.

Too many ideas

Some novelists spend years waiting for ideas to come to them. Novelists of this kind have difficulty finding ways to coax ideas into existence at all. Others have the opposite problem, and find that they have *too many* ideas. Perhaps they have been sitting on a number of eggs, and suddenly they have all hatched at once. These kinds of novelists have the opposite problem of deciding which of their ideas to go with. Having too many ideas at one time can be paralysing. You either end up trying to do everything at once, or else you find yourself unable to choose between your ideas.

TRYING TO DO EVERYTHING

There are sleek, streamlined novels based around very few strong ideas, there are gloriously baggy novels crammed full of ideas, and there are novels that represent every stage in between. But if a novel has *too* many ideas at work in it, these ideas may pull in different directions and eventually pull the novel apart entirely.

No one novel can talk about everything. If you ask yourself what your novel is about, and you find yourself answering that it is about the Russian Revolution, the mass extinction of the dinosaurs, the Big Bang, the nature of human frailty, and the crisis in global capitalism… then your novel is probably about too much. You may be biting off more than you can chew.

Focus point

Novels that draw upon too many ideas tend to fall apart at the seams; novels that draw upon too few ideas tend to lack depth and richness.

If you suffer from a surfeit of ideas (rather than too few), it can be better to think of these ideas as the raw materials for a lifetime's work, rather than cramming them all into a single novel.

Sometimes, if you are the kind of writer who has lots of ideas, you might even get to a final draft and realize that your novel is in fact *two* novels that have somehow collided and got tangled up with each other. When this happens, you have to get to work on the long, hard labour of prising them apart.

Snapshot: how many ideas?

If you suffer from an *excess* of ideas, try the following exercise. Write down a list of the major ideas in your book, the things that you want your book to be about. Now go through the list and ask yourself this question:

If I could keep only three or four ideas, what would they be?

Cross out any ideas that feel less central or important to you. When you have done this, see what remains. If you focus in on these few ideas and discard the rest, how will it change the shape of your project? Will it make your book stronger and more focused, or will it weaken your book?

INABILITY TO CHOOSE

Another problem with multiple ideas is that of choosing which one to go with. This is a common cause of writer's block: you have one perfectly good idea that is going to lead you in one direction, and another perfectly good idea that is going to lead you in wholly another direction, and you do not know which one to choose. Like Buridan's Ass – the famous fictional donkey who stands equidistant between a bale of hay and a pail of water, and cannot choose between them – you either starve to death or die of thirst. If you find yourself in this position, it can be useful to recognize that there is no single right idea out there. If two ideas seem equally good, it may be because they *are* equally good. Toss a coin, or go with the one that seems more intriguing or compelling. Don't worry too much about getting *the* 'right' idea; just decide on what the next project will be, and follow that as far as it will take you.

Are my ideas any good?

As I said at the opening of this chapter, there are not necessarily any *bad* ideas, but some ideas are more promising than others. Not only this, but ideas are promising in *different respects*. What makes an idea good or bad is partly the context in which it is evaluated, and partly about what you want your book to do and who you want to communicate with.

Snapshot: evaluating your ideas

Try writing out four or five of the major themes (both *subject-matter* and *guiding ideas*) that your novel is exploring. Now ask yourself the questions below.

- *Depth*: are your ideas simple and straightforward, or are they full of complexities? What deeper questions do they provoke?
- *Scope*: is your subject-matter fairly narrow, or is it quite broad?
- *Interest*: how interested are *you* in your ideas? Is there enough substance here to sustain you through the writing process? What is it that makes these ideas interesting?
- *Audience*: what kind of audience might be interested in these ideas? Is there a market for these ideas? Do your guiding ideas and your subject-matter relate to broader concerns that readers might have?
- *Scale*: is this enough material for a whole novel? Or would it be better off as a novella, a short story or a series of novels?
- *Familiarity*: How familiar or unfamiliar will your audience be with the ideas in your book?

If you can clarify some of this, then you can get a sense not only of the shape of your book, but also of how it might eventually fit with the publishing world.

Do I have enough material?

At the ideas stage, it can be useful to have an idea of the *scale* on which you are working. Some ideas are not quite full enough to be sustained throughout a whole novel. Others might be *too large*: perhaps you don't have just one novel on your hands but a whole series.

This raises the question of how long a novel should be. Most novels find themselves falling between 60,000 and 120,000 words. Some are shorter: if you write something beautiful and literary and poetic, you may get away with 30,000 words (although it may feel closer to a novella). And if your great family saga is 160,000 words, you will be lucky to find a publisher willing to take a chance: if this is your first novel, you might want to think about establishing a track record with something shorter. When Vikram Seth published his *A Suitable Boy*, weighing in at around 600,000 words (give or take a few), it was on the back of a substantial track record as a writer. It is to Seth's credit that many readers, when they finish his book, find themselves *still wanting more*; but it is to his even greater credit that he doesn't give them more, and leaves them still wanting. If you are writing anything on that scale, then at the very least think about publishing your book in a series of self-contained volumes. In general, however, the rule of thumb is this: your novel should be *as long as it needs to be and no longer*.

'Original' and 'outlandish' are not synonyms

One mistake that novelists can make early on is that of being over-concerned with 'originality', or misunderstanding what it means for a novel to be original. The struggle to be original can create startling new works of art. But the struggle for originality *for its own sake* more often leads to works that are more outlandish than they are original.

Originality and outlandishness are not the same thing. Originality is something that comes from following your obsessions, from honing your language and your own particular perspectives, from a commitment to the craft that you are pursuing, from close attention to the development of the ideas upon which you have settled. It is not something that can be 'bolted on' by simply making your story more and more outlandish and strange. This is not to say that you should *not* write outlandish novels; it is only that not all original novels are outlandish, and not all outlandish novels are original. If you find yourself deliberately introducing outlandish elements into your novel simply because you are worried that the story itself is not interesting enough, then instead of thinking about bolting on new elements, try exploring the elements that are already there in more depth, drawing out their contradictions and tensions.

Fattening up ideas

Once you have a set of ideas up and running – once the eggs have hatched, once the rabbits are breeding – your ideas may still need a long period of development and fattening-up before things come into shape. Do not feel that you have to launch straight into the writing. You need to be careful to get the balance right between neglecting your growing ideas and attempting to force their development.

Keep turning your ideas over in your mind, reflecting on them, reading about them, thinking about them and discussing them; and eventually they will take on greater shape, form and depth.

Where to next?

We have looked in this chapter at how to generate and evaluate ideas. Now these ideas need to be 'fattened up' and developed into something more sustained: you need to move from these initial ideas to the development of a full, fictional world. World-building is the subject of the next chapter.

5

Architecture and world-building

Every story has to happen *somewhere*. Whether this 'somewhere' is your home town, the other side of the world or the surface of a small planet light years away from earth, if there is to be a story at all, there has to be a world in which this story happens.

Sometimes people talk about this 'world' as 'setting', but this isn't quite right. 'Setting' suggests that the story exists already, and that it is just plonked down with the 'setting' acting as scenery. But the best and most convincing stories, the most powerful novels, are often those that grow organically out of a specific world. They are stories that could not take place – or not in the same way – anywhere else.

Think about the people you know, and think about your own life and your own history. Think about how influenced you are by the world around you: by your upbringing, by your friendships, by the landscape in which you live, by the culture in which you are immersed, by the weather and climate. All of these things not only shape *who you are* but they also shape *the kinds of things you do.* Of course, we can always go against these forces, and we often do. But the choices we make, and the kinds of people that we are, are profoundly fashioned by the world around us. What this means is that the possibilities of both *character* and *plot* depend on the kind of world we live in.

John Fowles

'There are many reasons why novelists write – but they all have one thing in common: a need to create an alternative world.'

'Writing a novel is a cosmological matter'

Umberto Eco had a surprise international bestseller with his dense, medieval detective tale set in a remote monastery, *The Name of the Rose*. Later, when he came to write about the book, he said that writing novels is a *cosmological* matter. What Eco meant was that writing a novel is about *creating a world*. When you read a novel, a world comes into being for you. When you write one, you have to build this world from scratch.

 Key idea

Writing a novel involves building an entire fictional world.

The dimensions of your fictional world

World-building is not just about getting the physical setting of your book right. Instead, it is that trick of pulling off the perfect combination of setting, character, plot, language and storytelling that will give your novel a sense of uniqueness, marking it out as distinctive and different from all other novels.

The world of your novel is not just a matter of physical detail. It is multidimensional and has many different aspects.

 Focus point

The different aspects of a fictional world include:
- physical environment
- language
- thought, values and beliefs
- culture, politics and society
- history.

PHYSICAL ENVIRONMENT

What is the physical environment like? What might it feel like to actually *be there* physically? We are physical beings who are strongly affected by the physical world around us.

You may have heard of the 'pathetic fallacy' – coming from the Greek word *pathos* meaning suffering, emotion or strong passion. As it appears in fiction, the pathetic fallacy refers to stories in which strong emotions are mirrored in the external world.

Key idea

The 'pathetic fallacy' is a term for the way that fictional characters' emotions and experiences are reflected in and attributed to the external world.

So, if your hero is feeling turbulent, you have a thunderstorm to show this; if your hero is feeling miserable, outside the window there is drizzle. The pathetic fallacy is often considered to be a mistake because the world isn't like this: however good I feel, my feeling good doesn't have any effect on the weather. However, before throwing the pathetic fallacy out altogether, it is worth remembering that it *does* work the other way: we *do* respond to the weather; and changes in the atmosphere *do* affect how we are feeling. Cats and small children go nuts when it is windy outside (ask any primary-school teacher or pet owner!). The sunshine makes us feel better about life.

Focus point

While the pathetic fallacy should be treated with care, it can be useful to have a sense of the ways in which the climate, weather and other physical aspects of the world interact with your characters.

We are intimately linked to the physical world. Our stories grow out of the environment in which we find ourselves. This will be the same for your characters as well. Try the following exercise.

Snapshot: the physical world

Ask yourself the following questions about the world in which your story is set. If you have already written some of your book, you can ask these questions scene by scene. If not, then use this exercise to get a *general* sense of your fictional world.

- What kinds of *things* are there in this world? What are they made of?
- How do people interact with these things?
- What do these things feel like in the hand? What are the tactile qualities of the world you are writing about?
- What is the lie of the land? What is the landscape like?
- What does this world *sound* like? What does it smell like?
- What is the quality of light? What is the weather like? What kind of atmosphere does your world have?

If you are not sure about the answers to these questions, you may need to pin things down a bit more. Ask what things you need to know that you don't already know. Some of this you might be able to fill in now. Some of it may need to wait until you have explored the next chapter on research.

LANGUAGE

Another aspect of any world is language. People speak differently in the boardroom and in the bedroom. In some cultures, chattiness is valued more highly than in others. The relationship between language and world is complex.

Snapshot: language and world

Here are some questions to ask about the place of *language* in your fictional world. Make notes for later, if you like.

- How do people speak? Is their speech casual or formal?
- Are there particular accents or dialects? What languages do they speak?
- How do the inhabitants of your world understand one another? How do they *misunderstand* one another?
- What are the influences that have shaped language in your world?
- If you are writing in English, but your characters are speaking a different language, how do you indicate this?
- How *much* do people in your world speak? Even if there is not much actual *speech*, does communication take place in other ways?
- Do they use jargon and clichés? As a writer you may want to avoid cliché; but if your *characters* use clichéd language, you may want to exploit this.

Again, if you are not sure how to answer these questions, more thought may be needed.

THOUGHT, VALUES AND BELIEFS

Different worlds have different landscapes of belief. You may need to take time to carefully sketch out these often complex systems of thought and belief. People in nineteenth-century France think differently, have different values and hold different beliefs from people in twenty-first-century Beijing. One of the central things that can generate conflict in stories is a clash of values, thoughts and beliefs. So this is an aspect of your world to which you should pay attention.

Snapshot: values and beliefs

Ask yourself the following questions about the role that belief plays in your fictional world.

- What values do people in your world have? What do they think is good or bad, acceptable or unacceptable? What things are considered important and what things are considered unimportant?

- What belief systems are there in your world? Does your world have one single belief system, or are there multiple belief systems in conflict with one another?
- What is reality like for the inhabitants of your world? Do they believe in ghosts? Spirits? UFOs? Gods? Money?
- How do people think about themselves and about the world of which they are a part? How does the world appear – not to you, the author, but to *them*?
- Do the values that people have lead them to act in particular ways?

CULTURE, POLITICS AND SOCIETY

Next, there are questions of culture, politics and society, questions about the broader social world in which your story is set. If you are inventing a world from scratch, this can be difficult. But it's worth persevering to make sure that you get it right. By 'politics' I don't mean the business of government. I mean the question of how people in your world organize themselves collectively. There can be politics in an office, in a school staffroom or in a playground.

Snapshot: culture, politics and society

Here are some questions about the cultural world of your novel. Remember, even if your novel is about a small household, there will be a 'political' system of some kind: somebody will be in charge, there will be power relationships, and so on. Similarly, there will also be an economic system, as well as various technologies, cultural activities and products.

- What is the political system of your world like? Who is in charge?
- How orderly is the political system? Is it very strictly and closely ordered, or is it disordered?
- How do people organize themselves? How do they make collective decisions?
- How does the economic system work? How does the society or culture sustain itself?
- What technologies are there in your society, and how do they work?
- What kind of cultural products are there in your world? What do people do for entertainment? Do they write books? Do they make art?

HISTORY

Lastly, the world that you are writing about is not just a single slice in time, but will also have a history. Again, this can be large scale (the history of the rise of a civilization), or small scale (the history of major events in the street where your story is set). So the world extends *both* in space *and* in time. We will be looking at history again when we look at storytelling and plot in later chapters. Here, what we are mainly interested in is the *broader history* into which the story that you are telling fits. The following questions may help you think about this a bit more deeply.

Snapshot: history

Ask yourself the following questions about the role that belief plays in your fictional world:

- What are the most important historical events that relate to your story? If your story takes place at a particular moment in history, what was going on in the world at the time? What background events will influence the story? If it is speculative fiction, what history does this imagined world have?
- In the ten years leading up to the beginning of your story, what has happened?
- Is there one single history that lies behind your story, or are there many histories?
- What kind of histories are most important to your story? World events? Local events? Political events? Personal histories?

 Focus point

All five aspects of your fictional world – physical environment; language; thought, values and beliefs; culture, politics and society; history – are bound up with one another. When you tweak one of them, you may find that you need to tweak the others, too.

A place fit to live in

Building a world is like architecture, and so you need to make sure that you build a world that is fit for your characters to inhabit, and into which you feel you can invite your readers without fear of things beginning to fall apart. You need to make sure that the foundations of your fictional world are firm, that the rain will not come in through the roof, and that the whole thing doesn't come crashing down around your reader's ears.

There are three things that you need to work on to make the world of your novel a fit place to live in. These are *consistency*, *coherence* and *concreteness*.

CONSISTENCY

'Consistency' means that your fictional world needs to be stable, so that it doesn't change (without very good reason) from chapter to chapter. If on page 17 you have a character called Susie who lives on the twenty-first floor, then it is a problem if on page 56 she opens the front door and steps straight on to the street. Consistency includes the following:

- Making sure that the physical details of your world remain unchanging, unless there is good reason for them to change.
- Making sure that your characters always act as characters *in this world*. Your characters are always constrained by the kind of world of which they are a part (it is

a constraint of Susie living on the twenty-first floor that she cannot step straight out on to the street, unless it is through the window, in which case it is going to leave a mess on the pavement).

- Being aware of the overall context of your story, in all five dimensions, and maintaining this throughout the story, scene by scene, unless there is good reason not to.

COHERENCE

'Coherence' means that the various bits of the world that you create must hang together as a whole, and this whole must be plausible. *Plausible* is not the same as *possible*. But if your story is going to be about impossible things – time travel, for example, or teleportation, or telepathy – you need to work out the logic of your world very carefully to make these impossible things seem plausible. This means being clear about the *logic* of your world. Coherence involves some of the following things:

- Thinking not just about *what* happens, but also about *why* and *how* things happen – under what conditions, and for what reasons.
- Asking yourself if this story *adds up*, if it is intuitively convincing.
- Reflecting on whether the things that happen in your story are *the kinds of things* that could happen in the kind of fictional world you have built.

CONCRETENESS

'Concreteness' means that your world must be fully imaginable *to the reader*. The last bit here – the bit about the reader – is important. As the writer of your novel, you may know masses of background information that doesn't actually appear *in* the novel. You may have in your head long family histories, a detailed knowledge of the place where the story happens, fluency in the 17 languages spoken by your various characters and an encyclopaedic knowledge of their record collections; but your reader may not need to know this. So concreteness involves some of the following questions.

- Assuming that the reader doesn't know what you know about the story, have you given the reader the information that they need to make sense of what is happening?
- Is the world drawn precisely enough that the reader can picture it clearly?
- Does your world feel like a *particular* world? Are the details well chosen enough that this feels not just like *a* seedy bar, for example, but like *this particular* seedy bar?

World-building for beginners

Umberto Eco's idea is that if you want to tell a story, you need to build a world in all its details. The more care you take with this careful construction, the more convincing the world of your story will be.

Umberto Eco, *Reflections on* The Name of the Rose

'What I mean is that to tell a story you must first of all construct a world, furnished as much as possible down to the slightest details. If I were to construct a river, I would need two banks; and if on the left bank I put a fisherman, and if I were to give this fisherman a wrathful character and a police record, then I could start writing... What does a fisherman do? He fishes... And then what happens? Either the fish are biting or they are not. If they bite, the fisherman catches them and then goes home happy. End of story. If there are no fish, since he is a wrathful type he will perhaps become angry. Perhaps he will break his fishing rod. This is not much; still, it is already a sketch.'

This is a good example of consistency, coherence and concreteness. Eco starts by making a series of *concrete* decisions. There is a river. It has two banks. The fisherman is on the left bank. He is angry by nature and has a criminal past. The fish either bite or they don't... Not only this, but he makes sure that *every decision* he later sticks to. His world is *consistent*. Finally, for each *new* decision, he takes into account the decisions he has already made. So his world is also *coherent*. Notice also how the story emerges almost *automatically* from this process of clear decision-making.

Key idea

The consistency, coherence and concreteness of your fictional world depend upon making clear decisions, and then sticking to them and following through the implications of these decisions.

You can try pushing Umberto Eco's thought experiment further. Why are there no fish? Perhaps there *are* fish, but the fisherman is incompetent. That's one kind of story. Or there are no fish, because there's a chemical plant which has recently opened upstream. That's another kind of story. Or there *are* fish, but a helpful duck that is fluent in the language of fish warns them away from the fisherman. That's a third kind of story.

Write: fishing for stories

Using Eco's approach of asking questions and finding answers, try to plan *three* different short stories that could arise out of the fisherman/riverbank scenario. Make sure that every decision you make fulfils the conditions of concreteness, consistency and coherence.

Now choose the story you like the most, and write it!

For Eco, if you build a world carefully enough, stories will emerge practically of their own accord. So, if your characters are milling around without any idea of what they are doing, perhaps it is because they are on a blank canvas, instead of living in a fully realized world. Once you make some clear decisions, you reduce the innumerable possibilities of the blank canvas down to a more manageable number of possibilities within a more fully imagined world. Then the writing process becomes far, far easier.

Breaking the rules

But what about those genres where things do not obey the rules of the everyday world? What about speculative fiction? What about fantasy? What about science fiction? What about magic? (And, as scientist and science fiction author Arthur C. Clarke famously said, 'Any sufficiently advanced technology is indistinguishable from magic.') The same principles apply. Even if you break the laws of physics, you need to break them in a fashion that is consistent and coherent (and, of course, you need to know what the rules are before you start to break them). If you want magic in your book, then you have to be clear about when, where and how it works, and when, where and how it doesn't. The more you depart from the shared sense of the world that we all have, the more you need to be careful about consistency, coherence and concreteness.

The following exercise is a way of exploring the approach to world-building above. It will involve putting your novel to one side and creating something new from scratch. Take three-quarters of an hour to an hour to complete it.

Write: furnishing a world

For this exercise, you will be exploring how character grows out of a sense of world. Start by choosing a world for a *new* story (preferably nothing to do with your novel) to take place in. If you are having trouble, you can choose one of the following: city, moon base, the back seat of a car, attic, cave, mountainside.

Using some of the questions above in the section on the five dimensions of your world, make a few notes to give a richer picture of this world.

Come up with a character. Just one. Again, don't be too specific. Don't give a whole biography, or even a name. Just think: *What kind of person might I find in this place?* Write down the character.

Now write down *where they are specifically* in this world. (Inside or outside the moon base? Halfway up the mountain, or at the bottom? Lying down on the back seat of the car, or sitting up?)

Now press on, asking yourself questions like the following:
- What does my character want?
- Why is my character where they are?
- What else do I know about this world?
- What happens next?

Write down every question that occurs to you, and write down an answer for each. You may find yourself making notes about aspects of this world: politics, culture, language, the physical world, thought, values and beliefs, and history… But make sure that your answers are all consistent with previous answers, coherent and concrete. Avoid vagueness.

When you have filled a page with notes, write either a very short story or the opening passage of a story (say 500 words) about this world.

Building a monastery: a case study

When he decided to write *The Name of the Rose*, Eco had a head start. As well as being a novelist, he was also trained as a medieval scholar, so he knew the world that he was writing about intimately. He already knew about the languages, thought, values, beliefs, culture, politics and history of the medieval world. However, the monastery where the book was set never existed; and so he had to build it.

Eco worked out the details of this world with all the care of a master architect. He drew maps (which are in the published book), he worked out the precise arrangement of all the parts of the monastery, he thought long and hard about every last physical detail. He knew exactly how far it was from one building to another, and so, if two characters were having a conversation while walking this route, he would know exactly *how long* this conversation should take. For every conversation had by two characters going for a walk, he *walked the same distance*, holding the same conversation with himself. When he had walked the full distance, he knew that the conversation had to stop, or change direction, or at least his characters had to stop walking. This attention to detail is part of what makes *The Name of the Rose* such a convincing book.

At the end of the novel, Eco wanted a terrible fire in the monastery library. But when he came to write this section, he realized that something was not right. Looking back at his maps, the construction of the library made him wonder about the feasibility of a fire. He couldn't be sure that inside those solid monastery walls there would be enough oxygen to get a good, roaring fire going. So, not wanting this blazing finale to burn out after a minute or two, he made some modifications to his architecture: to make sure there was enough oxygen to keep the fire nice and hot, he added slits in the library walls!

Knowing when to stop

This may all seem like overkill – and, in fact, for the novel you are writing, some of it might be. The trick is knowing how *much* world you need to build, and how much you can leave to one side. But just as even the most apparently miraculous of buildings have some kind of careful behind-the-scenes construction – struts and beams that no visitor ever sees – so even stories that seem to be written with a very light touch have considerable engineering behind them. In other words, even those things that are invisible in the final book may help give your story solidity and conviction.

But isn't there a time when you need to stop building a convincing world, and get on with writing? I think there is: given that any world is, in principle at least, infinitely complex, there must be point at which, as a writer, you decide that enough is enough.

When this point comes depends very much on the project you are working on. Some novels require more careful world-building than others. The crucial issue here is whether the world you are building is fit for your story to take place in, and for your characters to live in. You will get a feel for when you have enough in place for your story to be fully convincing. Every story takes place within particular horizons. You need to make sure that everything within the horizon of your novel as a whole hangs together, and you need to make sure that the reader isn't going to fret about anything that is *beyond* the horizon. If you can do these two things, then you have probably done enough.

Now have a go at the workshop task below.

Workshop: maps, timelines and thinking through your fictional world

This workshop is designed either to 1) help you build a convincing world for the novel you are planning, or 2) help you make the world of the novel you are working on more robust. You can complete as much or as little of the task as you like. Feel free to return to it as your novel progresses, to keep tweaking your world.

1 Getting the physical environment right

First, *draw a map of the world* in which your story is set. Think about the meticulous care that Umberto Eco used in mapping the world of his novel. Make sure that your map is clear and precise. If your novel is set in a kitchen, draw a map of the kitchen. If it is set in a town, sketch out the town, making sure that you note where all the important buildings that feature in the novel are. If your novel is set in a place for which you already have a map, make a copy of the map, and mark all the places that are important for your book. If your novel takes place in several locations, *draw a map of each.* You might find yourself using a pre-printed map of the (real) town in which the novel is set, marking locations on it, but inventing a map or plan of the (imaginary) house where much of the action takes place.

You can make the map as detailed as you need. Some novels will need a greater degree of detail. But make sure that everything that needs to be on the map is there.

2 Thinking about consistency, coherence and concreteness in five dimensions

For the final part of this workshop, if you have not yet completed the five 'dimensions of your fictional world' snapshots earlier in this chapter, complete them now.

Now go through these notes and use the chart below to ask about each of these five dimensions, and how consistent, coherent and concrete your world is. Give yourself a tick (✓) if you are confident that this dimension scores highly for, give yourself a cross (×) if you feel that it needs more work.

Dimension	Consistency	Coherence	Concreteness
Physical environment			
Language			
Thought, values and beliefs			
Culture, politics and society			
History			

When you have done this, you should have a strong sense of the problems and blind spots when it comes to building your world.

Where to next?

While thinking about world-building, you may have realized that there are gaps in your knowledge, that there are things you need to find out to really build a convincing world. This, then, leads us on to the subject of the next chapter: how to go about researching your novel.

6

Research

Writers are often told to 'write about what you know'. While this can indeed be good advice, the trouble with what we know is that, however deep and rich and extensive our knowledge is, the things that we don't know are vastly deeper, richer and more extensive; and there is a risk, in sticking determinedly to 'what you know' that you might miss out on this depth and richness. So this chapter is about research. It is about those things that you *don't* know but that you need to know to write the story that you want to write.

Why do research?

Robert McKee, *Story*

'Research is meat to feed the beasts of imagination and invention, never an end in itself.'

As a novelist, you are not researching to become an expert on your subject, or so that you can write learned, scholarly papers. You are researching, as Robert McKee points out, so that you can feed the beasts of imagination and invention. Stories feed off good research. Earlier we talked about fattening up ideas. Research is one of the ways that you can do this most effectively. Research is not window-dressing, stage design or just a matter of getting the period details right (although it may involve some of these things). Instead, it is about giving shape to your fictional world. Research is another aspect of world-building. It gives you a scaffolding for your storytelling, it opens up new possibilities for plot and action, it allows you to choose just the right telling detail to bring your world to life, it provides you with rich resources to draw in while writing your book, and it means that when your novel is published – if your research is good – you will not get into trouble with readers, reviewers and experts.

 Key idea

Whatever your genre – from family history to fantasy to literary fiction – at some stage in the writing process, you will need to get to grips with research.

Try the following exercise as a way of getting you thinking about research.

 Snapshot: what research is needed?

Jot down a few notes on the kind of research that you think you might need for the following novels. Alternatively, discuss this with a fellow writer. It may help to think about the five dimensions of the fictional world explored in the previous chapter (physical environment; language; thought, values and beliefs; culture, politics and society; and history). Here are the novels:

- a love story set in samurai Japan
- a science-fiction story set in the year 2379 in a Mars colony after the destruction of the Earth
- a thriller set during the Cold War
- a story based upon an incident in your own childhood
- a Western
- a story that took place last year, and that is set in your home town
- a story that took place ten years before your birth, and that is set in your home town.

Write about what you don't know

The earliest record I can find of the advice that you should write about what you know dates from 1865, when somebody called Date Thorne published a curious little article in the *Ohio Educational Monthly*. The article was called 'Something about Compositions', and dealt with the art of teaching children to write. 'Such hard work?' Thorne asks. 'I know it is. I know all about it. Many a time I have sat an hour, with a pen in my hand, and a great white sheet of paper before me…' She ends her essay like this:

Date Thorne, 'Something about Compositions'

'One day, somebody asked one of these same little boys why it was that he liked to write compositions so well. He twisted his button-hole with his fingers, and looked up at the clouds with his eyes, and, after thinking a minute, he said: "I guess it's 'cause I always write about what I know." Now, there's the secret for you, children. Always write about what you know, and it will not be such hard work after all.'

My argument with this as advice for novelists is that to write about what you know simply as a way of avoiding this hard work is to duck the issue. Whatever the starting point of your novel, if you restrict yourself *only* to what you know, your novel is going to be the worse for it. Besides, novel writing *is* hard work.

Focus point

Instead of writing about what you know, make sure that you know what you are writing about.

All novels are born out of an individual's knowledge, expertise, obsessions and accumulated experiences. As a novelist, all of this forms a rich repository of ideas. But this is a *starting point*. Once your story takes on its own shape, it will almost inevitably be necessary to go beyond the things that you know, and to venture into new territories.

You will need to do this not only to fill in specific gaps in your knowledge and to make sure that you are getting the story right, but also to open yourself and your story to new and as yet undiscovered possibilities.

FILLING IN THE GAPS

Sometimes there will simply be gaps in your knowledge that you need to fill in by research. This level of research is, more or less, a matter of fact-checking. It doesn't alter the framework that you have set out for your story; it only provides an extra level of detail. However, even if your research is restricted to this simply filling in the gaps, there is always a chance that a new piece of information, a new fact, will *force* you to make substantial changes to the story you are telling.

EXPLORING NEW POSSIBILITIES

If you are stuck with your story, if the world you are writing about feels a bit cramped and small, this may be a problem to do with lack of research. Research is not just about filling in gaps; it is also a way of opening up yourself and your story to the richness of the world, helping you to fatten up your ideas, and to enrich and deepen the world you are building. Without research, the beasts of imagination and invention can waste away.

Snapshot: experiences, gaps and possibilities

Take a sheet of paper and divide it into three columns. Give these columns the headings 'Experience', 'Gaps' and 'Possibilities'.

1   In the first column, write a quick list of all the individual experiences and the individual expertise upon which you are drawing in writing your novel.

2   In the second column, list down the specific gaps in your knowledge that need to be filled in by further research.

3   Finally, in the third column, list some areas of research that you think might be useful to help fatten up your ideas, even if you are not sure in which direction this research will take you.

For the third column, it can help to work alongside a friend – they don't need to be a fellow writer – to make suggestions about things that you could go off and explore to enrich your book.

The familiar and the unfamiliar

All novels take research, whether you are writing about subject-matter you know very well indeed or whether your subject-matter is more unfamiliar to you; and the craft challenges are slightly different depending upon the degree of familiarity you have with the material you are working on.

THE CHALLENGE OF THE UNFAMILIAR

One of the big problems with writing about worlds with which you are unfamiliar, or with which your readers may be unfamiliar, is that instead of really digging into the deeper realities in this world, you rely on a sense of the strangeness and difference of this world to make your story interesting. But when you start to dig beneath the surface, often worlds that at first seem exotic and different turn out to be strangely mundane: the surface gloss of the tourist visit doesn't last beyond a few hours. Writers writing about other places, about elsewhere, have to be more like anthropologists drilling down to find out deeper realities than they are like tourists hurrying on for the next photo-opportunity.

Key idea

When writing about that which is unfamiliar, the main risk is that you can end up relying on surface exoticism.

THE CHALLENGE OF THE FAMILIAR

If you are writing about somewhere familiar and close to home, then the challenge may be rather different. We often take that which is familiar for granted; we don't see how strange and singular it is. Often, we don't pay very much attention to the everyday details of the world with which we are most familiar.

Key idea

When writing about that which is familiar, the main risk is that you overlook what makes it strange, singular or unique.

There is another challenge when writing about worlds with which you are familiar, and that is that you can easily fall into the trap of assuming that your readers know what you know: you need to not take anything for granted. If you are writing about your home town, think about how strange and exotic it would seem to somebody who was from elsewhere. As you write, ask the kinds of questions that an outsider might want to ask. After all, your readers will almost certainly (unless they are close friends or family) be outsiders to some degree.

However familiar or unfamiliar the world about which you are writing, the crucial point is that *writing is an act of investigation*. It is about exploring the world. Research is how you as a writer become skilled at moving between the familiar and the unfamiliar, the known and the unknown.

When should I research?

It's easy to think that research is something that happens right at the start of a project. And, certainly, if the world were a tidy kind of place, novelists might find that they could do all their research before setting out on the writing. Having collected all the information they needed, they could get on with the writing. However, as the world is not a tidy kind of place (which is a good thing, because if it were, novelists would be out of business), things don't always work out like this.

My own suggestion is this: instead of seeing research as a *preliminary stage* in your writing, it can be more useful to see it as a process that takes place *alongside* the writing. It may be that you are the kind of writer who does more research up front. It may be that you alternate between drafting, research, redrafting and further research. And it may be that, close to publication, you find yourself having to conduct fairly intensive research to deal with problems raised by your copy-editor.

How to research your novel

Different kinds of novel require different kinds of research. You may need to go and spend some time in the locations you are writing about, your research may be entirely through books and the Internet, or else your research may involve meeting people or learning new skills. There is no single 'right way' to research a novel. Nevertheless, however you are going about your research, it can be useful – as a starting point – to think in terms of framing a few research questions: things that you need to find out to tell your story. Try the following short exercise.

Snapshot: framing your research questions

Get a new piece of paper and divide it into two columns. In the left-hand column, write down a list of research questions. If you tried the previous snapshot, then you can use the 'gaps' to help you come up with some questions. Try to make your questions specific: 'What was Paris like in the past?' is less useful than 'What were bars in Paris like when Toulouse-Lautrec was around?'

Now in the right-hand column, note down a few ideas about how you might go about answering each of these questions. Approaches that you could use might include.

- consulting libraries/archives/books/journals
- searching on the Internet
- contacting experts
- visiting places
- learning new skills.

This should give you a rough research plan on the basis of which you can start thinking about getting stuck into the research. We'll explore some of the ways you can do this in more depth.

LIBRARIES, ARCHIVES, BOOKS AND JOURNALS

Much of your research may involve haunting libraries and exploring books, journals and periodicals.

Make use of libraries

Libraries are wonderful and miraculous things. If libraries didn't exist, and somebody said to you, 'I've just come up with a brilliant idea for a massive book-house where you can go free of charge, and sit all day and read stuff, and take books home for short periods without paying a penny, and talk to knowledgeable, well-informed experts who will help you find just what you are looking for', people would say that such an idea would never catch on, and that, if it did, it would bring the entire capitalist world crashing down apocalyptically. But such utopian places do indeed exist, and for writers they are both havens and wonderful resources. Whether it is the Library of Congress, the British Library or your local lending library, libraries remain fabulous repositories of information, and as a novelist you should use them.

Caitlin Moran, *Moranthology*

'*A library in the middle of a community is a cross between an emergency exit, a life raft and a festival. They are cathedrals of the mind; hospitals of the soul; theme parks of the imagination.*'

In the age of the Internet, it might seem as if books are no longer as important a resource as they were in the past; but there is a level of *depth* of information in books that Internet resources still struggle to match. There is also a particular kind of serendipity that comes from browsing library shelves and finding books catching your attention. Libraries are good places to idle, to soak up ideas and knowledge, to get a sense of what kind of information is out there.

As well as public libraries, many *university libraries* are excellent. If you are not a member, check their websites to see whether they allow external readers or borrowers. Sometimes there will be a fee for this, but it can often be worth paying. You may not be able to borrow books unless you are a member of the university (or of another university), but you may be able to get permission to access the library and read on site. University libraries often have substantial collections of academic journals containing rich and useful information.

Make use of librarians

Libraries are not just about books. They are also peopled by librarians. The popular image of librarians is of stern women in tweedy skirts who are always saying 'Shhh…', or balding men in their fifties with thick spectacles who go home in the evening to play with their train sets while their mothers cook dinner. But while such characters still exist, many librarians (or 'information professionals', as they might prefer to think of themselves these days) are not at all like this, will do anything they can to help you, and are just longing for somebody to come along and ask them interesting questions.

Focus point

Librarians are professionals in the business of helping people research the information they need, so speak to them about what you are looking for, and they will be able to assist you.

If you come across an unhelpful librarian (it sometimes happens), then just smile, make your excuses, and go and talk to somebody else.

Getting hold of books from other libraries

If the library doesn't have what you are looking for, books can sometimes be ordered from other libraries, either through local arrangements or through using the Inter-Library Loan (ILL) system for a small fee. It can take a while for books to arrive and sometimes, after a long wait, you just get a note saying that it was not possible to get hold of the book, so patience is necessary. But if your library doesn't have the book you need, talk to your librarian to see whether they can track it down.

Archives

Many libraries will have extensive local history archives that you can explore. There may also be archives held by government organizations, record offices or other bodies, and many of these permit access by members of the public. Archivists are often highly qualified experts who can also be extremely helpful when it comes to tracking down information.

Other ways of getting hold of books

The Internet has made getting hold of obscure books easier than it was in the past. You can often get out-of-print or hard-to-find books at good prices through online bookstores such as www.abebooks.co.uk, www.amazon.co.uk or www.biblio.co.uk. Somewhat controversially, Google Books has also digitized many books (books.google.com) and you can search for content *within* these books, reading all or part of their contents. For out-of-copyright books, try project Gutenberg (www.gutenberg.org) and the Internet archive (www.archive.org).

Journal articles

Many academic journals and periodicals are useful for specialist information. The problem is that these can be crazily expensive (often a single article in PDF format costs more than the price of a hardback book). Increasingly, there is a significant movement towards what is known as 'open access' (OA), which makes academic journal publishing publicly available, so the amount that you can find online is increasing. One of the best places to track down articles on the subject you are interested in is Google Scholar (scholar.google.com).

Other library resources

Libraries may have significant holdings of other useful resources: films, music, TV documentaries and other things that you can use for your research.

OTHER INTERNET RESEARCH

The Internet is an amazing tool for research and is also, if you use it with good sense and care, far less unreliable than many people claim. But the crucial thing here is *if you use it with good sense and care*. There is a lot of misinformation out there. The online encyclopaedia Wikipedia (www.wikipedia.org) is a fairly decent first port of call for information on a subject; but it should be only a first port of call, a jumping-off site for finding rich and useful information elsewhere. There are also many well-considered blogs out there but, again, exercise caution. Books and magazines have editors; academic journals have 'peer reviewers' who approve the content for publication. But if I want to write a blog, nothing stands between the contents of my head and the wider world. There is no third-party quality control. So whenever you are using Internet resources, ask yourself: *How reliable is this information?* Ideally, you should do this with books, magazines and journals as well!

Key idea

When carrying out research, it is important to be able to evaluate how reliable your sources are.

Major newspapers also have searchable websites. *The Guardian* (www.guardian.co.uk) has a particularly comprehensive one, and *The Independent* (www.independent.co.uk) has recently made its online content freely available. The BBC's news pages are good, and they also have resources on various subjects (as well as copies of old radio shows to download, etc.). Go to www.bbc.co.uk for more information.

EXPERTS

Another thing that you may need to do for research is to talk to people who are experts. These may be people who have lived in the place you are writing about or have experienced the events you are using in your writing. They may be people who study the topics that you are exploring in your writing, either professionally as a part of their job or else as a hobby. If you are writing a novel based on your own family history, then the experts in question may be your own family members. If you are writing about things further afield, they may be strangers.

Often, other people will be very willing to help you with your research. In particular, many 'experts' – particularly academics – will be happy to talk to you. When getting in touch with anyone for your research, remember the following rules of thumb:

- **Do some preliminary research!** Make sure that you know who you are contacting and why they might be helpful. If they have written relevant books, read the books before you contact them, so that you can be sure that you are not just asking them for something they have already said.

- **Be sure about what you want.** If you know what you want from the person in question – to meet up, perhaps, or a specific piece of information, or to conduct an interview – this makes thing easier on them than a general 'I'm researching my novel on x; can you help?' request.

- **Be friendly but also professional.** You are researching a novel, not trying to find a new lifelong friend, a date or a potential marriage partner.

- If you end up getting published and they've been a lot of help, **send a copy of the book with a thank-you note.** It may be good to credit them in the acknowledgements section of your book, but it is good manners to check first whether they would like to be credited.

Snapshot: who can help with my research?

Write down several of the main themes and topics that you explore in your novel, and that could require further research. Now go online and see whether you can answer the following questions.

- Are there any *organizations* that might help you in carrying out your research?
- Are there any *individuals* who might be of assistance?
- Are there any specialist *sources of information* that might of use to you?

See whether you can find some contact details so that you can follow up these leads later. You don't need to make contact yet, unless you have a clear idea of what you want to ask; but it is useful to have this information on file.

MAKE A RESEARCH TRIP

You may decide that a research trip is in order and that, as the anthropologists like to say, you need to 'go out into the field' and really get your hands dirty, rather than just mucking round with books and spending time on the Internet. This can be a very useful way of doing research, and can both lead you in unexpected directions and also help enrich your novel considerably. Here are some reasons why you might want to make a research trip:

- to visit museums or specialist libraries
- to talk to experts who know about the subject-matter of your novel
- to see specific historical sites associated with your book
- to get a deeper sense of the landscape, culture and language of the place that you are writing about, whether it is a village down the road or a city on the other side of the world.

By immersing yourself in the physical details of a world, you can soak up a really rich sense of place. In addition, in travelling you often meet interesting people who can help you greatly with the research towards your novel. And while it is possible to write about places you have never been to, your novel will be strengthened by this first-person immersion.

Of course, travelling costs money, and the further afield your novel is set, the more this will be an issue. If your book is set on the moon, a research trip may be beyond the budget of most aspiring novelists, but you may want to make a trip to a planetarium or a science museum instead. In order to offset costs, there are various places that you can go to look for grants towards your research costs. For my second novel, *The Descent of the Lyre*, I received a grant from Arts Council England to travel to Bulgaria by train, where I spent seven weeks travelling through the mountains, visiting small museums and monasteries and making new friends. I could not have written the novel without this trip.

Focus point

A research trip – whether it is a day trip or a longer expedition – can help you in several ways. It can also be a lot of fun, and can help inject a new lease of life into your project.

LEARNING NEW SKILLS

You may want to go further, and learn new skills to help research your novel. If you are writing your novel about a car mechanic, apprenticing yourself to a real-life car mechanic for a month could tell you more than years of reading in the library. Similarly, I know a writer who learned how to pick both locks and pockets (although she insists that she never committed any actual crimes) while researching a crime story. Other things that you might find yourself doing are:

• learning a new language

• learning to play a musical instrument

• learning to play a sport or game

• learning new practical skills (house-building, baking, lock-picking, taxidermy).

Of course, you are doing these things *as a novelist*. You are not trying to become a world expert. But even a bit of experience can really help you get inside the world you are writing about. This is not to say that you *have* to learn new skills as a part of your research: careful research through books, journals, the Internet and multimedia, talking to people in the know, and a good dose of the imagination can all get you a long, long way. But learning new skills might help.

Finally, of course, you need to remember that you don't have to have first-person experience of everything you are writing about to make your writing convincing; otherwise the prisons of the world would be filled with crime novelists.

Organizing your research

If you are writing a novel that involves a large amount of research, you may need to think about how you organize it. The methods you choose will depend upon the kinds of research materials you are gathering. If much of your research is on paper, it can help to have well-organized folders, so that you can find what you are looking for. There are advantages to paper materials: you can spread piles of paper out on the floor and shuffle them around. On the other hand, electronic materials can be easily searched by keyword, and don't take up the same amount of storage space.

However you organize your research, remember to *keep track of your sources*. This means that for every piece of information, you should know where it came from and how reliable or unreliable this source is. For books and magazine or journal articles, note down the full title, the author and the page number. For interviews, note who the interviewee was, and when and where the interview took place. For websites, make sure that you note down the full web address or URL. For written resources, there is plenty of good bibliographic software that you can use to keep things in order. There are some suggestions for useful research tools and resources at the end of this book.

Knowing when to stop

 Zhuangzi

'My life has limits, but knowledge has no limits. Using that which is limited to pursue that which has no limits is perilous!'

The number of things that we *could* know about is infinite, and so research could in principle go on for ever. Knowing when to stop is important. There will always be more research that you could do, but remember that you are doing the research not for its own sake but for a particular job: to write as good a novel as you can.

Some books require much lighter research than others. Some require you to be more systematic and in-depth. You will need to use your own judgement here. Keep your eye on the point at which the research feels as if it is becoming an end in itself, rather than a means to an end. If you find yourself getting so lost in the research that you lose touch with the actual writing, try putting the research to one side and trying to write a bit more. You can always pick up the research later if you need to fill in more gaps or think through other questions.

Remember, too, that not all your research will make it into the final book. As you do your research, you may turn up all kinds of interesting facts, stories or ideas that may not fit into your novel. Don't try to shoehorn everything in, thereby doing violence to your story. If there is something wonderful that you have stumbled across in your research and that doesn't fit, save it for the next novel, or for a short story, instead.

 Focus point

Remember that not everything you research can, will, or should go into your final novel.

Workshop: planning a research day

In this workshop task, you are going to plan a day dedicated *only* to research. Although this workshop asks you to set aside a whole day for research, it actually involves a bit more than this, because you need to *plan* your research in advance, and then you need to make use of it. So think of this as a workshop over three weeks, divided like this:

Week 1 (2 to 3 hours)	Planning what you are going to do on your research day. Set aside two to three hours at least a week before your research day.
Week 2 (1 full day)	Actually doing the research. Allow yourself the luxury of a whole day to do this, if you can.
Week 3 (2 to 3 hours)	Going back over your research to see what use you can make of it. Set aside two to three hours, at least a week after your research trip.

Week 1: planning your research

Any piece of research starts with some questions. You will be using a table like the one below to keep track.

Question	Kinds of research needed	Notes

Start by writing down as many questions as you can think of about the world of your novel. It may help to get a friend to talk this through with, as often questions will arise in other people's minds (and these other people will one day be your readers) that haven't occurred to you yourself. Just jot down questions at random, without giving them too much thought.

When you have done this, take a short break. When you come back to the questions, choose the ones that seem most important, pressing or interesting. When you have done this, put them in table form. Under 'Kinds of research needed' you might put some of the following:

- Internet research
- Visit a library
- Conduct an interview
- Visit a particular location
- Learn a skill
- Get hold of journals, magazines or other publications
- Explore public archives.

Under 'Notes', make any notes that you need about practicalities (for example, contact details, addresses). You may need to do a bit of research to find out the best way of researching these questions.

Now that you have done this, make a quick plan of what you think you can reasonably achieve in a research day, and write a plan for the day.

Week 2: your research day

Now that you have done the hard work, this is where the fun starts. Give yourself a full day. Cancel all other engagements. Allow yourself this whole day to follow up these questions. Remember that research is inherently unpredictable. It is about moving from the known into the unknown; and so if you stumble across something that grabs your attention or takes you in new directions, just go with it.

A few rules of thumb for your research day:

- Make a clear, but realistic, timetable for your day, so that you don't end up frittering it away!
- Keep clear records of all the information you are gathering and where it comes from.
- Keep alive to unexpected possibilities.
- Don't try to research your *whole* novel in a single day: remember that research will be taking place at *all* stages of the writing.
- If you find one avenue of inquiry is not working, feel free to change direction.
- At the end of the day, leave your research on one side (unless you are too gripped by it to do otherwise), and come back to it a week later.

Week 3: looking over your research

Take a couple of hours. First, look over your research findings. Then have a look over your novel-in-progress (or, if you have not started writing yet, your plans for your novel). Ask yourself:

- Will this research lead to me having to change anything in my novel? Does the plot need to change? The characters? The world in which it is set?
- What sections of the novel should I write or rewrite in the light of this research?
- What further research do I need to do?

Where to next?

As you go on with your novel, you may find that you accumulate increasing quantities of research. But, however much research you have done, the reader is not going to be interested in this world unless something interesting happens there. So in the next chapter, we are going to look at the question of what happens in your novel. In other words, we are going to talk about plot.

7

Plot

In this chapter we will start to think about what actually *happens* in your novel. In other words, we are going beyond questions of world-building and research to look at plot. For the purposes of the present book, I'm making a distinction between 'plot' and 'storytelling'. 'Plot' is the question of how you build a story worth telling. 'Storytelling' is how you go about telling that story. Sometimes a novel will not quite work because, although this is a *story worth telling*, there are problems with the *way* in which you are telling it. This is a problem with storytelling. Sometimes you encounter the reverse problem: the way that you are telling the story is good, but the story itself doesn't have quite enough substance or structure. This is a problem with plot.

Basics of plot: what happens, why, and why we should care

 Kurt Vonnegut, *Palm Sunday*

'I don't praise plots as accurate representations of life, but as ways to keep readers reading.'

There are many complicated theories of plot out there, but for the time being I want to keep it simple. When somebody you know has read a book or seen a film, and you ask them what the plot is, what are you really asking? It seems to me that you are asking three things:

1 **What happens?**

2 **Why do these things happen?**

3 **Why does it matter that these things happen?**

So, you want to know what events take place in the world of the story. You want to know who lives and who dies, who falls in love and who falls out of love, and so on. But you also want to know *why* any of this happens. It may be slightly interesting to know that Igor is going to Paris to meet Isabelle. But it becomes a whole lot more interesting when we know he is doing so because Igor had his right kidney stolen, and he has discovered that this same kidney is now nestling inside Isabelle's slender back. Some plots are tied very tightly, some very loosely indeed. Some have no threads hanging loose; others have threads dangling everywhere. But whatever kind of plot you are writing, there needs to be *some* sense of causality or consequence so that these various events hang together – so that we know why they are in the same novel.

 Key idea

Plots are not just about events, but about events that are tied together by causality.

Finally, you want to know why any of this matters. This is, of course, also tied to the question of causality and consequence, because causes and consequences are tangled up with our caring.

WHAT HAPPENS?

At the most fundamental level, the question that you need to ask of your novel is this: *What happens in your story?* Stories are made up of *events* or *happenings*. These events do not have to be particularly elaborate. You may be writing a story that involves sword fights, sea battles and terrible monsters; but equally you may be writing a story about the shifting of the landscape of a set of personal relationships. Neither is more or less worthwhile as a choice of subject-matter, and neither has more or less plot. A quiet event can be just as powerful, sometimes even more powerful, than a noisy one. In fact, if your story is relatively high-octane, then, when you are plotting it out, you should think about introducing some quieter scenes. One high-intensity scene after another tends to have a numbing effect. If you can make sure that you alternate between scenes of greater and lesser intensity, the impact will be greater.

When I say that a story needs something to happen, what I really mean is that a story needs to have a transformation or change. This transformation may be a change in the *world* of the story. It may be a change in the *characters* or in their fortunes. It may also be a change in the perceptions of your *reader*. It may be all three. But by the end of the novel, things have to look different from how they looked at the beginning.

Key idea

Stories require some kind of transformation or change: either in the *world* in which the story is set, in the *characters*, or in the *reader*.

WHY DOES IT HAPPEN?

The next question you need to ask is: *Why does whatever takes place happen?* Although the world we live in may seem confused and sometimes arbitrary, there are regularities and patterns in the way events unfold. Certain events make other events more likely. Some happenings make other happenings *inevitable*. This is the art of tragedy: to set in course a train of events born out of the noblest intentions that seem, of necessity, to lead to the most terrible of conclusions.

When writing plot, it is necessary to think about *causes* and *consequences*. By causes, I mean what the things were *in the past* that led up to a particular event (events, of course, can have multiple causes). Consequences are the results of the events that happen, reaching into the future.

Key idea

Every event has both *causes* and *consequences*. The art of plotting involves being able to follow through this logic of causes and consequences.

Thinking through the causes and consequences in your story world is challenging, but it can open up all kinds of riches. You can go through your story point by point and ask: Why *does* this happen? Do the events feel arbitrary, or do they happen for a reason? If they feel arbitrary, is there a good reason for this arbitrariness?

In thinking about what happens and why, you will realize that plot is closely tied in with the world that you have built. Plots and stories are not entirely transferable from one context to another. They change and warp as you transplant them. They mould to the worlds in which they find themselves.

Snapshot: what happens and why?

Either take a novel you have read recently, or take your own novel. Ask yourself what the major events in the novel are. Make a list of five or so. Do not write more than a sentence for each one.

Now ask yourself for each event: *Why does this event take place?* Make some notes on this.

What you may notice is that, for some important events, you know that they *ought* to happen for the sake of your story, but you are not clear *why* they happen. This might be a weakness in your story (it might not, of course – but it is worth asking whether it is a weakness) that you will need to address.

For each event, ask yourself: *What consequences would this event have in my fictional world?* Make some notes on this.

You may notice here that there are some major events for which you haven't fully thought through the consequences. Again, this may point to a weakness in your plot that needs attention.

WHY SHOULD WE CARE?

These two elements – what happens and why – are not yet enough for a plot to be really successful. Even with a sense of causality and consequence, events that lead to other events are no more than events that lead to other events. Your reader also has to care enough about these particular chains of events to keep on reading (rather than getting out of their chair and going off to initiate their own chains of events somewhere out there in the world).

What do readers care about? Some people say that readers care about 'sympathetic' or 'likeable' characters. I'm not sure that this is true. Some of the most magnificent characters in literature are neither sympathetic nor likeable. What really makes us care, I think, is this: we care when we know that something is *at stake*.

 ## Will Self

'A party full of "likeable" people doesn't bear contemplating.'

Imagine that you see two people having a scuffle in the street. You don't know either of them, so you don't know whether they are likeable or not. You glance at them, and walk on past. Then somebody says, 'They're fighting over a gun.' Suddenly the stakes have shot up. You still don't know whether either character is sympathetic or likeable, but you know that there is now an element of heightened stakes. This is not just a scuffle. It could be a matter of life or death. Suddenly, you are interested.

Here we need to be cautious. For the stakes to be high in a story, there doesn't have to be high drama. The stakes can be trivial but still *matter* to the characters. Think of a child for whom it really *matters* that they have an ice cream – it matters so much that they will yell and wail until they get one. What makes the stakes high is that something really matters not to the reader but to the character. What the reader recognizes and what draws the reader's attention is the intensity of that character's desire.

Desire, I think, is central to plot, because it is at the heart of what makes us care about a story. This insight goes all the way back to the great philosopher of ancient Greece, Aristotle. In his *Poetics* – a book that is still read today by fiction writers and screenwriters – Aristotle writes that plot is the most important element of any story (he is talking about tragedy, but we can generalize more broadly). Plot is the armature, the backbone, on which a story hangs. What makes a plot, Aristotle says, is that it is an imitation (or representation) of an *action* that is 'complete in itself, as a whole of some magnitude'.

What Aristotle means by 'action' is best understood by thinking in terms of *desire that is played out in the world.* So the 'action' of a story could be the prince's desire to become king. Or it could be the bored wife's desire to leave her husband. 'A prince', or even 'the life of a prince', is not a story. 'How the prince strives to become king' *is* a story.

Key idea

The thing that drives your story forwards and that gets your characters moving is *desire* or *wanting*.

Why does desire matter? It matters because it opens up possibilities. It impels us (or our characters) through the world, makes us (or them) *act*, and drives change and transformation. Try the following exercise.

Snapshot: thinking about desire

This is an exercise to be left until you have either written – or at least planned – some of your novel.

Firstly, identify the three most important characters in your novel. Can you clearly articulate what they *want*, what they *desire* in the novel *as a whole*?

Now ask the same question at the level of individual sections or chapters. Go through your manuscript and for each chapter or section ask yourself: What does this character want?

Are these desires clear? Do they help to drive the plot? Do the characters act in accordance with their desires or not?

Constructing a plot: from the top down, or from the bottom up

Plotting is an aspect of world-building in that it involves asking about a particular series of events that is unfolding in your fictional world. You are extracting a single skein (or several skeins) of history, of time and space from the huge complexity of the world that you have built, and you are following the events of this history, through their twists and turns, until their necessary conclusion.

There are different ways of planning out a plot. There are some writers who plan everything out meticulously: their plot is *top-down*. Writers like these orchestrate all the details of their characters' movements, so that the plot fits together like clockwork (these kinds of writers tend to incline towards writing tighter plots). Other writers prefer to let the plot *emerge* from the desires of the characters and from the world that they have built. Their plot is bottom-up (stories plotted like this tend to be rather looser, baggier affairs). *Bottom-up* plots can often feel more organic and natural, and often rather messier as well. *Top-down* plots, conversely, often have quite a strong sense of necessity. They are often far neater than bottom-up plots.

Neat plots can be satisfying: you can admire the story for its craft and construction, for the sense of necessity that drives it, for the way that it does not stray off down side-alleys, for the incredible focus of the storyteller. But too much neatness also puts you at risk of the story feeling forced and unnatural. Messy plots, on the other hand, different virtues. Because life doesn't have tidy beginnings and ends, messy plots may have the virtue of being more like life itself. On the downside, messier plots can feel a bit *too* loose-knit and baggy.

In reality, most writers will work in both fashions at some point during the writing of their novel. And it can be good to have a mix of careful top-down planning, and also some bottom-up 'let's-see-what-happens', a mix of both the messy and the neat.

Raising and responding to questions

Thinking about the structure of your plot in terms of *questions* can be a useful way of exploring the mesh of cause and consequences that makes up your plot. It is your ability to raise questions that will keep your readers engaged in your book. Human beings are naturally interested in one another's business. They are interested in causality and in consequences. If you can hook your readers into asking questions about your characters and the world they live in – Why *is* she walking out on her husband? What *does* he keep in the box in the attic? Will the hero manage to defuse the bomb and save New York? What is the dark secret in her past? – they are likely to keep reading.

Milan Kundera

'The novelist teaches the reader to comprehend the world as a question.'

Thinking in terms of questions can be a good way of thinking about the structure of your plot. The earlier part of your story may be concerned with *raising* questions; the middle of your novel may be concerned with *deepening*, *complicating* and *multiplying* questions; and the end of your novel may be about *resolving*, *addressing* or *responding to* questions (but not necessarily answering them), or else it may be about raising the same questions again, *but in a new way* or *at a deeper level*.

Key idea

You are not obliged to *answer* every question that you raise. But you do need to *respond to* or *address* these questions.

Snapshot: questions

Go back to a novel that you have read some time in the past few years, and reread no more than the first chapter (or the first 15 pages, if the book has short chapters). Now go through page by page and note down for each page the questions that the novelist is raising for the reader. When you have done so, ask yourself the following things:

- Which questions are dealt with quickly, within the first chapter?
- Which questions are left open?
- Which questions feel like *major* or *important* questions?
- Which questions feel like *minor* or *unimportant* questions?
- Does the novelist answer the questions raised? If not, how else does the novelist address them?
- If the novelist answers these questions, is it in a fashion that you expect? How does the novelist play with your expectations?

In Nigel Watt and Stephen May's book in this series, the authors say that there are two kinds of questions that drive stories: *suspense* questions, which look forward to the future (consequences) for their answers, and *mystery* questions, which look back into the past (causes) for their answers. In other words, *suspense* questions are about *what is going to happen*, and mystery questions are questions about *what has happened*. A novel may include both, of course. You may neither know whether the bomb is going to go off (you want to find out what *will* happen – this is suspense) nor who planted the bomb (you want to find out what *has* happened – this is mystery). The way that you manage to raise and answer questions in your story is central to the way the story unfolds.

Beginnings, middles and ends

Aristotle, *Poetics*

'A beginning is that which does not itself follow anything by causal necessity, but after which something naturally is or comes to be. An end, on the contrary, is that which itself naturally follows some other thing, either by necessity, or as a rule, but has nothing following it. A middle is that which follows something as some other thing follows it.'

In *Poetics*, Aristotle writes that every plot should have a beginning, a middle and an end. This is another way of saying that, at the point of entry into the story, the major questions should be set up; at the point of exit, the major questions should be resolved or responded to; and in the middle of the story, the questions should be deepened, complicated or multiplied.

Beginnings	Middles	Ends
Raising or *posing* questions	*Deepening, complicating* or *multiplying* questions	*Resolving* or *answering* questions

Many writers I know, when they are writing novels, have strong ideas for the beginnings of their books – an image, a character, a situation. They also often have strong ideas about the ends of their books. They know where they want to end up. But how they are going to get from A to B is a different matter. There is some wisdom in this. If you have *only* a beginning, then you can wander off writing chapter after chapter, and never know whether you have got where you want to go. If you have *only* an end, then you can spend your time writing draft after draft of Chapter 1 and never getting any further. But if you have *both* beginning *and* end, then you have a clear itinerary that you have to take as a writer. You can settle into the ride, and have fun exploring the various ways of getting from A to B.

Focus point

One good starting point for building a plot is by clearly establishing both a *beginning* and an *end*. Often the middle can look after itself.

Let's now look at beginnings, middles and ends in more depth.

BEGINNINGS

There are people who claim that the first sentence of a book – the beginning of the beginning – is very, very important indeed, that somehow you need to make the first sentence so spectacularly wonderful that the reader is left gasping for breath. The first sentence, some people claim, needs to 'grab' the reader, needs to make them sit bolt upright in their chair, needs to astonish them so that they keep on reading.

Openings like this, whether sentences or paragraphs, are sometimes referred to as 'narrative hooks'. But while a good opening sentence can be wonderful and satisfying, I think that this tendency to over-emphasize the job of the first sentence, or even the first paragraph, is a mistake. Have a look at the following first sentences, culled more or less at random from the selection of books on my bookshelves.

- 'The summer she was fifteen, Melanie discovered she was made of flesh and blood.' (Angela Carter, *The Magic Toyshop*)

- 'At almost one o'clock I entered the lobby of the building where I worked and turned toward the escalators, carrying a black Penguin paperback and a small white CVS bag, its receipt stapled over the top.' (Nicholson Baker, *The Mezzanine*)

- 'What do you pack for the rest of your life?' (Lionel Shriver, *So Much for That*)

- 'It was an early, very warm morning in July, and it had rained during the night.' (Tove Jansson, *The Summer Book*)

- 'As Gregor Samsa awoke one morning from uneasy dreams he found himself transformed in his bed into a gigantic insect.' (Franz Kafka, *Metamorphosis*)

What you will notice is that some of these are startling or surprising and hook you in immediately. The Kafka opening sentence is breathtakingly strange. The Lionel Shriver sentence raises intriguing questions about what is to follow. The Angela Carter sentence is both rich and earthy. But not all these opening sentences 'hook' us in quite so determinedly. Tove Jansson's opening sentence is matter-of-fact, almost plain. Meanwhile, Nicholson Baker's opening sentence is deliberately, determinedly banal. Not all of these opening sentences could be called 'narrative hooks'. But all of them do the same job. That job is not to grab the reader by the lapels and yell into their face that they are in the presence of literary gold, nor is it to announce the book with a brash and abrasive fanfare. Instead, the job of the first sentence is simply this: to get the reader to read the second sentence. And the job of the second sentence is to get the reader to read the third sentence. And so it goes on until you get to the very last sentence of all. Some stories start with a bang, some with astonishing understatement. To get a feel for how different novelists deal with the problem of beginnings, try the following exercise.

Write: beginnings

Go to the library or a bookshop (online or bricks and mortar) and pick five or six novels off the shelves at random. *Go for novels that you have not read before.* Do not read the blurb on the cover. Copy out the first sentences. Do not read any further! Now answer these questions:

- What mood does the first sentence set up?
- From reading the first sentence, what expectations do you have as a reader?
- What do you already know about the kind of book that this is?
- Now take one of the sentences that interests you most and continue to write the remainder of a first chapter that could follow from this sentence.
- Finally, go back to the original book and read the first chapter in the original. How does your first chapter differ in mood, genre or feel?

Whether you use a narrative 'hook' or not, whether you start with a bang or with a murmur, by the time the reader has read a few pages, you should have raised a few questions in their mind, questions that will interest them enough to keep on reading. And of course, it is worth remembering that this will depend in part on your readers and the genre you are writing in: not all kinds of questions are interesting to all kinds of readers.

If you have succeeded in raising some powerful and intriguing questions at the beginning of your book, and if you have judged your audience well, then very soon your readers will find themselves in the thick of things, in the *middle*.

MIDDLES

 Russell Hoban, *Riddley Walker*

'But you never wil get to see the woal of any thing youre all ways in the middl of it living it or moving thru it.'

When it comes to the middle of your book, you have an awful lot of leeway. You have opened up some initial questions, but you are a long way from your destination. Even if you know where you are going to end up, there are a great many ways to get there.

The middle of your story is where you can deepen, complicate or multiply the stories you are telling. It is where a lot of the richness in fiction happens. One of the ways in which this deepening, complication and multiplication can take place is through the transformations in what your characters desire, and how they go about realizing (or failing to realize) these desires. If the questions that you set up at the beginning of your story are questions about what your characters *want* and whether they can get what they want, what gives your story a middle is *conflict*.

The easiest way of thinking about conflict in a story is that it is the thing that gets in the way of a character getting what they want.

 Focus point

Conflict is the thing that stops a character getting what they want.

Conflict is not necessarily about *confrontation*. Instead, it is the thing that gives a story its twists and turns. Think of the following story: 'Yesterday, I wanted a sandwich, so I bought one and ate one.' What's wrong with this story is that there's no middle. There's no gap between wanting the sandwich and getting it. Similarly, 'Yesterday, I wanted a sandwich, but I didn't have one' is not much of a story either. You need some complicating factors between the wanting and its resolution. 'Yesterday, I wanted a sandwich, but when I went to the shop I found my wallet had been stolen…' sets up a conflict. I want a sandwich, but something (my stolen wallet) is getting in the way of me getting what I want. From here, the story can go in all kinds of directions.

One way of seeing how you can cut dead passages in your work is by asking whether there is any desire or conflict, or whether your character is just mooning around. Look particularly hard at any sections of your book where characters are drinking coffee or tea, watching TV or going for a walk. We all know that people do these things; but what is it about this cup of coffee or tea, this evening watching TV, this walk, that makes it worth telling us about it?

Edit: in want of wanting

If you have already written some of your novel, go through the text and mark any scenes in which your characters seem to be just wandering around, but in which they don't really want anything. If your characters don't want anything, then these scenes will not have any conflict.

Ask yourself what these scenes add to the book. Do they help the story, or are they just playing for time or filling space? Are they serving another purpose, unrelated to plot, desire or conflict?

If you think that the scene needs to be modified, there are two ways in which you might be able to improve things:

1 Cut the scene altogether
2 Look more deeply at the scene and introduce an element of desire.

Remember that desire can be for something quite simple but that, if there is no desire, and hence no conflict, your audience may have difficulty maintaining their interest.

Conflict can be of several kinds. Here is an overview.

Kind of conflict	Example
External/physical	I want to go outside, but a landslide has blocked the door.
Interpersonal	I want to go outside, but you want to stop me.
Internal or psychological	I want to go outside, but I am afraid of what I might find.

Some kinds of conflict can be present alongside each other: if I am climbing Everest, for example, this may be both an internal conflict (my desire struggles against my fear of heights) and external conflict (I am physically struggling with Everest itself). It may also be interpersonal (I am on an Everest tour with somebody with whom I don't get on). This layering of different kinds of conflict often makes a story much more richly interesting. Think, for example, of a detective novel about a police detective who is trying to solve the mystery of a strange, ritual murder of a society heiress. There's one set of conflicts there already – the detective wants to solve the crime, but there are various things that get in his way. Now think about how it could be made more complex. Perhaps the detective is also struggling with a drinking habit (the old 'wrestling with his demons' story…). Perhaps he is wanting to retire and take up stamp collecting, but has been persuaded to stay for this one last case (the old 'too good to retire' story…). Perhaps he has a distaste for high society and so, alongside his desire to solve the crime, he is wrestling with his hatred of society heiresses and all their ilk. Whatever way you play it, it is clear that already the story has taken on a greater degree of complexity.

When actually *writing*, don't worry too much about this classification of different kinds of conflict. But if your writing goes a bit dead, ask yourself the following questions:

- Where is the desire?
- Where is the conflict?
- Can these conflicts be deepened, multiplied or made richer?

Conflict eventually leads to some kind of transformation or resolution. Not all the transformations that arise out of conflict are resolutions: some *deepen* or *multiply* the conflicts.

Focus point

One way of thinking of the basic unit of plot is as follows:

Desire → Conflict → Transformation

There are various kinds of transformation. Either your character gets what they want, or they don't get what they want, or they get only one of the different things they want, or else they get something *entirely different and unexpected* (whether welcome or unwelcome). In tragedy, of course, they get precisely what they were trying to avoid: Oedipus really doesn't want to kill his father and sleep with his mother; but that is that he ends up doing.

Write: a simple conflict scene

Try writing a conflict scene. Imagine that one character wants something objective and physical from the other. Meanwhile, the *other* character wants something intangible from the first. For example, Patsy wants Mike's chips, but Mike wants Patsy's heart. Now write about this conflict. Take two names, take two desires, and let the character and the story emerge from this.

ENDINGS

If the opening of your book sets up the problems and questions, and if the middle of your book complicates them, deepens them and multiplies them, by the end of your book you may want to have found a resolution for some of the major conflicts in your story.

Anton Chekhov once reportedly said – although it is hard to actually find a credible source for this – that if you introduce a gun in the first act (setting up a problem at the beginning), then by the end of the second act it should have gone off. This principle has since become known as 'Chekhov's Gun'. Some novelists follow Chekhov's Gun precisely, extending it to include not only the gun but every single object that they mention. I recently read a crime novel where *everything* had a part to play. When the heroine saw a rickety fire-escape and thought 'I wouldn't like to escape down there in a fire,' it was clear that by the end she would have to run for her life down those precarious steps. When she saw a cleaver in the kitchen, and admired the cook's ability with a whetstone, it was clear that by the end somebody would be getting the chop. The book was from one point of view an impressive piece of craftsmanship. But it was also a bit frustrating, because I read it with the growing sense that *life isn't like this*, that everything was just a bit *too* tidy, and the foreshadowing was too neat. On the other hand, there are books that are so loosely constructed (as life itself is loosely constructed) that, although they have a rich sense of life, by the end they feel somewhat unsatisfying because there is no real *shape* to the way the author has raised and answered questions.

My own feeling is this: with most novels, at least the *major* questions raised at the beginning should be addressed and the *major* conflicts should reach some kind of resolution.

Focus point

In most novels, the major questions raised in the first half will be addressed by the end and the major conflicts will reach a resolution.

Before moving on from endings, it is worth also saying something about two specific plotting problems. The first is the device known as *deus ex machina* and the second is what I call the 'problem-solving bloodbath'.

Deus ex machina

This literally means, in Latin, 'the god from the machine'. The machine was a device used in ancient Greek drama by means of which an actor, playing the part of a god, could be winched down on to the stage to resolve all the problems in the plot. Euripides was a particular fan of this approach. What this means in the contemporary setting is an ending in which something entirely outside the story turns up in the last few pages to resolve all the problems in the plot.

Aristotle disapproved of this kind of thing, as did the Roman poet Horace. But you can get away with it if you know what you are doing or if you are using it knowingly, perhaps for parodic effect.

The problem-solving bloodbath

What I mean by 'problem-solving bloodbath' is that your novel ends with an unanticipated and random act of violence that solves all the problems you have carefully set up in the beginning. It is fine, of course, to end your novel in a bloodbath, if this bloodbath is necessitated by everything that has gone before. If, on the other hand, this is a desperate measure to kill off your characters before they realize that they are living inside a story that is too full of contradictions to bear, then you should avoid this approach at all costs. This attempt to solve your problems by ultra-violence is, in a way, a form of *deus ex machina*. The final burst of excitement may be briefly engaging for the reader, but if you have not really addressed the questions your novel has raised, your readers will leave your book unsatisfied.

Workshop: thinking through plot

This workshop applies some of the ideas in this chapter to the plot of your own novel. There are two different tasks in this workshop, which follow more or less logically from each other. However, it is up to you to decide whether to do them both together or whether to treat them separately. This will depend, once again, upon the way you work as a novelist. If you have a full manuscript, this might take a morning's work.

1 Raising and addressing questions

Use a table like the one below to help you think through the process of raising and responding to questions in your novel. I recommend that you draw up your own table, as you will almost certainly need more than four rows.

What question is raised?	In which chapter?	How is it addressed?	In which chapter?	How important is this question (1–5)?

The way to use the table is this:

- In the first column, write down the questions that you are raising for the reader.
- In the second column, write down the chapter in which the questions are raised.
- In the third column, write down how the questions are addressed/resolved.
- In the fourth column, write down the chapter in which they are addressed/resolved.
- In the final column, write down how important these questions are to the story (with 5 being 'very important' and 1 being 'not very important').

This should give you a map of the overlapping questions in your book. If your book is not divided into chapters, you can work through your book by page number, or else by section or by scene. Feel free to adapt the exercise to suit your circumstances.

Remember that addressing a question does not mean answering it. It could mean returning to the question with a deeper sense of its significance and mystery.

2 Troubleshooting plot for consistency, coherence and concreteness

We saw in the chapter on world-building that a well-built world needs consistency, coherence and concreteness. These three aspects can also be applied to plot. Go through your plot outline (if you have completed the first task, then the table you have produced will function as a fairly detailed outline), and ask yourself the following questions:

- *Is your plot consistent?* Is this the kind of thing that could happen in this world? Are there any happenings or events that don't fit with the world you are building? Are the desires consistent with what we know about the characters?
- *Is your plot coherent?* Do things happen for plausible reasons? Can the reader make sense of why people are reacting in the way that they are? Is there anything that feels arbitrary?
- *Is your plot concrete?* Are you clear what the events in your plot are? Do you know what it is that your characters are doing? Do you know they are doing it? Are you clear why? Have you got concrete reasons for the conflicts that are taking place?

We have looked at consistency, coherence and concreteness in the context of your novel's *world*; but this exercise focuses not just on how the world is constructed but on how *events unfold* in this world. If you have completed the first step in this workshop, you might be able to simply go through your table row by row, making sure that you are confident that *all* the plot questions are responded to in a fashion that maintains the consistency, coherence and concreteness of your fictional world.

Where to next?

All these questions about motivation and desire naturally lead us on to the question of character. Character is, according to Aristotle, the next most important thing after plot. So in the following chapter we will move on to talk about how you might go about writing about other people.

8

The basics of character

Human beings are natural gossips. We are extremely interested in other people. We are interested in what makes them tick. We exchange information about others as a kind of social grooming. Gossip may be ignoble, but it makes us feel *good.* This natural propensity towards nosiness and gossip may be a large part of why we spend so much time immersing ourselves in stories about people who don't exist and never have existed: we are naturally attuned to take an interest in others.

Fiction is first and foremost about *other people* and about how they make sense of the world. This is why the way you write about the other people in your novel matters. For Aristotle, character is second in line to plot in terms of what is most important in the telling of a story. For some novelists, this is reversed, and character is the centre of the story, while plot takes a back seat. In the rich ecosystem of fiction, there is room for both character-centred stories and plot-centred stories; but wherever you fall on this continuum, you will need to think about how to write convincingly and compellingly about the people who populate the world of your novel.

Characters and caricatures

In this chapter I will be talking about 'characters' because this is the way that this aspect of writing fiction is usually discussed; but there are problems with thinking about the business of writing about people as writing about *characters*.

Ernest Hemingway, *Death in the Afternoon*

'*When writing a novel a writer should create living people; people not characters. A character is a caricature.*'

In this chapter and the one that follows I'm interested in explaining how it is possible to create 'living people' in the world of your novel. Although I'm going to use the term 'character' out of convention, what I am going to be talking about is how to draw upon the experience we have of living people so that we can populate our fictional worlds with people who will live in the minds of our readers.

Who is my story about? Protagonists and antagonists

In the jargon often associated with fiction writing, a 'protagonist' refers to your major character or characters. This term comes from the Greek word *protagonistes*, which means 'most important actor'. The word for 'actor' here derives from the term *agon*, meaning 'contest' or 'struggle'. So a protagonist is the character whose struggle is central to your novel. An *antagonist*, on the other hand, is one who your protagonist struggles *against*, the word coming from the Greek *antagonistes*.

Key idea

A protagonist is a major character whose struggles and desires are central to your novel. An *antagonist* is a character who stands in the way of your protagonist's desires.

It is always a good idea to ask yourself: *Who is my story about?* It may be that your story is about several people. This is fine. You may protest that your story is not, at root, about any one person. You may say that it is about a big idea like the birth of a nation, or the struggle between freedom and order, or the moral consequences of unfettered capitalism. And this is fine, too; but generally speaking, these themes will be explored by telling the stories of *people* who are giving birth to nations, or navigating between freedom and order, or wrestling with these moral consequences.

Snapshot: who is my story about?

First, write down the names of up to seven of the major characters in your book. Now try the following exercise.

- Try to identify who the *main protagonist* is, if you have one (you may not – in which case, don't worry. Not all novels need one).
- If you do not have a single main protagonist, try to identify who are the major protagonists and who are the minor protagonists in your novel.
- Jot down the primary desires of these major protagonists.

If you try this exercise and you find that you are not sure what your characters want, or you are not sure who the story is about, you may want to think through your story again to bring these things into focus.

Focus point

Even if your novel tackles big philosophical, political or social themes or ideas, what matters most is how these ideas are played out in the lives of individuals.

How many protagonists?

A novel need not have a single protagonist. Your novel may be a straightforward story of one person's journey. You can think of this kind of novel as being rather like a portrait painting. But a novel may equally well be like one of those big canvasses that seethes with hundreds of individuals all going about their business. Either way, you will need to think about how you will manage the storytelling; and the challenges are different with each.

SINGLE PROTAGONISTS

Many stories take this form. The main protagonist need not be a 'hero'. Some protagonists are much more deeply strange, unsettling and flawed. Your protagonist may be involved in external struggles, or their conflicts may be almost entirely internal. But if you can say firmly that your story is about one individual, then you have a story with a single protagonist.

The advantage of having a single protagonist is that the unfolding of your story will have a clear thread. If we engage sufficiently with the protagonist, we will want to follow this thread to the end. The disadvantage is that – in fiction as in life – it is possible to tire of one person.

Focus point

The challenge of a story with a single protagonist is maintaining the reader's sense of engagement, intrigue and interest in this character.

We have already raised the question of whether the reader should sympathize with, or even *like*, your main protagonist. Again, whether your protagonist is likeable or unlikeable is not the main issue. What is important is whether what happens to your protagonist matters to the reader.

Conversations with Don DeLillo

'I don't feel sympathetic toward some characters, unsympathetic toward others. I don't love some characters, feel contempt for others. They have attitudes; I don't.'

What matters to a reader is seeing the consequences of the protagonist's actions, and seeing how their desires are played out in the world in which they live.

MULTIPLE PROTAGONISTS

You can have more than one protagonist but, if you do, you will need to manage the switch in focus from one to the other.

Focus point

The challenge in a story with multiple protagonists is that of making your story coherent, and drawing together these multiple threads into something that feels like a unity.

Multiple protagonists might be bound together very tightly. It might be that their various desires are tangled up with one another and that they are immersed in the same plot. They may be mutual antagonists and have mutually conflicting desires, or else they may all be struggling for the same goal. But the relationship between different protagonists – and hence different plots – may be more subtle. It is possible to write a novel with stories that do not so much intersect as *echo* one another, in the way that separate strings on a musical instrument set one another vibrating.

There is nothing to stop your novel being braided together out of three completely distinct, but parallel, stories that take place in separate worlds. It is still a novel if it holds together enough, and is written convincingly enough, for your readers to *believe* that it is a novel.

Sometimes you may find that a character wanders into your novel for one reason or another, but at the redrafting stage you realize that they don't really belong there. If this is the case, you should cut them out. If they are an interesting enough character, they will wander back eventually – in a short story, or perhaps even in a novel of their own.

Snapshot: thinking about multiple protagonists

If your novel has multiple protagonists, ask yourself the following questions:

- How tightly interlinked are your protagonists' stories? Are they loosely knit, or are they woven together more tightly?
- How can you maintain your readers' interest in all these protagonists simultaneously?
- Are some protagonists more important than others? How do you want to reflect this in the way you tell your story?
- Are there any protagonists who do not belong in this story?

Character and world

At this point it may be useful to take a couple of steps back; because the question of *who* your story is about is intimately related to the question of *where* your story takes place. Character and world exist together. None of us exists in a vacuum. Our characters, our desires, our hopes, our beliefs and our behaviour are shaped by the world of which we are a part.

The people we are, and the people we become, are the products of a particular kind of environment. Our desires are both fashioned and constrained by the world in which we find ourselves. If I want to become a novelist, it is because I live in a world in which both novelists and novels exist. It is because I live in a world in which it seems to me that being a novelist might be a worthwhile thing, a world in which being a novelist *means* something. This is not to say that characters cannot *change* the world of which they are a part: they can, either in dramatic ways or in ways that are far more subtle. But it is important to remember that there is a symbiotic connection between character and world.

Key idea

Your characters are free to act, desire and make decisions, but only in the context of the world that you have built for them.

For you as a novelist, this means that when you are thinking about character, you need to do this in the context of the world that you are building. The desire to become a monk or nun might be a relatively common desire in the world of medieval Europe that Umberto Eco writes about in *The Name of the Rose*; but in the contemporary Western world it is rather more unexpected. The world of which we are a part both *offers us* choices and also *constrains* our choices.

One of things that can make a character unconvincing in a novel is when it feels as if the character doesn't *belong* to the world of the novel, and has instead just been plonked down in the middle of a world that is little more than a stage set for the character's desires. If you want your characters' desires to convincing, they need to be grow organically out of your fictional world. Try the following exercise to help draw out some of these connections between your characters' desires and the world in which they find themselves.

Write: the origins of desire

Take either your main character or one of your major characters. Ask yourself what it is that your character wants above all else.

Now write down two incidents in the past that have contributed to your character desiring this. These don't need to be in the novel itself.

If neither of these incidents appears in your novel, then write short scenes exploring these incidents in more detail. You don't have to use these in your novel, but they will help you investigate your character in more depth.

Where characters come from: inventing and drawing from life

So where do fictional characters come from? How do you go about beginning to bring to life characters on the page? There may be all kinds of starting points that you find for your characters. The Indonesian yeti-smuggling protagonist of my first novel came out of a chance meeting with a curious English entrepreneur adrift in East Indonesia, where he was planning to set up a factory manufacturing nutmeg soap. The protagonist of my second novel, the saint Ivan Gelski, came out of an image that I dreamed up one day of an Orthodox icon of a saint holding a guitar, his hands raised in a gesture of prayer. Meanwhile, the protagonist of my third novel came direct from Greek myth. Your characters may arise organically and almost mysteriously out of the world that you have built. They may be based upon people you know, or chance encounters that you have. They may be based quite closely on your own experience. They may be imagined or dreamed. Or they may arise out of literature, art, story or myth. But however they arise, all characters are built out of a combination of invention and experience.

Key idea

All fictional characters are based upon *both* experience *and* invention.

'ALL CHARACTERS ARE THE AUTHOR IN DISGUISE'

Because all characters draw upon a novelist's own experience, sometimes people assume that all characters are somehow the author in thinly veiled disguise. If you write a book with first-person narration, people will assume that the narrator is you, particularly if you write a book about a protagonist who is roughly your age and gender, and whose life is a little like your own. Even if your character is totally unlike you, you may have readers assuming that this character is the *real* you, your shadow-side. There is no way around this. If you write a novel in which there is a first-person serial-killer narrator, people will regard you with suspicion. You can either resist this, or embrace it. A friend of mine, the crime writer Jane Adams, introduces herself by saying, 'Hello, I'm Jane, and I kill people for a living.'

However, if you find that your first novel mirrors your life a bit *too* closely, you might want to play with increasing the distance between yourself and your character. As the writer of your story, you need to feel *free* to invent, and to follow the story where it needs to go. Being too slavishly autobiographical can give you less room to move.

Focus point

If the story that you are telling is quite closely autobiographical, one way of getting a bit more distance can be by writing in the third person rather than in the first person.

'I BET YOU'LL PUT ME IN ONE OF YOUR NOVELS…'

Sometimes, if people find out that you are writing a novel, they will confide in you and tell you their own stories, suggesting that you might want to write about them. Just as readers may assume that characters in your novels are *you*, they may also assume that you are writing about *them*. And, to some extent, you may be. This can be problematic, and it is worth being aware of the difficulties that this might cause.

If you draw upon real-life characters for writing your fictional story, you need to be very careful: you could risk falling out with people or, even worse, a libel case (there is more on libel law later on in this book).

Legal and ethical complications aside, there is another reason why you might not want to draw too closely upon life. In the same way that writing about characters that are too closely based upon your own life can be restrictive, so can writing about characters that are modelled too closely upon people you know. If you don't allow enough room for invention, your characters may be less full and less convincing.

Key idea

Regardless of how closely your characters are based upon real people, they need to be fully imagined within the context of your fictional world, independent of their existence in real life.

FICTIONAL EXCESS

There is another question about invention and drawing from life, and that is the question of how *realistic* your characters should be. It is often said that characters in novels need to be more starkly drawn than in real life, and that novels are a kind of heightened reality so that we can see things more clearly.

But sometimes the problem with fiction is simply that it is insufficiently alive to the strangeness and complexity of everyday life. Life itself is often pretty starkly drawn. People *are* strange and absurd and multifaceted and endlessly fascinating and – most of them, at least – deeply weird. There can be something glorious about fictional excess, something compelling and entertaining about taking the strange, absurd or unsettling aspects of everyday existence, and cranking them up to the highest degree. On the other hand, sometimes it can be a better strategy not to *heighten* reality so much as draw out aspects of reality that are already there.

Flat and round characters

This leads us to the famous distinction made by the novelist E.M. Forster in his book *Aspects of the Novel* between 'flat' and 'round' characters. This is a distinction that has been so often quoted that it has almost become a cliché. For Forster, 'flat' characters have only two dimensions: they have no *fullness*. They are cardboard cut-outs. 'Round' characters, on the other hand, have a dimension of depth and complexity.

 ## E.M. Forster, *Aspects of the Novel*

'We may divide characters into flat and round. Flat characters were called "humorous" in the seventeenth century, and are sometimes called types, and sometimes caricatures. In their purest form, they are constructed round a single idea or quality; when there is more than one factor in them, we get the beginning of the curve towards the round.'

What does it mean to say that a character is flat or has no depth? I think that what Forster means is that a flat character has no psychological complexity. We know how a flat character will respond in any circumstances. A flat character is like a dog that will always bark when it hears an intruder, or a police chief who always lights his pipe and sighs wearily when he is called to the site of a murder. Whatever situation a flat character is in, we know how they will respond.

You might think from this that you should avoid flatness; but Forster points out that, in fictional worlds, flatness has some uses. Flat characters are easy to recognize and are also often memorable. They are useful shorthands. And our *experience* of many people in the world is often very flat. There are many transactions that we undergo in the world in which we don't want or need a sense of the psychological complexity of the people with whom we are dealing. We want the bus driver to sell us a ticket, and we want to swiftly move on. The bus driver probably wants this as well. We don't want to know her entire life story, the reason for the scar on her cheek, or the fact that she is studying for a PhD in law in her spare time. All of this is interesting, but we don't have the capacity to take this level of interest in everybody we meet. Similarly, we don't want everybody to take this level of interest in *us*.

E.M. Forster, *Aspects of the Novel*

'The test of a round character is whether it is capable of surprising in a convincing way. If it never surprises, it is flat.'

In a work of fiction, we don't necessarily need to know this stuff about the bus driver who appears briefly on page thirty-seven, or the lawyer who clears her throat on page one hundred and nineteen and then never reappears: often we don't *want* these characters to surprise us. Nevertheless, a book with *only* flat characters will, Forster points out, be a book that lacks surprises.

Key idea

You don't want all your characters to be 'flat' but, just as we experience some people in the world as deep and complex, and some simply in terms of surface impressions, so also in your novel you can have a mix of flat and round characters.

Snapshot: flat and round

Make a list of all the characters in your novel in descending order of importance, with the most important first. If it is a very complicated novel, then make a list only of those characters who play a larger part in the story. When ranking your characters in order of importance, you do not have to be too precise.

Now give each character a score from one to five, as follows:

1   Very flat (one-dimensional, not complex at all)
2   Flat (not much complexity)
3   Neither particularly flat nor particularly round
4   Rounded (somewhat complex)
5   Very rounded (extremely complex).

Again, don't agonize too much about this; just go with your instinct.

Write the scores next to the characters' names. You should find that your scores tend to descend as you work down the list. Look for any anomalies. If there are any major characters who score highly for flatness, or minor characters who seem very rounded, then ask yourself whether you need to make any adjustments.

Remember, however, not to make changes mechanically. As always, you should go with your own best judgement when revising your work.

Unless you are making a satirical point, your major characters probably (note that I say 'probably') need a degree of roundness and complexity. If your major characters are simply a hero and a villain, and if the hero is relentlessly heroic and the villain relentlessly villainous, then your book may fail to intrigue the reader. There is no doubt that there are acts of heroism and of villainy within the world; and some of the greatest fiction is about these acts. But when you start to look more deeply, it seems that there is nobody who one can *reliably* depend upon to always act out of villainy, or who one can *reliably* depend upon to always act out of heroism. Indeed, a villain who is also capable of exhibiting acts of great kindness is a *more* unsettling villain than a villain who is simply evil in all respects.

Character and desire

We have already seen in the chapter on plot that desire is the driving and shaping force of plot. In relation to character, we should ask how we know what a character's desires actually are. Here we can see that things are rather complex. We can infer desires from *observation*. Characters can *communicate* their desires. Characters may also be aware of their desires through *introspection*, whether or not they communicate these desires. Finally, they may have desires of which they themselves are unaware, or which they have not acknowledged, but which nevertheless impel them to act in certain ways. There is a lot of scope here for complexity and for conflict. Desire does not have to be explicitly communicated. Not only this, but our desires are also not always apparent, either to ourselves or to others, nor are they always internally consistent.

DESIRE AND MOTIVATION

Desire is also related to motivation: if desire is *what* we want, motivation is *why* we want it. It is sometimes said that fiction writers need to be very clear about their characters' motivations; but motivations are often murky and multifarious. The fact of *wanting* is often very clear, but the question of why we might want what we want is often more difficult to establish.

 Key idea

Desire is a question of what I want to do. Motivation is a question of why I want to do it.

Sometimes you can use motivation as a strong plot device. We can know who the killer is from page 1, but we don't know *why* they killed. The exploration of the question *why* could take up the entire novel.

But even if a whole novel was about finding a character's motivation, by the end things could still be inconclusive. All of our actions are conditioned by countless things that have gone before. We are often unclear about the reasons why we act in the way that we do. We make up our reasons and our motivations, very often, after the event. So don't assume that your characters are accurate judges of the reasons behind their actions. They may be decidedly bad judges of their own natures.

A note on names

Annie Dillard

'Naming your characters Aristotle and Plato is not going to make their relationship interesting unless you make it so on the page.'

Another thing to think about is how you should name your characters. Different names have different resonances, and so you need to have a keen ear to make sure that the names you use have the right connotations. If you are stuck with names, then search the Internet for random name generators. Some writing tools like Scrivener (www. literatureandlatte.com) have built in random name generators. Whatever name you give your characters, make sure that you do your research so that the name is plausible and suits the character.

If you decide to change the name of your character at the last minute, a quick 'search-and-replace' might do it. But beware: there is a possibly apocryphal story about a writer who changed her character's name from David to Jeff using search-and-replace. She then sent the manuscript off to her editor. She got a reply several days later, asking her to clarify the reference to 'Michelangelo's "Jeff"'.

Snapshot: what's in a name?

Use a randomizing method to come up with several characters' names. You can either use one of the tools mentioned above or else, if you have an old-style telephone book to hand, you can flip it open and choose a name at random. Select four or five names overall and write them down.

Read all the names out loud several times. Then choose only one as a starting point.

Now think about who would have such a name. Are they male or female? How old are they? How do they spend their time? Where do they live? If you want to look up the history or the meaning of the name, feel free; but keep research to a minimum: this exercise is about how names can provoke the imagination, and not about research.

Give yourself 5–10 minutes to allow your imagination to play with the name. Make notes as you go along. Then write a very short story about this character. Allow 15–20 minutes.

When you have finished, reflect upon the connection between the name of the character and the story. What is it about the character's name that suggested this story, and not another?

Workshop: characters, time and history

This workshop is about how you can anchor your characters in the fictional world of which they are a part. If you have many characters, it can be hard to keep track of what they are up to, or to maintain a good overview of their interrelationships. This simple workshop aims to give you this overview. You might want to give a couple of hours to completing the workshop. It might be more or less, depending on the complexity of your novel.

1 Timelines

One way that you can do this is by making a timeline for your story, with a focus upon your characters. There are quite a few specialist tools that can be used to do this, some of which are mentioned in the Resources section at the end of this book; but often just a hand-drawn calendar, table, diagram or spreadsheet can do the trick. If you are doing it this way, you can put important dates down the side, and names of characters (if you know them already) along the top. My second novel, *The Descent of the Lyre*, was set in nineteenth-century Bulgaria and France. Part of the timeline looked like this (the original was rather more elaborate, but this is provided just as an example). Two of the characters named here – Karl Töpfer and Fernando Sor – are historical characters, so I built the story around what I knew of their history.

Dates	Historical events	Ivan Gelski	Fernando Sor	Karl Töpfer
1778			Born	
1791				Born
1794	Selim III on Ottoman Throne	Born		
1808	Mahmud on Ottoman Throne. Napoleon in Spain			
1810				In Breslau
1811		Bride-to-be kidnapped		
1812	Napoleon's Russian campaign	Becomes a bandit		
1813	Napoleon's armies leave Spain		Exiled in France	
1815			Moves to London	
1816				Performing in Vienna
1823		In Vienna, studies with Karl Töpfer	Leaves for Russia with dancer Félicité Hullin	Takes on Ivan Gelski as a pupil
1826	Mahmud eliminates Janissary corps	Leaves for Paris	Returns to France with Félicité	
...	...	...	...	

If you do an electronic version of your timeline, it is very easy to add extra dates, or extra characters, just by adding rows or columns.

This should give you a *framework* to allow you to think about your characters and how they are situated in time and space. It should also allow you to maintain consistency by cross-referencing entries. So if character A meets character B at a certain point, then we know that character B must meet character A at the same point.

2 Character biographies

Now that you have a sketch of some important moments in your characters' lives, imagine that you are writing a biographical dictionary entry for each your major characters. Select up to five characters and for each of them write a 300- to 500-word biography, focusing on the major aspects of their lives. Even if this does not enter into the novel, make sure that you give both birth dates and dates of death, so you have a sense of your characters' lives *as a whole*.

Where to next?

Now that we have looked at the basics of character, we are ready to go a little deeper. The next chapter explores the question of how we can know characters – through observation, communication, direct experience and introspection – and what this means for the craft of creating credible actors in the world of your story.

9

Knowing your characters

This chapter is about going deeper into the question of how to create fictional characters. We will be looking, in particular, at the question of what it means to *know* your characters. Sometimes writing textbooks say that you should know your characters *inside out*, that you should know absolutely everything about them: you should know what they have for breakfast, what they dream about, what their deepest desires are, and so on. But there is something decidedly unconvincing about the idea that you could know *anybody* inside out like this. If you find yourself having a *complete* knowledge of the people who populate your fictional world, then it is likely that your characters will feel closer to caricatures than to real living people. And if knowledge of other people is at best only ever partial, this applies also *within* the world of your novel, which means that *no character* in your book should expect to completely know and understand any other character.

W. Somerset Maugham, *The Summing Up*

'People are hard to know.'

Complete knowledge of your characters is not necessary. To fully know someone would be to know in advance how they might respond in every single context or situation. It would mean having a complete understanding of their past, possessing a total knowledge of their desires and motivations, and having a complete understanding of what they might do in any possible situation. But we struggle knowing these things even about ourselves. This, of course, is why we find ourselves saying things like 'What was I *doing* last night?', or 'That wasn't like me', or 'I don't know what got into me', or 'I hadn't thought that I was capable of doing *that*.' Those things that might seem most intimate to us – our mental activity, the bubbling cauldron of our own desires, motivations and wishes – are often obscure to us.

When it comes to writing, all you need is to know your characters well enough to be able to tell their stories as best you can. If their stories involve breakfast, then you should think about what they eat for breakfast. But, for many stories, this knowledge will not be particularly relevant or interesting.

 Key idea

You do not need to completely know your characters. You only need to know enough to be able to tell their stories.

To say that we cannot know our characters fully isn't to say that we cannot know them at all. Nor is it to say that we shouldn't attempt to get to know them better: in literature as in life, it pays to know who you are doing business with. But this knowledge will never be entirely complete.

There are four ways in which we can know fictional characters and communicate this knowledge to readers. These are: *observation, communication, direct experience* and *introspection*.

 Focus point

There are four main ways that we can get to know people:
- We get to know other people by 1) *observation* and 2) *communication*.
- In addition, we also get to know ourselves by 3) *direct experience* and 4) *introspection*.

This chapter will explore each of these in turn. As a writer, you have a certain freedom that you don't have in the everyday world. You can view characters both from the inside (by taking a first-person perspective on their experiences or by eavesdropping on their introspection) and from the outside (by seeing how others observe them or through observing their dialogue and communication with others). This allows for a considerable richness, flexibility and freedom of movement when exploring the various dimensions of your characters.

Knowledge from outside I: observation

Observation is one of the main ways that you can establish a character firmly in your readers' minds. Don't think about *description* so much as *paying attention* to how your character's distinctive traits, characteristics and ways of being unfold within your fictional world. Descriptions belong in police reports; but stories require a different kind of attention. Often, you can keep actual description to a minimum. In novels, a large part of how we come to know fictional characters lies not so much in long descriptions of their outward appearance but in seeing how they act and react, physically, mentally and emotionally. Through seeing them responding and acting in the face of the things the world throws at them, we understand what kind of people they are.

The closeness with which you describe your characters is, in part, a matter of personal choice. Thinking of an analogy with the visual arts, it is possible to draw a likeness of somebody with a few swift lines of the pen; but it is also possible to capture a likeness in much more meticulous detail. If, every time you introduce a character, you launch into a seven-page description, then you are going to stretch your readers' patience. There are better ways of going about observation of character. Think about the things that stand out, the things that single this character out from other characters. And think how through the action of the story we can learn more about any particular character: their appearance, the kind of person they are, their desires and drives and quirks.

When observing your characters, there are a number of things to pay attention to.

Focus point

When observing characters from the outside, some of the aspects to which you may need to pay attention are:

- how they dress
- their physical build
- how they hold themselves physically or how they move: their demeanour and gait
- how they respond to other people or things in the world they are in
- their emotional air: this might be betrayed by facial expression, posture, speech or action
- what they are doing: their actions.

If you observe well enough, you often don't need to be explicit about how people are feeling. If you see somebody having an argument in the street, you don't need a big sign above them saying, 'This person is angry.' You *know directly that* they are angry. You know because of how they act, how they speak, how they move, how they relate to the rest of the world. It is the same in writing. Good observation can free you from the necessity of explaining the emotions of your characters.

Write: observation and emotion

This exercise is a way of practising writing about characters' inner lives and experience without having to be explicit.

First, write about a character who is alone in the street at night, in the rain, and utterly miserable. Focus only on things that you can *observe* from the outside. Do not tell the reader how the character is feeling: just focus on how the character appears externally, and allow this to communicate the feeling. Don't introduce any other characters: just keep things simple and focused on a single individual. Write for about 10 minutes.

Now that you have done this, take another character (or the same character at a different time). This character is also in the street at night, also in the rain, but rather than being miserable is instead ecstatic with joy. In the same way as above, focusing only on external observation, write for 10 minutes about this character in such a way that you communicate this very different emotion.

One final thing to think about when it comes to external observation is that, if your character has important traits that matter for the story – they have red hair, they are missing a limb, they are seven feet tall or they walk with a limp – then you need to establish this early on. It is always disturbing for a reader to read on page 113 that the heroine 'tossed her russet-red hair', if by that time the reader has assumed that she is blonde or brunette.

Knowledge from outside II: communication

Joan Didion

'I don't have a very clear idea of who the characters are until they start talking. Then I start to love them.'

Another way that we know about people is through what they *say*, through how they communicate with each other. Human communication has multiple channels: we speak; we write letters, emails, instant messages and texts; we grimace, shrug, fold our arms, hug, push each other away; we tut, whistle through our teeth, sigh, titter, guffaw.

It can be useful to remember that communication is another aspect of *what people do*. *Saying* is a kind of *doing*; speaking is a kind of acting.

Key idea

Speech is a kind of action.

If you find dialogue difficult, remember that speaking is simply another of the things that your characters might *do* in the fictional world. Dialogue isn't really a specific, separate skill, totally separate from skills in storytelling, characterization or describing action. Instead, it is another *aspect* of these skills. Speech does not float free from the world. Instead, it is embedded in the world, a part of the whole maelstrom of action and desire that you are dealing with as a writer.

David Corbett, *The Art of Character*

'Characters are not shooting the breeze in dialogue, they're doing things to each other: persuading, teasing, mocking, challenging, probing, flattering, badgering, begging, deceiving, manipulating, pampering, scolding.'

If you are tackling dialogue in your writing, one of the things to do is to ask yourself what is going on beneath the surface. Even the most innocent-seeming conversation is actually simmering with all kinds of rich and interesting things. Take the following dialogue.

A: Would you like a coffee?

B: Yes, please.

Think about the different things that could be going on here. The question could be aggressive. It could be flirtatious. It could be bored. The answer could be cold, or over-eager, or laden with sinister intent. Our everyday conversations are full of subtexts such as these.

Write: several cups of coffee

Have a go at playing with the example above. Take this simple piece of dialogue about a cup of coffee, and have a go at writing a scene in which there are different subtexts. There are some suggestions below, but feel free to make up your own:

- A is in love with B; B is not in love with A.
- A has poisoned the coffee; B suspects that A is up to something.
- A has just got a job in a coffee shop and is very nervous. B is a confident and rather abrasive regular customer.
- A and B are driving down the motorway at night. They have just had a terrible argument. This is the first thing that anybody has said since the argument.

For the time being, keep as much as possible to external observation rather than exploring your characters' inner worlds. Don't add any extra dialogue; stick to these two lines.

Once you see that dialogue is a kind of action, you can see that it is not separate from the other aspects of your character – from their various desires, from their place in the fictional world, from their physical being. And when you see that writing dialogue is not a wholly separate skill but that it is embedded in the broader world of your novel, then writing dialogue becomes less of a daunting prospect.

WRITTEN DIALOGUE AND REAL-LIFE CONVERSATIONS

Even if writing dialogue is best not seen as a separate and distinct skill, nevertheless there are some things that are worth bearing in mind. If you have ever been involved in transcribing real-live conversations, you will see that the way people *actually* speak is rather different from the way they speak in books. People hesitate, they repeat themselves, they trail off towards the ends of sentences. When writing dialogue, it is not your job to slavishly transcribe every nuance of speech. Just as you don't have to give a complete account of what your character is wearing, or what the room in which they are sitting is like, so you don't have to give a complete word-by-word and blow-by-blow account of what they are *saying*. Instead, you need to convey an impression of everyday speech, while at the same time continuing to keep up the pace and development of your story. Writing dialogue involves a trade-off between veracity and economy. In this, it is the same as writing *any* aspect of your novel. You need a certain economy, otherwise your story will grind to a halt; but at the same time you need a degree of veracity, so that your readers will be convinced and won over.

Veracity and uniqueness

There are many ways in which you can give a sense of veracity to speech. The most convincing dialogue is often dialogue that gives the reader a sense of the individuality or the uniqueness of the character who is speaking. We all use language differently: we can recognize friends by the sounds of their voice or by the way they use language. If you attempt to reflect this variety in the way you have your characters speak, this can lend richness and a greater sense of veracity to your novel.

Snapshot: multiple voices

For each of your major characters, think about the following questions:

- Does your character tend to speak in longer or shorter sentences?
- What kind of rhythm does your character's speech have?
- Does your character speak in dialect? Does your character speak a foreign language? If so, how can you replicate this on the page?
- What kinds of words does your character use?
- What tone of voice is your character employing? Again, how can this be reflected on the page?
- How does *what is being said* relate to your character's body language, or the language of posture and gesture?
- How much does your character speak? Are they very garrulous, or do they prefer silence?

Changing patterns of speech

There is an idea that there is such a thing as a 'standard' speech, and then there are many 'dialects' that differ from this. But it can be more useful think about language as something that is rooted in individual and idiosyncratic lives. Every single person in the world has a different relationship with the language or languages they speak.

This means that, when writing dialogue, you should be alive to your characters' differing relationships with language and to how these relationships may change according to context and time. Your characters may not speak in the same way when they are in the dock for murder and when they are having sex. They may use different kinds of language with different people.

A character's relationship with language may also change as the story unfolds. There are a couple of striking examples of this. One is Daniel Keyes's novel *Flowers for Algernon*, in which the protagonist and narrator undergoes experiments that lead to a rapid development of his intelligence, and then a similarly rapid decline. Keyes reflects these transformations in the way his protagonist uses language. Similarly, Xiaolu Guo's *A Concise Chinese–English Dictionary for Lovers* starts out in broken English but, as the narrator, a Chinese woman in London, becomes more familiar with English language and culture, the language in which the story is told becomes increasingly sophisticated.

The art of attention

To be able to really reflect the complex and shifting relationships we all have with language, it can be useful to pay attention to actual speech patterns. Eavesdropping can tell you a lot about how people use language. The writer Helen Cross argues that travelling by public transport is a great way to pick up not only on how people use language but also on stories, ideas and possibilities.

Helen Cross

'I listen quite a lot. And I go on buses and trains. That's the best thing you can do to be a writer – go everywhere on public transport. People think that writing is about writing. Actually it's mainly about thinking and listening.'

Snapshot: eavesdropping

Go somewhere public with a notebook and, without making yourself obtrusive, simply listen to the conversations that you hear around you. Pay attention to how people are communicating, not just by means of words but also by gestures and expressions, by things that they *don't* say and so on. When something takes your attention, find a quiet place to sit and write the scene as faithfully as you can.

You are not your characters

You may have a strong investment or interest in your characters, but your characters are to some extent independent of your own voice and your own concerns. You need to give them freedom, rather than seeing them as ventriloquist's puppets.

One thing that novelists can sometimes do is fall into using their characters as a mouthpiece. If you have strong views – about politics, about philosophy, about society – you may be tempted to get your character to act as a conduit for these views. But your readers will be attentive to the change in mood and pace if they feel that they are being lectured to. It is fine to have a character in the story giving a lecture to another character, but it needs to be the *character*'s lecture, not the author's lecture.

Another way that you can make this mistake is by using your characters to fill in plot details, back story and other information, effectively getting your character to do your job as a storyteller for you. If you find your characters simply filling in this kind of information about the story, then you need to think about how you as a narrator can convey this information differently.

 ## Key idea

Dialogue should not be overused as a means of exposition.

One way of telling whether you are at risk of using dialogue simply as a means of exposition is by asking what the character is attempting to do to the other characters in that section of dialogue. If the answer is 'nothing', then it is probably the case that the character is simply trying to do something – in this case, pass on information – to the reader, and so that section should probably be cut.

The following exercise might be useful to try to see whether you can put some distance between your own voice and the voices of your characters.

 ## Snapshot: changing voices

Choose one of your characters. Now imagine that you and your character have both shared the same experience: a meal, a movie or a journey, for example. First write an account of this experience in your own voice. Now take a short break, and come back to write about the *same* experience, but using the voice of your character.

Direct and indirect dialogue

There are, broadly speaking, two ways of tackling dialogue on the page. You can show it *directly*, or else you can report it. *Direct speech* looks like this:

'It's alive,' she said.

Reported speech, on the other hand, looks like this:

She said it was alive.

Reported speech may allow you to be a lot more condensed, and to move much more quickly. 'She told him about the car crash,' may be much more economical than transcribing all the things that she said about the car crash on to the page. But the trade-off here is that reported speech may have a greater air of generality and less of a sense of immediacy.

If you are using direct speech, don't be afraid of overusing the verb 'to say'. Don't feel that you need to inject added variety into your prose by using 'he proffered', 'she whimpered' and (heaven forbid!) 'he ejaculated', instead of 'he said' and 'she said'. Of course, you can have your characters proffering, whimpering and (*in extremis*) ejaculating – if that is what you want them to do; but if you use alternative verbs just to avoid the repetition of 'said', then you will end up distracting the reader. You can always leave out the 'he said' and 'she said' from passages of dialogue, as long as you are sure that the reader can follow who is speaking.

Knowledge from inside I: direct experience

As a novelist, you are free to shift your perspective so that one moment you are standing outside your character looking in, and another moment you are standing inside looking out. In everyday life, you have inner access only to yourself, and you have access to other people by seeing how they act and what they say. As a novelist, you potentially (depending on the point of view you are using) have *both* inner and outer access to your characters. Not only this, but you can play with the tensions between these two different perspectives. The view from within and the view from outside never seem to fully match up.

Robert Burns

'*O wad some Power the giftie gie us*
To see oursels as ithers see us!'

Robbie Burns's famous poem points to these strange mismatches between the view from within and the view from outside. As a novelist, this provides rich material.

This knowledge we have of ourselves from the *inside* has two aspects. The first aspect is *direct experience*: the feeling of the wind on our cheek, the taste of coffee or strawberries, the shiver at the touch of a lover, the sensation of snow underfoot. The second is *introspection*, the thoughts that we have, the strange complexities of our inner mental world, our mind's own *commentary* upon our experience.

When you start asking about the nature of direct experience, you find that you become rapidly tied up in philosophical knots. Direct experience is maddening to the philosophers because it seems so very self-evident (we *know* what coffee tastes like), but it is very hard to grasp more precisely. Here we can leave the philosophers out of it. What matters to you as a writer is that your first port of call when thinking about the direct experience of your characters is by correlation with your own direct experience. If your character is suffering from insomnia, then think about what it is like if you have ever been sleepless. We understand our characters' experience by extrapolating from our own.

Everybody is different, but we have similar bodies, brains and nervous systems, and so drawing on your own direct experience to explore the experience of your characters can be really useful. Pay attention to your character's physical experience. What does it feel like to live inside their skin? How does your character move? If your character is cold, how is this experienced *in the body*? How does it affect your character's thoughts? Thinking is not just abstract, but is expressed through the body. If I am stuck as to what to write next, my eyes gaze off into the middle-distance. If my thoughts are agitated, my body too is agitated. If I am anxious, I pace around.

Write: your character's experience and your own

This exercise is designed to get under the skin of the characters in your novel. Take up to three key scenes from your novel. Note down for each scene experiences you have had that may correlate loosely with this experience. They do not have to be the same experience (if your character has committed a murder, then you shouldn't go and commit one yourself), but experiences that you think are somehow related. Now write first-person short pieces exploring these experiences that you have had. Make them as rich and detailed as possible.

When you have done this, read your accounts of the experiences that you have had, and then return to the original passages in your novel. Do they seem as convincing? As vivid? Do they feel plausible in the light of your own experience? Make any changes you can to enrich these aspects of your novel.

Knowledge from inside II: introspection

The other aspect of knowledge from the inside is introspection. By *direct experience* I mean the physical, embodied *What is it like?* of existence; by *introspection* I mean the inner world of thoughts and ideas that your character may have. As a novelist, you can simply *tell* the reader what your characters are thinking – you can eavesdrop on their thoughts – although this will depend upon the point of view that you choose to use. If you are using a rigorous first-person point of view, then you cannot eavesdrop on anybody's thoughts except the narrator's own: you can only *infer* what other characters are thinking. But if your point of view is less restrictive than this, you can move much more freely. When drawing upon introspection, you can give accounts of a character's internal monologue, of their thoughts and silent judgements and perspectives upon the world.

The thing to remember about introspection, however, is that despite our claims to know ourselves, it's pretty dark in there. We are not necessarily reliable guides to our own inner worlds. We often act out of motives that are obscure to us. We do not know ourselves as well as we think we do. Here there is huge scope for greater psychological depth and richness in your storytelling. You have heard, of course, about unreliable narrators. The term was coined by the scholar Wayne C. Booth, in his 1961 book *The Rhetoric of Fiction*. An unreliable narrator is a narrator who tells stories in such a fashion that the boundary between truth and untruth is no longer clear.

Key idea

An unreliable narrator is a narrator who cannot be trusted. Whether deliberately or unwittingly, the unreliable narrator gives an account that cannot be relied upon.

Unreliability might arise out of delusion, or malice, or necessity, or out of any of a number of reasons. The unreliable narrator is a useful device in fiction: your characters, and your narrative voice, can play with the truth in all kinds of ways. But there is something more fundamental about unreliable narration, I think. To the extent that we are not reliable guides to our experiences, we are, all of us, the unreliable narrators of our lives and worlds.

A final thought on these four dimensions of characterization – observation, communication, direct experience and introspection: you do not need to employ all four dimensions equally. Some characters you might want to talk about only from the outside, while with others you might want to plunge into their inner worlds. Remember, too, that in reality the four dimensions overlap in many different ways, and in fiction (just as in real life) they cannot be fully disentangled.

Drawing on tacit knowledge

We are *all* experts on human psychology and human behaviour. We are experts because we have grown up in a world populated by other human beings, and because we are naturally good at learning how to read the motives and thoughts and desires and intentions of others. Through years of going about the business of being human, we have accumulated a lot of what is sometimes called *tacit* knowledge (the term comes from the philosopher of science Michael Polyani). What this means is that we know an awful lot about how human beings act and behave, without being aware of how much we know and without being able to communicate all of it.

Michael Polanyi, *The Tacit Dimension*

'We can know more than we can tell.'

When we are writing, we draw upon this body of knowledge that we have built up over the years. This is perhaps the reason why many novelists report that their characters 'take on a life of their own'.

It might be useful to end this chapter by looking at this strange claim. It can all sound rather mysterious. The novelist John Cheever once complained that, 'the idea of authors running around helplessly behind their cretinous inventions is contemptible'. But there is something in this idea that characters have their own life and logic that we should take seriously. Cheever is right in that you should have *some* control over your characters and what they get up to. On the other hand, if you move around your characters too strictly, they may become as uninteresting as chess pieces. The reason for this is simple: if everything is too planned out, you are not allowing any of that tacit knowledge to play a part in how your characters develop and how they act. By all means carefully think through who your characters are. By all means plan them meticulously. But also give them some space to move.

 Focus point

To be able to allow this tacit knowledge – and the richness of this tacit knowledge – to filter into your writing of character, you will need to make sure that you don't keep *too* tight a rein on your characters.

Workshop: the actions beneath the words

For this workshop, you can use either your entire work-in-progress or a smaller extract. I recommend beginning with a chapter or a scene to see whether the workshop is useful. If it helps resolve some problems, then think about extending it further. If you working with a single chapter, it will take a couple of hours. If you are working with your whole manuscript, it will take considerably longer. Go through the text and clearly mark the points where there is dialogue, whether this is direct or indirect speech. You are going to be focusing only on these sections. If you haven't yet written any of your manuscript, start by sitting down and drafting out a dialogue scene.

Next, read the sections of dialogue that you have chosen out loud. This is a way of familiarizing yourself with the speech in this dialogue as a series of *spoken actions*.

Now go through the dialogue *line by line*, and for every line note down what is going on beneath the surface. What is the character trying to do to the other character? Here are some of the things that your characters may be up to:

- Challenging
- Probing
- Manipulating
- Flirting
- Persuading

- Teasing
- Scolding.

Note in the margin what the character is *doing* to the other character or characters. In other words, what is the *action* that lies behind the words? Use either single words or very brief sentences. If it is not clear what the action behind the words is, then simply put a mark in the margin to note this (an X, for example).

When you have gone through the whole text, you should have a skeleton or outline of the changing actions that are going on beneath the surface of your dialogue.

Now look back over your annotations. If there are whole sections where the characters do not seem to be doing anything to each other, you have two options:

1 Cut these sections entirely.
2 Rewrite these sections, changing the dialogue so that it is much more strongly underpinned by action.

You may also find that there are sections where the unfolding of action is not entirely clear: where the characters' actions change arbitrarily and for no good reason. If this is the case, then go back and revise these sections.

Where to next?

Now that we have covered the basics of building a convincing world, developing convincing plot ideas and peopling your world with characters, in the final chapter in this part of the book, we are going to look at the question of how you go about telling the story of your novel.

10

Storytelling

There is a tension at the heart of storytelling. When we tell stories, we are making things up; and yet we are asking our audience to trust us *as if these things were true*, or as if they *could* be true. In this chapter, we will be looking at the complex business of how we go about navigating the choppy seas where truths and falsehoods meet and intermingle.

Jeanette Winterson, *The Passion*

'I am telling you stories. Trust me.'

Jeanette Winterson's plea to the reader, taken from her novel *The Passion*, is a nicely ambiguous place to begin. The moment Winterson says 'Trust me', we are on our guard. We *know* that we are going to be led into a world where truths, half-truths and lies all jostle with one another. But, at the same time, we find ourselves putting ourselves willingly in the storyteller's hands. We want to be deceived; but we don't want our trust to be betrayed.

Lies in which not everything is false

According to Susan Feldman, in her book *African Myths and Tales*, Sudanese storytellers were once accustomed to beginning their tales like this:

Storyteller: 'I'm going to tell a story.'

Audience: 'Right!'

Storyteller: 'It's a lie.'

Audience: 'Right!'

Storyteller: 'But not everything in it is false!'

Audience: 'Right!'

A novel, too, is built up of lies in which not everything is false. It can be useful when working on your novel to think of yourself as a storyteller, as somebody who has at their disposal all the tricks that an oral storyteller might use to persuade, to convince, or to win over those who are experiencing the tale.

When writing a novel, you are dealing in *fictions*. The word 'fiction' suggests making or fashioning. If you trace back the etymology or the family tree of the word 'fiction', you find that it is a close cousin of the word 'dough', and that both words come from an ancient Proto-Indo-European root meaning 'to knead dough' or 'to fashion clay'.

 Key idea

The word 'fiction' derives from ancient roots meaning 'to knead (dough)' or 'to fashion (clay)'.

A novelist, in other words, is like a bread-maker or a potter, somebody who *makes* things. Even a novel that seems to closely mirror life is something that is constructed with a considerable amount of skill, artfulness and artifice.

Same story, different tellings

There are all kinds of ways of telling a story, and a convincing *telling* can profoundly affect the reader. A famous example is Nabokov's unreliable narrator Humbert Humbert in his novel *Lolita*. However much we dislike Nabokov's narrator, we nevertheless find ourselves drawn in and carried along by him. It is possible to imagine other tellings of the same story that would not be quite so compelling, that would not have the same tension between fascination and repulsion that Nabokov manages in his classic book.

> ## Key idea
>
> A *story* is different from any particular *telling* of that story: the same story can be told in very many different ways.

As an example, we could take '*Little Red Riding Hood*', a story that has been told and retold a million times. There are multiple versions of the story, some more bloodthirsty than others, but, even if we stick with one single version, there are all kinds of ways that this story could be told. It could be told by Little Red herself ('So, there I am walking through the forest one day, taking some cakes to my grandmother, when I hear a growling behind a tree…'), or by her grandmother ('Once I had climbed out of the wolf's still quivering belly, and wiped the gastric juices from my spectacles…'), or by a jackdaw watching from a branch ('"Caw! Caw! It's that girl again," I said to myself. "She is so reckless, wandering through the forest like that…"'); or it could be told by a godlike 'omniscient' narrator, in the traditional style ('Once upon a time there was a little girl who wore a red riding hood…').

> ## Key idea
>
> The same *story* can be *told* in a multitude of different ways.

There are two things to notice here. The first is that the telling of stories can differ in terms of the 'who' of the telling; the second is that they can differ in terms of the 'when' of the telling. We can look at these in turn.

The 'who' of the telling

This is a matter of *point of view* and *narration*. By 'point of view', I mean the position from which a story is being told. If we take the analogy of cinema, point of view could be seen as analogous to the camera angles that the director takes, and the characters upon whom the camera choses to focus. It might be, for example, that your main focus is on the wolf in the 'Red Riding Hood' story, in that you are telling it from his side of things: you are seeing what goes on in Wolfie's head, you are watching him as he creeps up on the girl who is skipping along the path. Point of view is about *the position from which the story is being told. Narration* is slightly different (although the two often overlap, sometimes quite closely). Narration is about *who is doing the telling.*

Catherine Brady, *Story Logic and the Craft of Fiction*

'Simply put, point of view provides us with a means for messing with the reader's head.'

We could take the wolf's point of view – it could be *his* story – but we could choose to narrate this either in the first person, as if the wolf is telling the story (perhaps from beyond the grave, given that he ends up dead!), or using a third-person 'omniscient' narrator (I have mentioned this strange beast – the 'omniscient' narrator – twice now, and I will have more to say about him or her a bit later on), or even as narrated by Little Red as she imagines herself into the perspective of the wolf.

The 'who' of the telling	
Point of view:	Narration:
• Whose story is being told?	• Who is telling the story?
• From whose perspective (or perspectives) does the reader have access to the story?	• Is the person telling the story inside the story, or an observer?
• Who is the focus of the storytelling?	• If the person telling the story is just an observer, what is their relationship to the story?

Playing with point of view and different approaches to narration can be a good way of uncovering hidden possibilities in your story.

THIRD-PERSON NARRATION

The third person is perhaps the most common way that stories are told. In the third person, the story is about 'he' or 'she', rather than about 'I' or 'you'. Some of the oldest literature of all, for example, *The Epic of Gilgamesh*, is told in the third person.

Third-person narration often gives your work a kind of distance. It makes both the narrator and the reader spectators of the action, rather than participants. If you are telling a story in the third person (this is a decision about *narration*), then you must still decide the perspective you are taking on the story (this is a decision about *point of view*), and this will affect the degree of distance. Here we'll look at three kinds of third-person narrator:

1 omniscient narrators

2 single-perspective stories

3 multiple-perspective stories.

1 Omniscient narrators

Omniscient (literally 'all-knowing') narrators are perhaps the most powerful, but they are also the most distanced. Like deities, they have access to absolutely everything in the fictional world: every last thought of every single character, every angle and every perspective upon every single action. As a writer, this kind of heady power can be intoxicating; but this is an approach that needs to be handled with some care. In particular, the sense of distance that comes with an omniscient narrator may make the reader feel less fully and intensely engaged in the action of your story. There is a trade-off between the power that the omniscient narrator gives you as a writer – the ability to move where you wish within the story – and the muting of the impact of the tale you are telling.

In reality, the idea of an omniscient narrator in its pure form is something of a myth. There are two reasons for this. The first is that all stories are told from a certain angle: in *narrating* your tale, you are having to choose some perspective or other. The second is that no writer has a god-like total knowledge of the world they create. However meticulous you are in building your world, there will be all kinds of things that you do not know.

Focus point

Omniscient narrators attempt to pull themselves away from the fray – from the mess and muddle of the tales they are spinning; but they never fully succeed.

In the end, omniscience is not so much a *position* from which to tell a story as a way of allowing yourself permission to move between third-person perspectives in the story. We can't have a true 'view from everywhere', but we can shuttle between different views from different perspectives.

Neal Stephenson, *Quicksilver*

'Each painter can view the city from only one standpoint at a time, so he will move about the place, and paint it from a hilltop on one side, then a tower on the other, then from a grand intersection in the middle – all in the same canvas. When we look at the canvas, then, we glimpse in a small way how God understands the universe – for he sees it from every point of view at once. By populating the world with so many different minds, each with its own point of view, God gives us a suggestion of what it means to be omniscient.'

2 Single-perspective tales

If viewpoint is rather like camera angle, you can think of a single-perspective tale as a tale in which the camera angle remains relatively fixed.

If you decide to tell your story from a single perspective, it needs to be the *right* perspective. The position from which you tell the story will need to be a strong one. The character upon whom you focus will have to be particularly strongly drawn and convincing if this is going to sustain you throughout the entirety of the novel. Not only this, but a single-perspective approach will work only for certain stories. If your story has a single thread focused upon one individual, this might work very well indeed. But if your story gives equal weight to a number of individuals, and the story as a whole is not so much a single thread as a braid made up of multiple threads, then a single perspective will probably not work for you.

 Focus point

Single-perspective approaches to storytelling often work best when the story is relatively simple, or when you have a very strong central character.

3 Multiple-perspective tales

Another way of telling the story is from multiple perspectives, with shifts in camera angles, but with each perspective being limited and partial. These perspectives, taken together, add up to a full picture of what is going on in the story. Most third-person stories are *to some extent* tales told from multiple perspectives. Even single-perspective tales tend towards the multiplication of perspectives if you look closely: all stories are, to some extent, braids.

Rather than worrying about which category your story falls into, perhaps the better question is that of how, point by point as your story is unfolding, you manage the various perspectives available to you.

 Philip Roth

'The shifting within a single narrative from the one voice to the other is how a reader's moral perspective is determined.'

There are a number of strategies open to you in playing with multiple perspectives. You can switch perspectives rapidly to give your story a sense of dislocation and pace. You can suddenly inject a passage from a wholly other perspective. If you tell your story from too many perspectives, a kind of blurriness descends over the world that you are writing about, and you risk losing the reader's concentration. But if you limit your perspectives too much, you may narrow down the possibilities of your story.

FIRST-PERSON NARRATION

First-person storytelling is immediately more intimate than third person. Take, as an example, this famous opening passage from Herman Melville's *Moby Dick*.

> *Call me Ishmael. Some years ago – never mind how long precisely – having little or no money in my purse, and nothing particular to interest me on shore, I thought I would sail about a little and see the watery part of the world. It is a way I have of driving off the spleen, and regulating the circulation...*

Let's try putting this into the third person:

> *They call him Ishmael. Some years ago – never mind how long precisely – having little or no money in his purse, and nothing particular to interest him on shore, he thought he would sail about a little and see the watery part of the world. It was a way he had of driving off the spleen and regulating the circulation…*

A few things have happened here. The second version is much more distanced. The narrator is split apart from the subject of the story. There are more subtle shifts, too. In rewriting this passage, I could not stop myself from making a few other changes. The addition of 'They' at the beginning seemed necessary to establish the third-person narrator, and the change of tense that worked fine in the first person ('I would sail… it is a way I have…') felt wrong in the third person, so I changed the beginning of the final sentence to the past tense.

If the first-person perspective gives more immediacy, it has the disadvantage of limiting what you, as narrator, can talk about. You are stuck with the knowledge and thoughts of the person you have chosen as a mouthpiece. This shouldn't be a massive problem (after all, I have been stuck all my life with *my* knowledge and *my* thoughts, and I have more or less got by); but it does mean that certain kinds of stories, certain kinds of plot devices, are going to be ruled out. Unless your character knows about, hears about, or sees the body in the library, then there is no way that you can talk about the body unless you break with this first-person perspective.

Multiple perspectives in the first person

One way of getting round the difficulties and limitations of first-person perspectives is by moving between *multiple* first-person perspectives. There is a wonderful example of this in *My Name Is Red* by the Turkish novelist Orhan Pamuk, in which each chapter takes a different first-person perspective. The first chapter of Pamuk's novel, which has the title 'I Am a Corpse', reads like this:

I am nothing but a corpse now, a body at the bottom of a well. Although I drew my last breath long ago and my heart has stopped beating, no one, apart from that vile murderer, knows what's happened to me. As for that wretch, he felt for my pulse and listened for my breath to be sure I was dead, then kicked me in the midriff, carried me to the edge of the well, raised me up and dropped me below. As I fell, my head, which he had smashed with a stone, broke apart; my face, my forehead and cheeks, were crushed; my bones shattered, and my mouth filled with blood.

SECOND-PERSON NARRATION

There are two ways you might use second-person narration in writing your story. The first is by having your characters using the second person among themselves. A good example is what is often called an 'epistolary' novel: a novel that is made up of letters exchanged between individuals.

But there is another kind of second person that is much stranger, and that is when the author directly addresses the *reader*. This direct address to the reader is by no means a new trick. In fact, it is as old as oral storytelling itself. Writing in the second person gives your reader a little frisson that comes out of being put on the spot, just as if you were sitting by the fire listening to a storyteller, and suddenly you find that you were singled out from the audience.

A striking example of this is Iain M. Banks's novel *Complicity*. The novel is about the way in which we are all complicit in injustices and horrors that we may never even dwell upon. Throughout the book, we see a number of acts of extreme and brutally cruel revenge perpetrated upon those who are involved in these injustices. Banks writes these passages in the second person, so it is *we* who are carrying out these brutal acts. In other words, we, too, become more deeply complicit in the complex moral web that he is weaving.

There are some books that sustain the second person throughout (for example, Bill Broady's *Swimmer*). If you are tempted to try this, ask yourself *why* the story needs to be told like this. Think about how the second person is used in everyday speech. It can be used as an invitation. It can be used as a challenge. It can be used as an accusation. What do you want to convey? What benefit will there be in writing your story in this way? In other words, a second-person perspective should be more than a simple gimmick: it should add something to the storytelling.

Snapshot: thinking about narration and perspective

Take a chapter of the novel-in-progress (if you have started writing) or of a short story that you have written. Alternatively, take a chapter of a novel you are reading.

- Working through sentence by sentence and paragraph by paragraph, work out the perspective from which the story is being told.

- When the perspective changes, mark this also on the text and note down how and why it has changed.
- If the perspective remains exactly the same throughout, ask yourself what new possibilities might be opened up by introducing changes in perspective.

The 'when' of the telling

The 'when' of the telling can also be broken down into two parts (as always, there may be different ways of breaking these things down – so this isn't a fixed rule, only a suggestion as to how it might be helpful to think about your story). Firstly, there is the question of what might be called *the time of the story*; secondly, there is the question of what might be called *the time of the telling*.

This may seem a little complicated, but it is really quite straightforward. All stories are made up of events that take place in a particular order. But, *as a story*, these events are often shuffled about. Think of Little Red Riding Hood again. We could start the story at the beginning, with Little Red being sent on an errand; and we could end with the bloody – but, in most versions, happy (unless you are the wolf) – finale. However, we could start in the middle, with Little Red traipsing through the woods ('It's a lovely day, Little Red Riding Hood thought, as she wandered off the forest path…'), or at the end ('It would take a lot of cleaning up, but at least the wolf was dead…'), or at the very moment that the wolf swallows the poor little girl ('As she slid down the wolf's gullet, Little Red Riding Hood regretted that she had forgotten to bring her hunting knife with her…'). The workshop at the end of this chapter will allow you to play with some of the ideas here.

> ## Key idea
>
>
> You do not need to tell stories according to the chronological ordering of events. You are free to start in the middle of events, at the end, or anywhere you like

The 'time of the telling' is a little different. This is about the relationship between the time of the story and when the story is being told. Folk tales that begin, 'Once upon a time…' put the time of the story a long time before the time of the telling. Sometimes you will want to give the feeling of the story unfolding in real time, and so the time of the telling will unfold alongside the time of the story. Imagine a story made up of letters and emails, in which the story unfolds as the apparently 'real-time' correspondence unfolds. Or, more commonly, a story might be told from the perspective of the more recent past: 'Several years ago, when I was employed in the diamond mines…'

The 'when' of the telling	
The time of the story:	**The time of the telling:**
• In which order do events in the story unfold?	• When is the story being told?
• Where do you start? In the beginning, at the middle, or at the end?	• Is the telling of the story happening as it unfolds, or after the event (or, exceptionally, before it has all happened – although this would be hard to sustain for a novel)?
• How do you weave different series of events (which may take place simultaneously) together into a coherent story?	

FEELING TENSE

One other aspect of time in your storytelling is the question of *tense*. Tense is a matter of the relationship between the telling and the events within the tale. The *traditional* way of telling a story is in the past tense and, if you choose to tell your story like this, almost certainly nobody will complain: it is so very common, so much a part of how stories have been told for centuries on end, that your readers will hardly notice that this is a choice you have made. However, the past tense is not the only option. Since the middle of the twentieth century, there has been an increasing fashion for telling stories in the present tense. It is often said that present tense provides a greater sense of immediacy: instead of being told what happened *in the past*, we see it unfold before our eyes *here and now*. And it is true that using the present tense *can* do this. But there is also a danger that it can have a numbing effect on the reader, making the story feel like simply 'one damn thing after another'.

 Philip Hensher

'Writing is vivid if it is vivid. A shift of tense won't do that for you.'

There is also nothing, in principle, to stop you changing tense throughout your story, and using *both* present-tense and past-tense narration alongside each other.

 Write: changing tenses

In this exercise, we will be looking at *retelling* a page of your novel – or, if you prefer, a part of somebody else's novel – in a different tense.

- First, select a page. If you haven't started writing yet, you can use a page of somebody else's novel.
- Now read the passage out loud to get a feel for it.
- Note whether the story is written in the present or the past tense, or whether it moves between the two. After this, rewrite the passage so that if it was in the present tense it is now in the past tense, and vice versa.
- Read the passage out loud again.
- Finally, reflect upon how this transformation of tense affects the feel, mood and possibilities of the story.

Showing and telling

I have been talking about 'storytelling' here; but the notion of 'telling' is one that is often, in books on creative writing, treated with some suspicion. There is a common slogan that is often repeated by creative writing teachers: 'Show, don't tell'. But what does this mean?

When you are telling your story, there are various ways you can do it. You can summarize what is happening in the story (this is what is meant by 'telling' when people say 'show, don't tell'), or you can paint a scene for your reader (this is 'showing'). The approach you take depends on how you want to balance immediacy against pace. Sometimes showing is much more effective than telling: I can tell you as much as I like about how to ride a bike, but in the end, you are better off with me showing you. Sometimes showing is just long-winded, and telling is better. For example, you can spend three pages showing a character waking up late and stumblng around the room looking for her socks, or you can just say, 'Deborah woke up hung-over again.'

Focus point

'Showing' may communicate in a fashion that is more visceral and immediate; 'telling' may communicate in a fashion that is more economical. You will need a balance of both in your writing.

In general, the extent to which you show and the extent to which you tell will be a matter of your own judgement. But however you decide to exercise this judgement, remember that one of the pleasures of being a reader is the pleasure of *drawing inferences*. Through what you show, what you tell, what you do not show, and what you do not tell, you need to leave readers the space to draw their own inferences, to come to their own conclusions, and to engage more deeply with the world of your story.

Breaking the frame

John Gardner, *The Art of Fiction*

'Fiction does its work by creating a dream in the reader's mind.'

The great writer and writing teacher John Gardner wrote in his book *The Art of Fiction* that novels should be like vivid, continuous dreams in the reader's mind, and that anything that interrupted this sustained dream should be avoided. I certainly agree that vividness (which I would prefer to call 'clarity') is vitally important in fiction. This is why the previous few chapters have taken such trouble asking about the *what*, the *who* and the *where* of the story that you are telling. You need to be sure what it is that you are doing. But this doesn't mean that a novel must *necessarily* be a kind of sustained illusion. There are many more ways that a story can be told than this, and sometimes one of the pleasures of storytelling is precisely that the storyteller intrudes on the tale.

Imagine your ancestors at the very dawn of history, sitting by a fire as a storyteller weaves tales. What the storyteller is doing is not just creating a vivid, continuous dream, but also making jokes, comments, asides, addressing the audience directly, and interacting with the audience in all kinds of ways. Spinning illusions is only *one of a number of things* that a storyteller might do. If you want to break the 'frame' of your novel to address your audience directly ('Reader, I married him…'), you should feel free to do so. Some readers may protest, but others may take additional pleasure in these tricks and games.

And remember, just like the storyteller by the fire, in addressing your audience directly, or in breaking the frame, you are not taking a break from spinning fictions: instead, you are making the fictions you spin even more complex and intriguing.

Workshop: same story, different tellings

This workshop is about playing with different ways of telling the same story. It is divided into two parts. Read through the whole exercise first before beginning. You are free to do either part separately, although they should follow on from each other well.

1 Old stories and new tellings

First, find a story that you can retell. This could be a folk tale, a story from the news, or a short story by a writer you like. The important thing is that this story should be relatively short and that it should have between three and six main characters. You can use 'Little Red Riding Hood', if you are not sick of this tale already.

Now get a piece of paper and divide it into eight frames as below. Number each frame.

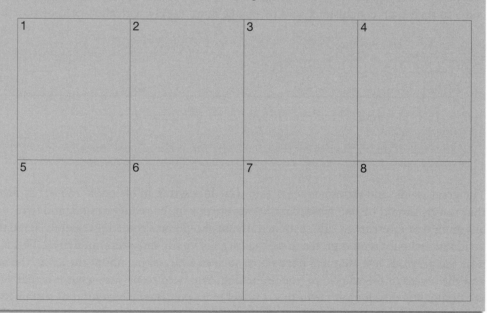

This is a storyboard for your story. Your job now is to sketch out, using words or pictures, the events of the story in the order in which they happen. If you are using 'Little Red Riding Hood', frame one might be her mother warning her not to step off the path, frame two might be her straying off the path to pick flowers (and the wolf behind a tree) and frame three might be the wolf hurrying to Grandma's. *Use no more than eight frames.*

- When you are done, give each of the characters in the story a number at random, from one to six.
- Cut up the storyboard into individual frames and shuffle them around. Lay them out in a line in front of you, in random order.
- Now roll the dice to choose a character. If you get a number that doesn't correspond to a character (say you get a five, and you've only got four characters), roll again.
- Now you have a new order of events (the 'when' of the telling) and a randomly selected character to focus on (the 'who' of the telling).
- Finally, retell the story from this character's point of view, following the order of your new, reorganized storyboard.

2 A different telling?

Now you can apply some of this to your own novel – or if you haven't got that far, to something that you have already written. Draw up another chart, numbering each frame. Then storyboard *either* your novel as a whole *or* a section of your novel, keeping it to eight frames as a maximum. What you are storyboarding are the events as they unfold in your fictional world, so you should ignore the order in which you have chosen to tell them in the novel.

Tear up the pieces into separate squares, and shuffle them in front of you *face up.* See if you can find at least *three* different ways of reordering the frames that make sense. It will be useful to record these three different ways of telling your story by simply writing down a list of numbers (e.g. 3, 2, 4, 5, 6, 7, 1, 8).

At this point it might be a good idea to work with another writer or friend. Explore the advantages and disadvantages of these different ways of telling the same story. Which one works best, and why? Is the order that works best the one you are already using, or do you need to change the way you are telling your story?

Where to next?

We have explored how to move from initial ideas, through world-building and research, to the intricacies of plot, character and storytelling. This should give you the tools you need to put together a first draft of your book. But you may have a lot of redrafting to do before your novel is finished. The next section of this book explores the most effective way to turn your raw material into a book worth publishing and reading.

PART THREE

Redrafting

11

Introduction: why redraft?

Part three of this book is about redrafting. Although redrafting may seem to some like a rather unglamorous business, it is in fact often intensely demanding, fascinating and creative.

For the purposes of this book, I'm going to distinguish 'redrafting' from 'editing'. When I talk about 'editing', I'll be talking about preparing the final version of your manuscript for publication, and all the processes that your book goes through to get it into a publishable state. When I talk about 'redrafting', I'll be talking about the process of taking the very first version of your manuscript and turning it into a final version ready for the attention of external editors. Of course, this distinction is a little artificial. What seems like a final draft often is not. I have often written a 'final draft' of a book only to put it to one side, have second thoughts, and find myself redrafting my final draft to produce a *final* final draft. Nevertheless, it is useful to think of these two stages as separate.

Focus point

It can be useful to think of 'redrafting' as the often solitary process of reworking your manuscript until it is as complete as it can possibly be, and 'editing' as the more collective process of taking this manuscript and fashioning it into something that is ready to be published.

There are four chapters in this part of the book. This reflects the fact that many novelists, myself included, spend a significant amount of time turning their first drafts into finished novels. Once again, there are always exceptions. Some writers do not redraft very much at all. Others redraft a fair amount. Often (but not always), there is an inverse ratio between the amount of redrafting and the speed that writers write. Writers who write 500 words in a morning may find that much of the close attention that, for other writers, takes place in redrafting is already there in the first draft stage. Meanwhile, writers who write thousands of words a day may find that they redraft rather more. Either way, it is good to remember again that what matters most is what the book eventually looks like rather than how you get there.

This chapter will look at the question of why redraft at all, and at some of the general principles involved. The next chapter will look at redrafting for structure, pace and rhythm. Then, in Chapter 13, we will look at what I am calling 'redrafting for logic', thinking hard about how your story and world hang together. Chapter 14 will then turn to questions of language, and how to effectively hone and sharpen your prose style.

Why and when should you redraft?

Key idea

Needing to redraft is not a sign of your failure to produce a perfect first draft. Instead, it is a sign of your success in producing a first draft at all, however imperfect.

Sometimes writers feel as if they *shouldn't* have to redraft, that they should be able to get everything right first time. But this almost never happens. Expect to redraft numerous times, refashioning and polishing your work until it is ready for the next stage.

Focus point

Redrafting can be a very long process. Expect to go through *multiple* drafts before you have your novel right.

SEPARATING WRITING (FIRST DRAFT) AND REDRAFTING PHASES

One reason why you need to redraft is that *novel writing is unpredictable.* Even for the most meticulously planned project, you do not know for certain where your story is going to take you. Many things can change along the way. If you change direction in Chapter 20, this will send ripples throughout the entire novel, so you will need to go back and rethink Chapter 1 or Chapter 5.

The second, related, reason why you might need to separate writing first drafts and redrafting your novel is that *a novel is an organic whole.* Every part of a novel is linked to every other part. Every part of a novel has to work with every other part. And you don't know what all the parts are until you have a first draft.

A third reason why you might want to separate writing first drafts and redrafting is that they are very different processes that require different kinds of attention. Think of Kerouac by his typewriter, bashing out his novel in three weeks. Had he stopped every five minutes to go back to tweak a word or two, he probably would not have got very far.

Key idea

There are three reasons why you need to redraft:

1 Writing novels is unpredictable – at the outset you don't know where you are going to end up.
2 Novels are organic wholes. As you add words, this will affect the words you have already written.
3 Writing and redrafting are different processes that require different kinds of attention.

So, when writing a first draft, don't think about writing a *perfect* first draft. Think about writing a *finished* first draft. This means thinking of writing a draft that starts on page one and ends where the story ends. Think about writing a first draft that you can look at and say, 'That is a whole novel.' At this stage, it may not be a *good* novel. The job of first drafts is not to be *good*, it is to be *complete*. Almost always, a first draft will be a mixture of the good and the bad and the indifferent. It will have passages that work really well and passages that have no place in any self-respecting novel. The redrafting process is, in part, about distinguishing one from the other.

Focus point

Your first draft can be as messy or untidy as you like. But it is often wise to work on developing a *complete* draft before you start intensively redrafting.

Once you have your first draft written, put it to one side and do not think about it for a while. Writing a first draft is often a heated and impassioned process; but when you come to redraft, you may need to be a lot cooler, more level-headed and more objective.

If you've been involved in an intense relationship with your book, you may need a bit of time apart so that when you meet up again, things don't get too messy.

How long should you put the book aside for? No more than a month or two is usually what I would suggest. It will help you cool off a bit, think about other things, get more perspective. But you don't want to leave it so long that you feel out of touch with your book.

 ## Focus point

It can help to leave a gap between drafting your novel and coming back to the manuscript to redraft it. Don't leave it more than a couple of months, however, or you may lose momentum.

When you come back to your book, the first thing to do is to get a copy printed out. It is good to get your drafts printed out on paper, to feel their heft in your hand, to be able to leaf back and forth, to *physically* feel the difference between 10 pages and 30 pages. Now read the book *straight through*, making notes in the margin as you go. Don't get bogged down. Again, your first reading should be more like an aerial photograph: a snapshot of the whole territory. If you make sure that the first read-through is fairly swift and breezy, you will have a sense of the *whole*. Later on, you can parachute into your manuscript and hack your way through the jungles on foot.

When you get to the end of this read-through, two things may happen. The first is that you may succumb to despair and think that your book is so *terrible* that it should never see the light of day. The second is that you may succumb to excitability and think that your work is such a work of *genius* that the only thing standing between you and the Nobel Prize is time. On either count, you *may* be right. But it is more likely that your book is simply a mixture of good and bad. Your job now is to eradicate the bad and to make the good better.

 ## Focus point

If you have identified many problems in your manuscript, this is not a sign that you are a bad writer. Instead, it is a sign that you are on the right track. Bad writers do not identify problems. They do not even notice problems.

Redrafting for...

One reason that it can help to think in terms of multiple drafts is that 'redrafting' is a general catch-all term for numerous different processes. When you are redrafting, you may be thinking about any of the following things:

• Are there any parts of my novel that are boring? Are there any sections that are irrelevant?

- Where does the story slow down? Where do I move too quickly over important aspects of the story?
- Is the story told in the right order? Do the chapters need to be rearranged? Is the structure right?
- Does the point of view work?
- Are all the details accurate? Does the world as a whole hang together?
- Is the language effective? Is it precise? Are there bad habits, tics or clichés that I need to address?
- Does the story start in the right place? Does it end in the right place?
- Are my characters convincing?
- Does my dialogue work?

Because these are all very different questions, it makes sense not to try to do everything at once. If you think about doing *multiple* redrafts, then you can think about focusing each redraft upon a particular set of questions or concerns. In this book, I have divided redrafting into three separate, but linked, areas: structure, logic and language. So you might think about having *at least* three phases of redrafting your text, one phase for each of these.

A circular process

Because your novel is an organic whole, the redrafting process is often circular. Even a tiny change in one place can cause you to make big changes elsewhere. If a butterfly flaps its wings on page 1, it can cause a tsunami on page 31. Think of redrafting as a process of circling around your ideal novel, the novel that your novel *could*, *should* and hopefully *will* be, but that it isn't quite yet. Each time you go through your manuscript, you may come a bit closer to this ideal novel.

BOLDNESS, IMAGINATION AND CREATIVITY

Some writers and writing teachers like to distinguish the 'creative' process of writing first drafts from the 'analytical' or 'critical' process of redrafting. This can give an inaccurate view both of the process of writing initial drafts and of the process of redrafting.

Mario Vargas Llosa

'I think what I love is not the writing itself, but the rewriting, the editing, the correcting... I think it's the most creative part of writing.'

Redrafting is an intensely creative process. It requires as much boldness, imagination and audacity as did your first draft – sometimes even more. One of the biggest problems that many novelists have when editing their first novel is that they are not bold enough in their willingness to make changes. Remember, no change is terminal. As long as you keep copies, if you make a change to your manuscript that you later think the better of, you can always go back to an earlier draft.

Redrafting is not just about making small changes. It can be about huge, bold moves, great flights of the imagination and intensely creative solutions to problems in your work.

Expansion and contraction: finding the right length

Two things may happen while you are redrafting. One is that your novel may find itself *contracting*, that you may find yourself losing words at an alarming rate. If you redraft with sufficient boldness, you may start with 90,000 words, and after a week of redrafting you are down to 75,000. After another week you may find yourself down to 60,000 words. And you start to panic and worry that your novel will be reduced to nothing, or to a short story, or to a single paragraph of flash fiction.

On the other hand, you may find that the reverse happens. As you start asking questions about your work, and solving problems, you may find that your slim novella of 40,000 words grows and grows and grows until you worry that you might have a trilogy on your hands.

This expansion and contraction is normal and it is not something to worry about. Through successive redrafts your novel might expand and contract several times. And if your interesting but not-quite-working doorstop of a novel *does* dwindle away to a stunningly good short story (although this is unlikely), then a stunningly good short story is a better than a not-quite-working doorstop of a novel.

How do I know I have reached my final draft?

If drafting is a long process, and if you are going to find yourself going through multiple drafts, you may be wondering at this stage how you will *know* when you have reached your final draft. There is no clear answer to this question. Sometimes you may think you've reached a final draft, get up from your desk, go for a walk, and then realize all of a sudden how much more there is to do. The answer, in the end, is that you have reached your final draft when you are happy that your work is ready for the next stage.

Keeping track of drafts

It can be very useful to keep track of your various drafts, so that you can refer back to earlier versions. You may make a change in draft number five, and cut out a whole chapter; but then, after successive changes, you may return in the tenth draft and think about putting that chapter back in, in a different place. But if you no longer have a copy of draft number five, then you are stuck.

If you are working on a computer, one of the very worst ways you can keep track of drafts is by calling your drafts: 'FinalDraft.doc', 'FinalFinalDraft.doc', and 'ReallyFinalDraft.doc'. This is a recipe for confusion. Similarly, calling your file, 'MostRecentVersion.doc' is not very useful if you end up with another file in the same folder called, mysteriously, 'LaterVersion.doc'.

Snapshot: keeping track of drafts

There are several ways of keeping track of multiple files. Here are two that I favour:

1   Marking files with date completed

    If you have your drafts saved as file names including dates in them, this can help you see at a glance which document is the most recent. For example, you could have files called '2015_March3_Novel.doc', '2015_June5_Novel.doc' and so on.

2   Marking drafts by number

    Even more straightforwardly, you could mark your drafts by number, so that you have 'NovelDraft1.doc', 'NovelDraft2.doc', etc. Then, each time you start a new draft, you can make a copy of the file, give it a new file name, and work on it afresh.

Depending on the software you use, there may be built-in ways of keeping track of drafts. For example, Scrivener – which I use for all my writing projects – not only allows you to keep 'snapshots', or multiple drafts of the same document, but also to compare drafts and to roll back to earlier drafts and so on.

If you prefer to work on paper for your drafting, rather than on a computer, then keep hard copies of your drafts for reference. Even if you work exclusively on your computer, it can be useful to print out hard copies of major revisions for reference.

Where to next?

Now that we have looked at redrafting in general, we can move on to consider the specifics of redrafting in more detail. We'll start by looking at how you can redraft to improve the pace, structure and rhythm of your novel, so that you can sustain your reader throughout the journey from the first to the last page.

12

Redrafting for pace, structure and rhythm

Each book has its own unique rhythm. This depends not only on the story and how it is told, but also on how the text itself is structured, how it is broken up and how it looks on the page. When we pick up a book, we do so with a sense of the book's magnitude. We don't read a slim novella in the same way – with the same expectations, with the same internal rhythm – as we read a thousand-page tome.

This chapter is about how you can redraft for pace, structure and rhythm. It is about how you can tell your story in such a way that it engages your readers more deeply, drawing them in and sustaining their interest. In this chapter we will begin by looking at reading as a physical activity that takes time and that has a particular rhythm. We will then move on to consider the first thing that will strike your reader when they open your book, before they have even read a single word: how dense or airy the text looks on the page, how weighty the book feels in their hands. Then we will look in greater detail at the particular structural issues that will face you at various points in your text. The chapter ends by moving from the broadest structural questions – how you divide your text up into sections and chapters – to the most fine-grained questions about how you keep pace, movement, structure and rhythm by working at the level of sentences.

The rhythm of reading

The Italian novelist Italo Calvino begins his novel *If on a Winter's Night a Traveller* by addressing the reader directly in the second person. 'You are about to begin reading Italo Calvino's new novel,' he says. Then he launches into an extended passage about the ways you can read the book, whether in a hammock, upside-down in a yoga posture or on horseback, the book secured to the ears of the horse with some specially contrived harness. As an opening passage it is funny, but it also reminds the reader that reading is a physical activity. We have to adopt a certain posture, get comfortable, focus our eyes, cut out external distractions, turn the pages (or click forwards on our ereaders) and maintain this focus and attention as the words conjure images and stories in the mind.

 Key idea

Reading is a *physical* activity.

Because reading is a physical activity that takes time, there is a certain rhythm to reading a book. Unless your book is very short or your reader is very committed, this rhythm will be broken up over a number of sittings, so that your reader will find time to read the book between the other activities that make up their lives. Your job as a writer is to make your book unfold in a fashion that keeps your reader engaged, and that brings them back to the book between sittings, as they journey from the first to the last page.

Every book has its own rhythm, or its own set of rhythms. Some may be compulsive page-turners, some may invite a slower and more contemplative reading, some may move between moments of great pace and focus and longer, more meandering passages. But the way that you manage this is central to the feel and flavour of your novel.

 Virginia Woolf

'Here I am sitting after half the morning, crammed with ideas, and visions, and so on, and can't dislodge them, for lack of the right rhythm. Now this is very profound, what rhythm is, and goes far deeper than words.'

It can be useful to think of novels as being like pieces of music in which there are multiple rhythms at play: from slow pulsing bass-notes to rapid *pizzicato* passages in the treble. The art of rhythm in orchestrating your novel is to make sure that there is a sense of unity throughout, so that this feels like a single, coherent novel, but also to make sure that there is sufficient variety to keep the reader engaged.

Physicality: heavy and light, dense and airy

Books, even ebooks, are objects that are rooted in the physical world. A long, heavy, weighty book sets up different expectations from a slim, light book. When thinking about redrafting your work for pace, structure and rhythm, it can be useful to think about the physical being of your book: is it meant to be weighty or light? Is it a breezy novel that your readers can zip through, or something more dense and tangled?

One aspect of the physicality of books is the way that text is laid out on the page. Some books have a high ink to page ratio, while some have astonishing amounts of white space. The density of the text on the page, the way that it is carved up into paragraphs and sections, will have an effect on the way that the reader reads. The density or airiness of a book depends in part upon structural matters – the way you break up your text into chapters, the length of paragraphs, the way you lay out speech on the page, the length and rhythm of your sentences – and in part upon design choices made by your publisher (or, if you are self-publishing, the choices that you make yourself), such as the kind of font you used, the size of margins and so on. The way a book looks on the page will signal to the reader the kind of attention that you are expecting from them. Ask yourself whether this is the kind of feel that fits your story. Do you want to introduce more breathing space? Or do you want to close up the space, to make the experience of reading the book more intensely focused?

With the rise of ereaders, this physical dimension is perhaps less of an issue, as the reader has some control over the layout of the page and the amount of breathing space that they prefer when it comes to how the text is laid out.

Beginnings, middles and endings (again)

When it comes to questions of pace and rhythm, it can be useful once again to think about beginnings, middles and ends. We have already looked at this in terms of the shape of the story – that is, in terms of the events in your story-world; but there is also the question of where your book begins and where your book ends.

WHERE TO BEGIN

We have already seen that there is no need to have a blistering beginning that will make your readers' gasp in wonder: some novels can do this, but others are much quieter in the way they begin. Either is fine. Nevertheless, it can be very useful to think about your beginning, when you are redrafting, from the perspective of a reader who is as yet unfamiliar with your fictional world.

Many films begin with what is sometimes called an 'establishing shot'. This is a shot or a scene that sets the tone of the world of the film as a whole, that gives us the sense that we are watching *this* kind of film rather than another kind of film. Such an establishing shot allows the audience to settle into the film, to tune up their expectations.

Snapshot: setting the scene

Read through the first chapter of your novel, or even just the first few pages, and ask yourself the following questions:

- Are you giving the reader the information they need to engage with the book?
- Are you setting the mood of the book?
- Is there too much information too soon, information that you do not need to tell the audience just yet?
- Do these opening pages set up the right kinds of expectations, or are they misleading?
- Have you introduced the main character or characters? If not, do you need to?
- Are you setting up questions that will draw the reader onwards through your book?

You may want a beginning that plays with your readers' expectations. Iain M. Banks's book *The Player of Games* opens in the middle of what seems like a serious conflict; only after we have read on for a few pages do we realize that this is a simulation in which his characters are merely players. When you realize this as a reader, there is a kind of lurch, a shifting of expectations. But Banks knows what he is doing: he uses this device to set up questions about the relationship between games and reality that become central to the entire book.

Focus point

Remember that the beginning of your novel will be the place where you will be setting up the major questions that you want to explore.

False starts

It is a relatively common experience among novelists that their opening pages are less to do with *the reader* and more to do with *themselves*. As a writer, you may spend several pages working your way into a story: the first few pages may simply be what you need *as a writer* to get up to speed. I have heard some writers saying that, if you are writing a poem you should throw away the first stanza, if you are writing a short story you should throw away the first paragraph, and if you are writing a novel you should throw away the first chapter. This is not a hard-and-fast rule, but it can be instructive to ask yourself what happens if you *do* cut the first chapter, or the first few pages. Does your novel become more tight and focused, or does it lose something?

MIDDLES

Once you are up and running, then there are questions about how to maintain the pace through the middle of your story. You are asking your reader to commit a lot of time to your story, and so you need to make sure that this commitment is rewarded in some way or other. The middle of your novel is the meat of the story; it is where all the interesting stuff happens – all of the richness and complexity, all of the insight and excitement. If you have a strong beginning planned and a strong ending, the middle should not just be the quickest way of getting from A to B. Bear in mind the old cliché that the best journeys are not those that get you to your destination quickly, but that get you there by itineraries that are interesting, surprising, thought-provoking or moving.

When reading through your novel in the redrafting phase, develop the ability to be ruthlessly honest about when your attention flags or wavers. There will be moments when your eyes lift from the page, when you gaze out of the window, when you are reading the words but are no longer engaged in the story, or when you find you have skipped a page or two – or even more. Often when we are reading, we do not notice these moments. Our brains fill in the gaps. But when redrafting your novel, these lapses in attention may point to areas where your story is lacking in richness and depth.

Focus point

When editing your work, notice any points where you lose focus and attention. These points may be the very same points that lose your *readers'* attention

There are reasons why you may find the middle of your novel to be slack and lifeless. Many of these are to do with plotting. Some examples you may have to deal with are as follows:

• The plot is insufficiently complex.

• You are not continuing to raise new questions to keep the reader engaged.

• There are not enough concrete actions leading to changes in the direction of the story.

• You are not managing to deepen and complicate the questions that you have already raised at the beginning.

Resolving many of these problems may involve *cutting back*, but the solutions to some of them may also involve *adding more material*.

Focus point

Remember that the *middle* of the novel is the place where you will deepen, enrich and multiply the questions that your novel is raising.

There are also a number of smaller issues that may lead to a slowing of pace in the middle. Here are some things to look out for.

Stating the obvious

One of the most useful questions you can ask when editing your work is this: *What do I not need to say?* You should assume that your readers are intelligent people, that they will be able to understand what it is that you are getting at. Much of what you want to say or suggest in a novel is going to be by means of implication and indirectness. You do not need to ram your points home. If you find that you are doing so, if you are pointing out something that is already obvious from the unfolding of the story, then cut it out.

Irrelevancies

When you start out writing a novel, you may find that at every point you are presented with a huge number of possibilities. You set various threads in motion, you open up various questions, and so on. But a novel is not infinite in scope, and so you cannot follow them all up. If you think of your novel as a branching river, some of these branches will dry up, while others will continue to flow all the way to the end. When you go back over the manuscript, you may find that there are branches of the river that have gone nowhere, questions that you have raised and lost interest in, sideshows that had seemed interesting at the time but that now seem beside the point. Are there characters who have no place in it, but who would be better off in a different novel? Are there subplots that you could cut out without adversely affecting the novel in any way whatsoever?

Be rigorous about what is not needed.

Edit: what job is this doing?

One exercise you can do while editing your work is go through paragraph by paragraph, or even sentence by sentence, and ask yourself: *What job is this doing?* If you cannot find a good answer to this question, then cut the section at issue.

Sometimes you can agonize for hours over getting a paragraph right, and then you realize that the paragraph is doing nothing useful anyway: in such cases, you can solve the problem simply by cutting the paragraph altogether!

Digressions and lectures

Laurence Sterne, *The Life and Opinions of Tristram Shandy, Gentleman*

'Digressions incontestably are the sunshine; – they are the life, the soul of reading.'

I personally enjoy digressions. I appreciate it when Herman Melville takes the time to explain why white is such a terrifying colour, or why a whale is, in fact, a fish. But (whatever Laurence Sterne may say), many readers may not be that tolerant. There is always a danger that as a novelist you will get carried away by the sound of your own voice, that you will use the fact that you have the attention of an audience to present a lecture on whatever it is that preoccupies you. Audiences may not take this kindly: if they wanted a lecture, they would have signed up for one.

There are all kinds of ways in which you can explore your obsessions without preaching to your audience. If your novel is heavy on the research, then you may want to demonstrate to your audience how hard you have worked to get everything right; but not everything that you have researched should go into your novel. If it is not needed for the story, leave it out. This other research is not wasted: it is part of an invisible substructure that holds the story together, even if this is not apparent to the reader.

Back story

We do not need to know everything about somebody's past to be able to deal with them. There are people whom I know well, and with whom I interact day after day, but about whose past I actually know very little. Back story is not necessary to be able to relate to and engage with the people we encounter. This goes for fictional characters as well. By all means introduce back story if it is relevant to the story that is happening now; but if it is not relevant, keep quiet about it.

Sometimes, however, there is the reverse problem: the character is presented a little *too* baldly, without sufficient back story. When this happens, it can be useful to think about how this character can be brought into sharper focus as a living, breathing character.

There is also often a tendency to introduce a character's back story *all at once*. So the moment you meet a character, there are two or three pages explaining who this character is, where they come from, and so on. This kind of extended introduction is fine, but it can break the forward motion of the plot. Sometimes you can give back story in fragments, so that as the story rolls forward in time, so does the reader's sense of the history that underpins it.

ENDINGS

In terms of structure, endings matter a great deal. You will know the experience of reading a novel or watching a film that seemed compelling and interesting until the disappointing ending. There are several reasons why the end of a novel may be disappointing. Here are a few of them, and some suggestions for how you might remedy them.

Focus point

Remember that the *end* of the novel should usually address and resolve in some fashion (but not necessarily answer) the questions that you have raised at the beginning.

Premature climax

There is nothing more disappointing than a premature climax (except, perhaps, no climax at all). What I mean by this is a high point that comes too soon, without sufficient time to build up the tension. This may be a problem with the end of the novel, but it may equally be a problem with the middle – in that you may have not paid enough attention to developing the tension and the conflict throughout the novel so that the climax, when it comes, feels decidedly unimpressive.

False summits

If you are the kind of writer who likes to go walking up in the hills, you will know about false summits. You climb and climb, and you think you are getting to the top of the hill; and then when you almost get there, you see that what you thought was the summit was only a little hump along the way. So you climb further, the summit in sight, and when you are just about to get there… once again you see the *real* summit looming behind. Suddenly you are taken by a great weariness: *Will this hill ever end?* you think. This experience can happen in books as well. If you have signalled to the reader that this is the end of your story, then you need to make good on this.

Final exposition

Another problematic ending is when you find that you have resolved all the main questions that were raised in the earlier part of your novel, but then mysteriously you find that you have another 20 pages of discussion about the economy of Napoleonic-era France, or else a long description of what your main protagonist has for breakfast on the morning after the crime is solved. You are no longer exploring the questions that matter in the novel, you are just playing for time – filling in detail, or saying all the things that you have forgotten to say as you are going along. This is the opposite problem to the problem of false starts. Sometimes these final expositions can be the result of a loss of nerve: you don't believe that you have really communicated what you want to communicate, so you pop up at the end to drive the point home. If you find yourself doing this, then go back to the middle of your book and see how you can enrich it so that you don't *need* to drive the point home.

Time and intensity

We saw in the chapter on storytelling that there is a distinction between the time in which the story you are telling unfolds in your fictional world, and the way you manage the telling of this story. This means that it is possible to spend 15 pages talking about something that happens in two minutes, and then spend two pages skipping lightly over the next 15 *years*. If you have passages of time in your tale during which nothing happens, then you are by no means obliged to simply fill them by explaining that your character wanders around, drinks a beer, has a think about life and so on. You can skip lightly over these periods of low intensity in the story, and then you can unfold periods of high intensity at much greater length.

Key idea

To maintain pace, give more room in your text to events that have a greater degree of intensity, and ease off on events that have a lesser degree (even if they take up more time).

Showing, telling and pace

As we saw in Chapter 10, there is a distinction between 'showing' – allowing a scene to be played out in front of the reader's eyes – and 'telling', or reporting on what is happening. This matters for how you pace your story. Showing slows things down, and means that you cannot move quite so speedily; telling allows you to move things forward quickly and efficiently. When you are thinking about your novel in terms of pace, you can work with varying pace through asking which aspects of the story you want to *show* and which aspects of the story are better *told*.

Edit: showing and telling

Choose a few pages of your text, and take two different-coloured pens. Now go through the pages and outline the sections – whether they are sentences, paragraphs or pages – where you are showing in one colour, and the sections where you are telling in another colour.

Now answer the following questions:
- Do you incline to show more or to tell more?
- How do you move between showing and telling?
- How does this affect the pace of your writing?

Now take a single chapter and alter the pace by changing at least two instances of telling into showing, and vice versa. How does this affect the feel of your work?

Chapters

Not all books are divided into chapters. There are novels that are simply huge blocks of text, and novelists who believe that chapter breaks somehow interfere with the reader's immersive experience of the world about which they are writing. Other novels have a large number of short chapters. There is no rule about how many chapters your novel should have. The average probably floats somewhere between 15 and 20 chapters for a 90,000-novel, with each chapter being between 3,000–4,500 words long. But this is an average: it is not a rule.

LONG CHAPTERS VS. SHORT CHAPTERS

If you do break your book into chapters, remember that both *the book as a whole* and *each individual chapter* must have a shape of its own. A chapter break cannot be arbitrary. It will mark a pause for the reader. The end of the chapter will be the point where your reader gets up to make a cup of tea. I remember growing up, nagging my parents to come and do something more interesting, and they would say, 'I'll come and play when I've finished the next chapter.' The fact that a chapter break offers the reader a chance to disengage with your novel may seem like a disadvantage; but it is also an advantage, because it is easier, in general, for a reader to *re*-engage with your book when they return to it if they are picking up a new chapter rather than just continuing to plough through unbroken text.

Key idea

If you divide your book into chapters, each chapter must have its own shape and structure. Chapter divisions should not be arbitrary.

Snapshot: getting a feel for structure

Pull a number of novels off your bookshelves: five or so will do. Make sure that they are novels that you have read fairly recently. For each of them, jot down how many pages the novel has as a whole, and how many chapters each novel has. Write out results in a table like the one below (I've rounded the calculations to the nearest integer).

Total number of pages	Number of chapters	Average chapter length (pages)
256	24	11
420	16	26
256	24	11
230	62	4
360	49	7

Now ask yourself:
- Why has the author divided up the book in this fashion?
- How does this affect the pace of the novel?
- How would the novel have been different had the chapters been longer? What about if they had been shorter?

My own preference – and it is only a preference – is for shorter chapters. As a reader, I appreciate it. And, as a writer, I think of it as a courtesy to my readers, who may have cups of tea to make or nagging children to see to. But at the same time I can appreciate the opposite argument for longer, more immersive chapters, or for no chapters at all. My second book has very short chapters indeed, often no more than two pages long. I'm surprised by how many readers have come up to me and thanked me for this.

In part, the decision will depend upon the complexity of your story. For some stories, you may find that if you make chapters too short, you simply don't have enough room to move. On the other hand, you may find that if your chapters are too long, you start to lose focus.

Within certain genres – thrillers, for example – there are quite common tricks that novelists play with chapter breaks. If there are a number of threads to a narrative, you can keep your reader engaged by raising questions at the *end* of a chapter (for example, by placing a character in jeopardy, by introducing a new element to the plot, or by an unexpected turn of events), and then by changing the subject and picking up another thread. The reader will keep reading because she will want to know the answer to the question. And, of course, in the chapter in between, you can raise *another* question, so that by the time the reader finds the answer to the first question, she is desperate to learn the answer to the second. This braiding of questions in your story can be a very effective strategy.

CHAPTER TITLES

Another question that sometimes vexes novelists is whether their chapters should have titles. Chapter titles are strange things because they stand outside the narrative itself. They act as an extra layer that helps direct the reader, or raises questions in their mind, as they read the chapter. If you are thinking about using chapter titles, it can be useful to ask yourself what, if anything, the titles add to the story. If they are simply a word or a phrase that reflects the action of the story, they may not be necessary. But if the chapter titles do something *in addition* to the rest of the text, this may be more interesting.

CHAPTERS AND PARTS

You may also decide to divide your book into parts. Again, there is no strict rule for this. But the way you split up your novel will have an effect on how your reader approaches it. A book with three parts may fall more naturally into the reader's expectations of a three-act structure of beginning, middle, end – or a set-up, unravelling and denouement. A book with two parts may feel more like setting up two sides of an argument. A book with four or more parts may feel like an ongoing saga. Again, it is good to develop a feel for how other novelists use these structural devices. There are no rules for how you should do any of this. But the more you can develop this feel for how other novelists make use of these various strategies, the better.

Paragraphs

Jack Kerouac

'Every paragraph is a poem.'

Looking more closely at the structure of your novel, we come to the question of paragraphs. Paragraphs serve to break up large chunks of text, to introduce more space into your reader's experience of reading. The spaces between paragraphs are something like pauses and rests in a piece of music; and the way you play with these pauses and rests will have a strong effect on the pace and rhythm of the reading. Ideas and images that share the same paragraph will feel closer to each other than ideas and images that are divided into separate paragraphs. When writing essays, you may have been taught all kinds of things about paragraphs: about how each paragraph should convey a single, self-contained idea, or about how each paragraph should have a beginning, a middle and an end. But this is not strictly true when writing fiction. Think about paragraphs in terms of rhythm, in terms of the texture of your novel. Paragraphs are a way of tightening and slackening the attention of the reader, of alternating focus and relaxation.

Sentences

E. Annie Proulx

'You should write because you love the shape of stories and sentences and the creation of different worlds on a page.'

The final structural unit to look at is the sentence. For present purposes, I'm going to say that a sentence is any chunk of text that is self-contained, that begins with a capital letter and ends with a full stop, question mark or other appropriate punctuation mark. This is a sentence. And this? Sure. Why not? This is not a grammatical definition, but a practical definition. According to the rules of grammar, a sentence might need a main verb. But you don't need to worry about any of that. Think instead of a full stop as a pause, a break in the sense of what you are saying.

The feel of your novel will depend in part on how you manage sentences. Do you have long, luxuriant sentences with multiple clauses? Or do you go for short and snappy sentences? You may find that you have not even thought very hard about these questions while drafting your novel: you have just written what you have written. But when you redrafting, pay attention to what your own tendencies are, and whether these are working in your favour or not.

SENTENCES, BREATHING AND EMOTION

Sometimes it can be good to vary sentence length as a way of keeping variety in the rhythm of the book. Sentence length can also mirror the action in the story. Suddenness, danger, excitement or rapid action may be more suited to shorter, choppier sentences, while more languid passages may suit longer, more luxuriant sentences. This happens naturally in speech: if you are excited, or in danger, your breath comes and goes much more quickly, your sentences are shorter, simpler and more abrupt. Not only this, but you are more physically alert, you lean forwards, you are more attentive.

If you are relaxed, on the other hand, you will speak in longer, more meandering sentences. Physically you lean back, you slacken off the focus of your attention. There is a connection between the length of the sentences that we use, the kind of attention that we have, and the physical experience we have of the world. As a writer, you can reverse this: you can use longer, more drawn-out sentences to give the reader a physical sense of languor; and then you can use shorter sentences to ramp up the excitement. As a reader you may notice that at certain times you settle into a book as you would into a warm bath, at other times you sit up and lean over the page, your heart beating faster. Have a look at the following table:

Physical experience	Focus	Posture	Breathing	Sentence length
Relaxation	Broad, wide	At ease, horizontal, slack	Slow, steady	Longer, complex
Excitement, tension	Sharp, narrow	Alert, upright, tense	Fast, choppy	Short, simple, often broken

Part of the pleasure of reading is the alternation of slackening and tensing, an experience that is not just mental but also physical. What keeps a reader engaged is the way that you play with different levels of *intensity*. This is partly an issue of plot; but also playing with sentence length can subtly affect your reader, so that they remain engaged in your unfolding story.

Write: sentences, pace and emotion

Think up two scenes for one of your characters. Use fresh scenes, not scenes that you have in your novel-in-progress. You will need one scene that is low intensity (your character sinking into a bath at the end of a long day, or falling asleep on a train, for example), and one that is high intensity (your character hanging from a cliff by the fingernails, or desperately ransacking the waste-basket for a lost phone number).

Write each scene in the way that feels most natural. Take ten minutes per scene. Don't go back, edit or cross out.

When you have done this, read over both scenes and look at the sentence length. Are the sentences in the low-intensity passage longer and more luxuriant? Are sentences in the high-intensity piece shorter and choppier?

Now try this:
- Rewrite the story to make the sentences in the high-intensity piece shorter. Then rewrite the low-intensity piece to make the sentences longer.
- What does this do to the mood of each piece? How does sentence length affect intensity?
- If you want to, you can finish by rewriting a second time to make the sentences in the *low*-intensity piece shorter and the sentences in the *high*-intensity piece longer.

Does this feel strange? Do you experience any tension between the sentences you are writing and the subject-matter? The following workshop takes the idea of editing for pace further, and can be an interesting one to work on, and discuss, with another writer.

Workshop: editing for pace

This workshop consists of three different tasks that will help you edit for pace. The first task is about thinking about the intensity of the story as a whole. The second looks more closely at paragraphs and how working with breaking your text into paragraphs can affect the pacing of your story. The third looks at sentences.

1 Thinking through intensity

Take a section of your novel, and print it out. Mark breaks in the manuscript where there is a clear change in scene or focus. When you have done this, go through and write down a name to identify each scene, a rough word length for that scene (don't count every word, just estimate), and a score from one to five to indicate the intensity of this scene, where 1 is 'low intensity' and 5 is 'high intensity', as in the table below.

Scene/focus	Words	Intensity

If you like, you can do a graph of changing intensity, scene by scene, like the one below:

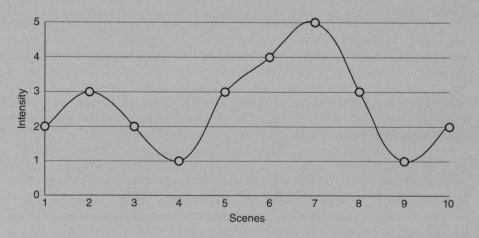

This gives you a map of your story in terms of degrees of intensity.

Now think about the following issues:

- When do you want to build intensity slowly? When do you want moments of shock or surprise (moments of high intensity bursting into moments of low intensity)?
- Are you effectively moving between passages of lower intensity and passages of higher intensity?
- If there are long passages of low intensity, how do you maintain your readers' interest?
- You can also try this exercise with books where you think the pacing works well, to see what you can learn.

2 Playing with paragraphs

In the second part of this workshop, we will be looking at paragraphs.

Firstly, take two or three pages of your novel and copy them into a new document (I'm assuming that you have an electronic version of your novel). Print out the copy as it stands. Call this Version 1.

Now double the number of paragraphs by finding places in the text where you can insert new paragraph breaks. Don't worry if some of these feel a bit artificial. This is Version 2. Print out a copy of Version 2 with extra paragraphs.

Having done this, return to Version 1 and cut out as many paragraphs as you can, so that you have a version of the document with as few paragraphs as possible. This is Version 3. Print out a copy.

Now you have three versions of the same text. Place the texts in front of you, side by side. How do they feel different? Read each version out loud. How does the change in paragraphing affect the rhythm of your reading? Does the extract work better with more paragraphs or with fewer? How does the way that you break up the text into paragraphs affect the changes in intensity in your story?

3 Sentences

Taking the understanding of the relationship between emotion, physicality, the breath and sentence length that you have developed in the previous snapshot exercise, take the same section of your novel that you have looked in in part 1 of this workshop, and explore the way that you write sentences. Read the passage out loud, so you can feel the coming and going of your breath. Now select a few consecutive scenes of varying intensity, and look at the sentence length. Do the higher-intensity scenes have shorter sentences? Do the lower-intensity scenes have more languid sentences?

Now see whether you can hone and tweak the intensity of these passages by playing with changing sentence length.

Where to next?

In this chapter we have covered quite a lot of ground about pace, structure and the rhythm of your work. Now we are going to turn to look at another aspect of redrafting: the logic of how your world hangs together, and how you can make sure that, beneath those wonderful sentences and paragraphs, there is a rigorously well-engineered framework.

13

Redrafting for logic

We saw in Chapter 5 that the architecture of your fictional world matters. Readers will feel confident and in good hands if your fictional world feels solid and well drawn, if your characters respond to things in a fashion that is consistent (even if it is sometimes surprising) and if there are no areas of fuzziness. If, on the other hand, your novel is filled with problems and inconsistencies, if it appears a bit fuzzy, or if there are obvious errors in continuity, or anachronisms, or other logical problems, then your reader will feel less at ease.

Readers often pick up on inconsistencies and logical problems intuitively, even if they do not do so consciously. If you have too many problems in your book, your readers will read it with a nagging sense that *something isn't quite right*, even if they cannot quite put their fingers on what it is that isn't right. So in this chapter we will be looking at how to tighten up your plot and how to troubleshoot some common problems.

Engineering and poetry

José Saramago

'Just as someone who builds has to balance one element against another in order to prevent the whole from collapsing, so too a book will develop – seeking out its own logic, not the structure that was predetermined for it.'

I should say something about what I mean by talking about the 'logic' of your novel. For some novelists, the notion of 'logic' may seem a bit cold and chilly. You may want your novel to be about human emotions and interactions, you may be concerned about exploring large existential themes, you may want to tell a heart-rending tale, you may want to make your audience laugh… but you may think that this does not have much to do with logic. However, it is often the case that the novels that are most heart-rending, that make us laugh best, that most successfully explore existential themes, that most deeply plumb the depths of human emotions and interactions, are those that have a strong and consistent internal logic.

This logic is not something that is imposed on the book from outside. Instead, as Saramago suggests, it is the story that dictates its own logic. Your task as the writer is to seek out this logic, and to follow it through as rigorously as you can.

In his famous *Poetics*, Aristotle lists plot and character as the most important aspects of successful storytelling. After plot and character comes what he calls 'thought', or *dianoia*. At the risk of annoying the philosophers, I'm going to go suggest that 'thought' in this context could be understood more broadly as the overall logic of your story. In Greek philosophy, *dianoia* might be said to be thought itself, and *logos* – the word from which 'logic' derives – the expression of this thought in words. So, for present purposes, I am going to take these as two sides of the same coin. One reason why Aristotle puts this *after* plot and character is that the logic of your story should be something that *arises out of* these things.

Key idea

Logic is not something you impose upon plot and character. Instead, it should emerge organically from the world, events and characters of your novel.

Think of a novel as being like a coach and horses. You can see plot as the horses that are galloping up front, keeping up the momentum. The plot is the driving force. Character is the coachman who drives the plot onwards. But then there is the machinery of the coach itself – the wheels that turn smoothly on their axles, the engineering that ensures that the whole thing doesn't fly apart, the suspension that ensures a comfortable and not-too-bumpy ride – that enables any of them to move at all. If your story lacks *logos,* it will grind to a halt or it will fall apart. And if you are riding in the coach (let's stretch the metaphor to breaking point and suggest that the people riding in the coach, the passengers, are your readers), not only are you interested in the destination, but you also want to get there in one piece. As a writer, if your book is badly engineered, the horses of plot may end up galloping to the end, and you may not realize that the carriage has collapsed on the road and that the readers have all clambered out, dusted themselves down, and hailed another, better-made vehicle that might take them somewhere more interesting, and in more comfort and style.

Focus point

Logic matters to your readers, not because all readers are pedants who love logical consistency, but because if you make too many logical slips, your readers will be repeatedly jolted and shaken like passengers in a badly made carriage.

There is, of course, a great deal of artfulness and poetry involved in writing a novel. But a novel is also a piece of engineering, a rigorously constructed bit of kit that allows you to take your readers where you want to take them.

Research and the redrafting process

It might seem as if research is something that you do at the beginning of a project, but that you leave behind once you start your writing. Or, at least, it is something that – once your novel is drafted – you no longer need to think about. However, this is usually not the case. Until your novel has reached its final form, research will remain of central importance. If you forget about research while you are redrafting, you may let all kinds of problems slip through the net.

Focus point

At the redrafting stage, you may need to go back and do quite a lot of research. This may be straightforward fact-checking, or it may be more in-depth research that will mean making considerable changes to your story.

When you are redrafting, it can be a good idea to go through your novel, chapter by chapter, and ask yourself whether the information you are drawing upon is accurate, or whether you need to do further research. Details matter. Place names change, lakes that exist today may not have existed in the past, whole landscapes shift and mutate over time. Technologies and ways of speaking and thinking also change in different times and places. A final read-through to make sure that your facts are fairly secure and backed up by solid research will be of great benefit.

Of course, *you will inevitably make mistakes.* You will get things wrong; there will be gaps and glitches. All fictional worlds are built on artifice, and there is *always* a point at which the cracks begin to show if you look hard enough. Your job is to make sure that these cracks are not too glaring or fatal, and to fill them in as far as possible so that there is no risk of the novel collapsing into them.

Who knows what? Troubleshooting point of view

As the creator of your fictional world, you will inevitably know things that your characters do not know. It may be clear to you that Florence has been having an affair with Mo, but it may not be clear to Giles. Your fictional world will be a world in which your characters all have only partial knowledge. This means that you need to keep track not only of everything that is happening, but also of who knows what. And if you have ever been invited into anybody's confidence and told that you can only tell certain people this or that, you will know that remembering who is party to what information is a difficult thing.

 ## Focus point

Things can go terribly wrong in your story if you lose track of who knows what.

When redrafting, make sure that you are clear chapter by chapter about what each of your characters knows, and make sure that they are acting *only* in accord with this knowledge. Keeping secrets is hard: you can easily let things slip. If you have a novel with multiple characters, all of whom have different knowledge, and if your plot depends on what your characters know, then you are effectively going to have to keep track of which secrets you have let which characters in on.

What a coincidence!

Coincidence literally means the coming together of two events or actions. But when people talk about coincidence, they usually mean the significant coming together of events that are in some way improbable, or between which there is no obvious causal connection. What interest us as human beings are not coincidences themselves, but coincidences that seem unlikely, improbable or meaningful.

 ## Paul Auster

'When I talk about coincidence, I'm not referring to a desire to manipulate… No, what I'm talking about is the presence of the unpredictable, the utterly bewildering nature of human experience.'

When we use the word 'coincidence' in everyday life, what we can sometimes mean is that there really *is* no connection between these two events; but what we often more frequently mean is that although there is no *obvious* connection between two events, there is perhaps a *hidden and mysterious* connection. Some writers – Paul Auster is a good example – thrive on tales of coincidence. But you need to be careful. Coincidences in real life can be strange and intriguing; but in fiction you need to make sure that you are not just employing coincidence as a lazy way of solving plot problems (this is a form of *deus ex machina* – see Chapter 7). In general, you should not overuse coincidences, or else you should use them as *starting points* in chains of causality. A novel might begin with a 'coincidental' encounter – for example, two people who knew and hated each other years ago find themselves pressed up together in a crowded commuter train – and then follow through the logic of what happens from that. But if you used a further coincidence to resolve this tricky situation, then your readers might be less impressed.

On the other hand, if you are writing a book that revels in the absurdity of multiple coincidences, by all means go ahead and pile up coincidence upon coincidence – as long as you are clear about what you are doing.

Breaking the laws of physics (and chemistry, and biology...)

As we saw in Chapter 5, you can't *arbitrarily* break the laws of physics, chemistry or biology in your fictional world. If you do break these laws, you need to do so in a way that is consistent and coherent.

Here it might be useful to distinguish between two kinds of laws: on the one hand, moral or socially constructed laws; and on the other hand, laws of nature. The law against stealing cars is not a law that makes it *impossible* to steal cars; it only means that you *ought not* steal cars, and that as a result, *if* you steal cars, there may be consequences. These are moral or socially constructed laws. But the law that says that, if the stolen car careers off a cliff edge, it will fall into the abyss below is not simply a moral or socially constructed law. It is a law of nature. Whatever our morality, whatever our legal system, we are all at the mercy of the law of gravity.

Of course, you can do anything you like in your fiction. You *can* have a stolen car that careens off a cliff and then simply floats away. You are not bound by the laws of physics. But if you *are* going to have a levitating car, you should be clear that you *are* breaking the laws of physics, and you should have a good reason for breaking these laws. The decision to break the laws of physics is a weighty one. It will have consequences throughout your story. If cars can float, then you will need to ask *how*, *why* and *when* they can float. You will need to ask why it is that the stolen car can do this, but not the police vehicles that are following. You will need to know precisely under what conditions, in your fictional world, floating cars are possible, and under what conditions they are not possible.

Your fictional world must be plausible through and through. This goes not just for the laws of physics. Say you are writing a crime drama, and the hero finds a DNA sample that points to a particular suspect. You need to know that the discovery of identifiable DNA is plausible under these conditions. If your hero plucks a coal out of the fire, cools it down, and then finds identifiable DNA on the now-cold nugget of charred, fossilized wood, then you need to think again. Your readers, if they are sufficiently well informed, will cry 'Foul!'

Redrafting for consistency and coherence

It can be useful to go through your work redrafting to make sure that it is both consistent (it is stable and it doesn't change) and coherent (the various parts of your world hang together).

Snapshot: busting blockbusters

A very good place to hone your skills in picking up inconsistencies and incoherencies is through watching big-budget blockbusters: particularly poor-quality blockbusters, or blockbusters that somehow bombed at the box office.

This exercise is simple. Your job is to get out one of these movies and watch it, notebook in hand, keeping an eye out for any plot holes, glitches, inconsistencies or moments of incoherence. You are watching out for any points where the story does not add up.

To do this, you need a cool and dispassionate eye. You are not watching the film to get *caught up* in it. Instead you are watching it with the detachment of a craftsperson, to see if you can find out where the logic of this fictional world breaks down, and what you can learn from this.

This exercise is best done with friends (and refreshments!).

When redrafting for consistency and coherence, you need to be clear whether your fictional world contains any elements that the real world does not (or at least, that the real world does not *uncontroversially* contain). If you are writing a historical novel, and you introduce a fictional character into history, then you are tweaking the fabric of reality. If you are writing a contemporary novel, the same thing also applies. It is what I like to think of as the Soap-Opera Paradox: a soap opera attempts to mirror reality, but the one thing it cannot do (unless it is a very postmodern kind of soap opera) is have the characters in the show sitting down in the evening and *watching themselves*.

Key idea

However closely fictional narratives mirror reality, there are always points where they will diverge and show themselves to be fictions.

If your fictional world has elements that do not exist in the real world – advanced technologies, magic and other kinds of causality – the following exercise might be useful.

Edit: altering the fabric of reality

- If your world differs from the everyday world in any respects, note down *how* it differs. This may involve advanced technologies, magic or other strange kinds of causality.
- Now make some notes about *under what conditions* these different forms of causality apply. What you need to do is set out the constraints upon this kind of causality. For example, if you have a character who can see into the future, then you need to know how this happens, when it happens, how far into the future your character can see, and so on.
- Try to turn this into a set of cast-iron rules that apply *throughout* your fictional world. Write down the rules in a list, as concisely as you can. These rules will act as a supplement to all the usual laws of causality in your fictional world.

Redrafting for concreteness

It may be that your fictional world is perfectly clearly worked out. You may have a strong notion of how everything fits together. It may be that everything is, in theory at least, perfectly plausible within the parameters that you have set (even if it is impossible in the real world). But still readers may not quite *buy* it. Why not? Because you haven't made the logic clear enough. You haven't been quite precise enough about how things work. So you can also go through and redraft for concreteness. Remember from Chapter 5 that concreteness means that your world must be fully imaginable *to the reader*. It is the last bit that is most important here. It is not a matter of whether *you* buy what is going on, but whether the *reader* buys it. As the author of the text, your understanding of it will have an elaborate scaffolding formed from all of the thinking, writing, research and experience that has gone into putting the book together. But an external reader will not have this scaffolding. As a result, you may not be the best judge of whether you have made the logic of your world fully concrete.

Focus point

Send your work out to trusted readers. If they come back to you and say they don't understand an aspect of your story, then it is not their problem, but yours.

If events unfold for too long without any apparent logic, the reader may well get bored. When this happens, the problem is often either that the writer is in fact confused and not sure what they are doing (a problem with the logic of the story being insufficiently thought through) or that the writer has just not given enough information to make sense of the story (a problem with how the story is told).

However, to say that the logic of your world should be fully concrete is not to say that you should not make use of ambiguity, mystery and intrigue. Some of the richest resources can be found in exploiting ambiguity and mystery. Fiction shouldn't necessarily be entirely clear and transparent. As we saw in the chapter on plot, a novelist's job is to raise questions, but there is no obligation to fully answer these questions.

Ambiguity and mystery, however, are not the same as logical fuzziness or unclarity. Ambiguity doesn't work if it is 'bolted on', or if it is the result of insufficient thought.

 Key idea

Ambiguity is a source of richness in your storytelling, but you shouldn't use 'it is ambiguous' as an excuse for inconsistencies, indecision, or lack of thought and care in writing.

Making the machinery invisible

A final thing to point out here is that, although your novel needs to be well engineered, this engineering needs to be done with a light touch. If the machinery of your novel is too obvious, your readers may be distracted from the journey you are taking them on. The coach is a means to an end, not an end in itself.

In mathematics lessons, I was always told by my teachers to show my workings. When it comes to writing fiction, this is not necessarily the best approach. If you, like John Gardner, want to create a 'vivid, continuous dream' in the mind of the reader, then you will have to make the machinery invisible, in the way that a skilled magician can make people levitate or produce live rabbits from hats, without any of the machinery being on show. However, this is not an absolute rule. Some books make their machinery much more explicitly visible – a good example is *Tristram Shandy* by Laurence Sterne, another is the *Lemony Snicket* series by Daniel Handler – and part of the pleasure of books such as these is the way that they play with the machinery of storytelling and of the book. The logic of most stories if *implicit*. If you want to make it *explicit*, then you are free to do so – you will have some noble predecessors; but if you do it at all, make sure you are doing it consciously.

Workshop: getting logical

This workshop has two stages. You are going to be looking at your entire manuscript (again!) and thinking about troubleshooting it for logical problems in the light of what you have learned in this chapter. In the first stage, you will be looking at troubleshooting for consistency and coherence. In the second stage, you will be looking at troubleshooting for concreteness.

1 Troubleshooting consistency and coherence

First, read over your list from the edit exercise above ('altering the fabric of reality') to remind yourself of the ways in which your fictional world differs from the real world.

Now read through your manuscript carefully. Look for any points where you can identify any of the following problems:

- The story does not adhere to the rules that you have set out in the earlier exercise.
- The physical details of your world change without reason.
- Your characters act in a way that is not appropriate to the fictional world you have built.
- Your characters act in a way that is inconsistent with their own behaviour elsewhere.
- Events occur that seem unlikely, improbable or impossible in your fictional world.
- It is unclear exactly what happens in your fictional world, or why and how things happen.
- Your story feels intuitively unconvincing.

Write out a list of problems that you need to solve by redrafting. These may be minor problems (for example, tweaking the finer details of a scene) or more major problems that you have not noticed before that require substantial revision. Go through the list and mark these problems according to their seriousness, based on the following chart:

Score	Seriousness
5	*Very serious problem:* requires major revisions of manuscript, and perhaps significant rethinking of the plot, characters and storytelling.
4	*Serious problem:* will require some significant changes and may have wider effects throughout the manuscript.
3	*Problem:* this requires serious attention, but it is likely that you can solve it without making sweeping changes.
2	*Minor problem:* light editing needed.
1	*Glitch:* small, local problem that can be solved without affecting the rest of the story.

When you have a list, work through it, solving all the problems systematically. Start with the very serious problems that you have marked with a '5', and work through these first. Some of the major revisions that you make may mean that the smaller problems disappear. Work through the entire list, finally ironing out all the glitches (the problems marked with a '1').

2 Troubleshooting concreteness

This next part of the workshop is one that can best be done by somebody else. If you can, find a friend who has a sympathetic ear, and who is likely to be able to give you good advice (you can work through this yourself, but it is much easier to get an external 'eye' on your work). Bribe them if you have to or, if your friend is a fellow writer, offer to work through their manuscript in the same fashion.

Ask your friend to write a list of anything that is either unclear, or that they don't understand, or that they find confusing. These questions might help them:

- Are there any crucial pieces of information about this fictional world that the reader needs to know, but that are not in the text?

- Is there any ambiguity that is unnecessarily confusing to the reader?
- What is the reader not told that would be useful for them to know?
- Does this fictional world feel like a particular world – does it have its own unique feel? Or does it feel a bit too generalized? How could it be made more particular and specific?

You are looking for a simple list of *things that don't make sense*, or of *things that don't add up*. When you have the list, the temptation will be to go to your reader and *explain* to them why they have misunderstood. But this is a mistake. You need instead to go back to the text of your novel and see what you need to do to solve the problems there.

Where to next?

If you have thoroughly redrafted for consistency, coherence and concreteness, made sure that your plotting does not rely on implausible coincidences and are fairly confident that the machinery of your novel is working, the next question to look at is how you can work on refining the language of your novel. This is the subject of the next chapter.

14

Redrafting for language

Now that you have nailed down the big issues in terms of the logic of your novel and the fictional world in which it is set, and now that you have dealt with the big structural issues, it is time to focus in on the language that you use to tell your story. In this chapter, we will be looking at how you can take a promising manuscript and really bring the prose to life.

What remains in the memory?

 ## Patrick Süskind, *'Amnesia in Litteris'*

> *I've been able to read for thirty years now, and I've read quite a bit, if not much, and all that's left is the very vague recollection that in the second volume of a thousand-page novel someone or other kills himself with a pistol...'*

In a very funny essay, the German novelist Patrick Süskind, author of the bestseller *Perfume*, writes about looking at his bookshelves and realizing that he has forgotten almost *everything* that he has ever read. In this, I suspect, he is not alone. Most books, after we have read them, will fade from memory. That is why I was so awed as a teenager by the ending of Ray Bradbury's novel *Fahrenheit 451*. Bradbury's book is set in a world where books are burned and a group of dissidents resolve to become a living library by memorizing books word for word. I was entranced and impressed by this ability to remember *entire books* word for word.

In reality, while we writers labour over finding just the right words, most of our words are soon forgotten. Go to your bookshelves and pull a novel down. Can you remember a single sentence from that book? For most novels, I would have to answer 'no'. In fact, the *words* are the first thing that I forget when I put a novel back on the shelf.

The next thing I forget is the *story*. Often, stories stay with me a bit longer. But if I look at the novels that are on my shelves and ask for how many of them I would be able to relate the plot in outline, I would have to guess *less than half*.

What might stick in the memory longer are specific events, scenes or characters. Sometimes I remember a single scene or character and nothing else: something about a train in Tolstoy's *Anna Karenina*, something about somebody (was she called Melanie?) in a wedding dress climbing out of the window and into the garden at night in Angela Carter's *The Magic Toyshop*... and that is all.

But what sticks in the memory the longest, after you have forgotten words, stories, plots, characters, scenes and events? What remains, I think, is a mysterious sense of the novel's *mood* or *atmosphere*. As I look at a novel that I read about a decade ago – and can perhaps barely remember – this mood or atmosphere seems to surround me, drawing me back in. *Ah, yes,* I think, *that was a good novel...*

 ## Focus point

The usual order in which we *forget* about books we have read is something like:

- words and sentences
- plot
- characters, individual scenes, events
- mood or atmosphere.

This is important, I think, because, if you want your book to linger long in the mind, then it is perhaps mood that is the most fundamental – as well as being the most intangible – thing.

> ## Key idea
>
> All books have a particular 'mood'; every book, if it is successful, conveys a particular and idiosyncratic sense of life.

Mood is a strange thing. It creeps up on us (the philosopher Martin Heidegger says that it 'assails' us). It is hard to grasp or define. You can think of it as the particular *flavour* or even the *odour* of a book: some books are pungent (like Süskind's *Perfume*); some have more subtle and delicate flavours. Mood arises out of many different aspects of writing, but two of the most powerful are the environment of the story (the world that the writer has built) and the *linguistic* environment of the storytelling (the language that is used to convey the story). We have already looked in detail at the first of these. Here we're going to focus on the second.

Style and voice

All of us, whether we are writers or not, spend our lives swimming in a sea of words. Words are all around us, and when we turn our attention to our inner monologues, debates and discussions, we find that they are inside us as well. Language surrounds us from birth. And like fish in water, often we take all of this for granted. We do not often think about the language that we use. We do not often *listen* to ourselves.

Our own relationship with language is unique and idiosyncratic. This relationship is formed by the books that we have read, by the people we have known, by the surroundings in which we have grown up, and by the languages with which we are familiar. As a writer, you may spend your first few years trying to get to grips with your distinctive voice.

> ## Miles Davis
>
> *'Sometimes you have to play a long time to play like yourself.'*

By 'voice', I don't mean anything too mysterious. Your voice is simply your unique relationship with language. Your voice is a matter of both *how* you use language and *what* you use language to talk and write about.

> ## Focus point
>
> We all have a unique relationship with language, a relationship that arises out of our history, the worlds we have inhabited, the books we have read, the people we have known, and the things that we have done.

If you worry too much about your style or your voice, you may find yourself straining a bit too hard. Often, the best writing is writing that keeps a connection with the rhythms of the spoken language. In the same way that, if you think too much about what you are saying and how you are saying it, you find that your throat dries up and that you are incapable of speaking at all (the classic first date ailment!), if you find yourself thinking too much about your voice on the page, you will find yourself hitting a brick wall.

There are, of course, differences between spoken and written language. When we communicate face to face or by means of the spoken word, our 'voice' – our particular style of communication – also involves things such as facial expressions, gestures and other non-verbal aspects of communication. The *gestural* nature of our communication is lost on the page: if I say something deadpan, but have a half-smile on my face, you may realize that I am employing heavy irony. But if I do the same in print, I need to find other ways to communicate this irony.

To have the impact of spoken language, written language may need to have a bit more vigour; it may need to somehow exemplify these gestures, these nods and winks, these dramatic pauses. As you develop as a writer, your skills in this respect will increase.

The problem with cliché

 Eugène Ionesco

'Banality is a symptom of non-communication. Men hide behind their clichés.'

Clichés are overused phrases or habits of thinking and writing that have become so well worn and hackneyed that they have lost their precision. The notion of cliché does not apply only to language, but also to plot and character: a cliché is an idea, a phrase or an image that is off the peg rather than bespoke. But cliché is a matter of degree. There is a continuum or a spectrum between the clichéd and familiar, on the one hand, and the new and unfamiliar on the other hand. Writers who write only in well-known clichés are as exhausting as writers who believe that every sentence should be somehow sparkling and new. Sometimes the well worn and the off the peg will be less obtrusive than something that is newly minted (and, of course, 'off the peg' and 'newly minted' are themselves both rather clichéd expressions!). And sometimes things are well worn for a reason: if there are two paths that head towards the same place, it can be wiser to take the path that is more well trodden than the path that is tangled and overgrown with brambles and nettles.

In other words, clichés that are used out of laziness, as a way of not really *thinking*, tend to be jarring; but clichés that are used because they are more efficient ways of doing what you want to do tend to become almost invisible. When editing and redrafting, read through your text and, if you find yourself relying on ideas, thoughts or phrases that risk being accused of being clichéd, ask yourself firstly whether this is *really* what you want to be saying, and secondly, whether there are *better ways* of saying what you want to say.

Clarity and complexity

Another question to ask is: *How clear and precise is my prose?* This doesn't mean that there is no place in the world for *difficult* writing, for writing that makes the reader work hard, or that places demands upon the reader. There is a virtue to clarity but that is not to say that clarity is the only thing that matters. Language is not just a window on to a world, or a way of conveying information to the reader. It also has rhythmic, sensory and visual aspects.

> ## Key idea
>
> There is no such thing as absolutely clear language. Language has ambiguity and complexity built in.

When writing, you may want to play off the ability of language *to tell a story* against other aspects of language such as *rhythm*, *sound* and *complexity*. Some kinds of language describe or represent *nothing* but are nevertheless powerful: think of spells and curses!

> ## Write: language and music
>
> It is sometimes hard to get beyond what language means to a sense of the rhythm and mood of language. If you have ever learned a foreign language, at first it may have sounded strange and alien. But little by little those curious sounds will have turned into something that conveys *meaning*.
>
> For this snapshot, you will need a friend who speaks a second language well, and it will need to be a language that you don't speak. Ask them to select a novel that they like in this second language, and get them to read a page out loud to you. Don't ask them to explain anything about the book.
>
> When you have listened to a page, write for 10 minutes about the text that you have heard. What is it about? What is the mood and the feel? What kind of story is it? If you want, you can try to 'translate' it by making up a passage of your own that reflects your impression of the mood and feel of the piece you have listened to.
>
> Finally, read what you have written back to your friend. When you have done so, get them to tell you what it is that they have been reading you. How close are you in mood and feel to the original? You may be surprised!

Adjectives, adverbs and other issues

Now we are getting down to the fine detail of honing your prose, to the question of what words to leave in and what words to leave out; and so it is time to tackle the question of those much-scorned parts of speech, adjectives and adverbs. There are some writers who recommend, at the editing stage, the ruthless pruning of adjectives and adverbs. Stephen King is one.

 Stephen King, *On Writing*

'I believe the road to hell is paved with adverbs.'

But before you start chopping out all your adverbs and adjectives, it might be worth stepping back and asking what is wrong with adjectives and adverbs. After all, they must exist for a reason, so why should you turn your back upon them? It seems not only rather unreasonable, but also rather *weird*, to hold a grudge against a part of speech. What are the problems with adjectives and adverbs, and how do they matter to you as a writer?

ADJECTIVES

We can start with adjectives. Adjectives modify nouns. Look at the following sentence.

He climbed the steep, crumbling, moss-covered staircase.

Now, what is wrong with this sentence? You might say that there are too many adjectives. But don't cut them just yet. After all, they are telling you *something* about the staircase. They are filling in details about the world. If you cut them, you would get,

He climbed the staircase.

While this might be better in some contexts, the disadvantage is that it gives us a much more general and non-specific image of the staircase. What if you *do* want to point out the moss, and the decay, and the age of the staircase?

Let's go back to the initial sentence and look at it differently. If there is a problem with this sentence, it is that we don't know that we are talking about a *staircase* until the very end. So we know that he climbed, and that what he climbed was something steep, and that it was crumbling, and covered in moss… but there is a noticeable pause between the knowledge that the protagonist is climbing and knowing *what* he is climbing.

One trouble with adjectives is that, in English, the thing that they modify usually comes *after*. So the reader has to wait to know what the *thing* is – the noun or the object – about which you are talking. When you multiply adjectives, this becomes a problem.

Now look at the following.

He climbed the staircase. It was steep, crumbling, covered in moss.

Now, it is possible to argue over whether the second sentence here is any good, or whether you need to know all this information. But leaving this question to one side, it is clear that this has solved the delaying problem. The reader *first* knows that there is a staircase, and *then* this knowledge is modified by knowing *what kind of a staircase it is.*

Key idea

Piling up adjectives before a noun creates a delay for the reader in knowing what it is you are talking about.

There may be circumstances in which you do decide to play a little delaying game, stretching things out for the reader a bit: but do be aware that this is what you are doing.

Snapshot: auditing your adjectives

Instead of encouraging you to set about your adjectives like a crazed pest controller going at an infestation of vermin, the following exercise aims to get you to think more clearly and calmly about what work, if any, they are doing in your story. Take a page or two of your work and try the following.

Firstly, ask yourself if your adjectives are needed. Remember that adjectives may have multiple functions within a sentence: they may not be there just for description; they may also be there for style, rhythm, sound and so on.

Secondly, if you have more than one adjective together, ask yourself whether any of them are redundant. For example, 'cold and icy' could be substituted for 'icy' with little loss in meaning (although you may still prefer the *rhythm* and *emphasis* of 'cold and icy').

Thirdly, if you use adjectives and nouns together, ask whether your adjective adds anything to the noun. If you say 'the striped tiger', this may be redundant, because we already know that the tiger is striped (while 'the hungry tiger' may give us some useful information).

Fourthly, think about *placement* of the adjectives. Do you need to place them before the noun they modify, or after? Should they go in a new sentence? How does placing them differently change the feel of your text?

ADVERBS

For many writing tutors, if adjectives are permanently under suspicion, then adverbs are often assumed guilty before they have even been arrested and tried. But many of the things we have looked at with adjectives apply to adverbs.

Adverbs modify verbs, just as adjectives modify nouns. While adjectives talk about particular qualities of subjects and objects (hence '*ad-jective*'), adverbs talk about the particular qualities of actions (hence '*ad-verb*'). Like adjectives, there is nothing at all wrong with adverbs in themselves. As with your adjectives, the question to ask is whether your adverbs are really doing the work that you want them to do. Are they helping to add intensity or nuance or richness to your story? Or are they slowing the pace, providing redundant information, or otherwise getting in the way?

Look at the following two sentences:

She suddenly burst through the door.

She burst through the door.

The second sentence, to my mind, is much more sudden, because we get to the verb – the action of the sentence – much more quickly. The sentence that announces its suddenness is *less* and not *more* suddenness. On the other hand, look at the following two sentences.

She slowly opened the bottle.

She opened the bottle.

In the first sentence, the reader is in the dark for a little longer as to what the protagonist is doing. But here you may want this effect: the slowing may suit your purposes. So there really are no rules about whether you should or shouldn't use adverbs, or how many you should use. However, as with adjectives, there are a few questions that you can ask.

Snapshot: auditing your adverbs

Now you are going to do the same thing that you have done with adjectives, but with adverbs: calmly go through your text and ask what work they are doing. Here are the questions to ask.

Do your adverbs add anything to the verbs that they are modifying (in 'run swiftly' the adverb doesn't say anything that isn't there in the verb itself, similarly in 'cry sadly', or 'scream loudly')? If they do not, you may need to cut them.

Can your adverbs and verbs be replaced by more precise and telling verbs? For example, 'to breathe quickly' might be better replaced by the single verb 'to pant' or 'to gasp' – both of which are much more precise than the initial verb and adverb.

Is the placement of your adverbs right? As with adjectives, adverbs can slow us down getting to the meat of a sentence. Can they be placed differently?

The virtues of simplicity

Because your novel matters to you, and because you want to write the best novel that you possibly can, there can be a tendency to 'overwrite', to make your prose unnecessarily complex. When you are redrafting, you may be spending a fair amount of your time paring back on your earlier excesses, losing unnecessary bloat and bagginess in your prose and paring down your sentences so that they work as well as they possibly can.

Focus point

Simplicity is often a virtue. Avoid, as far as possible, unnecessary over-complication. Your prose should be no more complicated than it needs to be.

There are a couple of problems that we need to look at here.

THESAURUS ADDICTION

If you find yourself resorting perpetually to a thesaurus, your novel is almost certainly overwritten. A thesaurus can be a useful kind of book, but you should not be using it to systematically replace straightforward words with flowery alternatives. If you find yourself using your thesaurus more than every ten pages or so, think about locking it away in a cupboard, far out of reach. Remember, too, that the alternatives that your thesaurus may provide have different shades of meaning: they are not equivalents.

ECONOMY AND OVER-ELABORATION

Another problem that you may pick up on is a tendency to long-windedness, or to over-elaboration. If you want to say something, it is often better to say it as economically as possible. This can often mean paring back your sentences to make sure that they do not have any slack in them. Remember, however, that meaning is not the only thing that matters. There is also sound, rhythm, the physicality of language. If you simply edit for *meaning* and remove anything that does not contribute to meaning, you risk missing out on all these other aspects of language.

Nevertheless, when going through your work, it can be useful to ask the question: *What can I get away with not saying?* Often, subtraction makes your story stronger, not weaker. If you elaborate *too much*, you may find that your images and sentences lose their clear focus.

Reading out loud

Saint Augustine, *The Confessions*

'When he read, his eyes scanned the page and his heart explored the meaning, but his voice was silent and his tongue was still.'

The story goes that, when Saint Augustine went to visit Saint Ambrose, the bishop of Milan, he was astonished to see the bishop reading *silently*: silent reading was something that Augustine had simply never encountered before. Although these days silent reading is the norm, it has not always been so. The novelist Alberto Manguel points out in his history of reading that it was only starting to become common in the tenth century; and even up to the nineteenth century – before radios, TV, cinema and the Internet – people would often share books by reading them out loud.

Daniel Pennac, *The Rights of the Reader*

'Didn't Flaubert bellow his Bovary *till he nearly burst his eardrums? And wasn't he then definitively in the best position to appreciate how sense comes through the sound of words, releasing meaning? Didn't he know better than anyone else, having wrestled with the arrhythmia of syllables and the tyranny of cadences, that meaning needs to be articulated out loud?'*

Despite the fact that most of us, these days, read silently, it is really worthwhile to try out your entire book *out loud*. This can allow you to get a sense of the music of your language, and to pick up on some of the following problems.

WOULD I (OR ANYBODY ELSE) ACTUALLY SAY THIS?

When you are reading your work out loud, one of the things to ask yourself is whether you or anybody else would actually ever use these sentences. Of course, the language in your book may be removed a little from the language of everyday life: a novel is a kind of artifice. Nevertheless, if when you say your sentences out loud they seem strange, alien and utterly divorced from our everyday speech patterns, this is often a sign that you need to simplify your sentences (see the section above on simplicity) and bring them more in line with our everyday sense of language.

RHYTHM, SOUND AND PACE

Some words are sharp and spiky ('clank, clank, clank'); others are more round and soft-edged ('thump, thump, thump'). If you read out loud, you will get a sense of the physical *feel* of the language you are using, and you will get a sense of the rhythm and music of your text that you simply cannot get by reading silently.

When you read out loud, you will notice where the slack passages are in your text, the places that will be less engaging to a reader or where the forward momentum seems to be lacking, and the places where you are just wandering off on digressions that the book may not need.

PUNCTUATION

Reading out loud is a useful way to pick up on problems with punctuation. There are, of course, rules of punctuation; and it makes sense to equip yourself with a good style guide so that you can fully understand these rules (see the recommendations in the Further Reading section). Nevertheless, punctuation is not *simply* a matter of following rules. It is also about the logical structure of your sentences, and about the music of your prose. A comma tells the reader that they can pause, take a short breath. A full stop is like the close of a musical phrase.

Snapshot: paying attention to punctuation

Select a page or so of writing from five of your favourite writers. Read each page out loud to get a feel for the unique rhythm of the prose. When you have done so, go through the pieces one by one, and look at the punctuation that each writer uses. Now answer the following questions:

- How does each writer punctuate their sentences?
- Which punctuation marks does the writer use?
- Are the sentences long or short?
- When read out loud, how does the punctuation affect the rhythm and music of the writer's prose?
- How do the five writers use punctuation differently from one another, and to what effect?

LOGICAL GLITCHES AND AMBIGUITIES

A final thing that reading out loud can do for you is that it can help you pick up small errors with logic or sense. When reading out loud, you can be surprised by what you have actually written. As you read, bear in mind the question: *Is this what I really meant to say?* If not, then revise or edit.

There are also issues here about word choice. I once read a book where, on the first page, somebody looked through the window to see two people 'rowing'. It was while the Olympics were on, and so I imagined the two characters on rowing machines, in their sitting room, working up a sweat. Only when I had finished the first chapter did I realize that they were not 'rowing', as in engaging in water-based sports, but 'rowing' as in having an argument. This kind of ambiguity does you no favours as a writer: it gives the reader a jolt when they realize that what they thought was going on was not going on. So be aware not just of logical glitches, but of moments where your words could be misconstrued or where they could be interpreted in different ways.

The feel of words

If you are writing in English, you should be aware that English is a rich language with multiple roots. Words with Latin roots often have a more 'high culture' feel, while words with Anglo-Saxon roots often have an earthier feel. This is because, at the time of the formation of the English language, the language of the court was French while the language of ordinary people had Anglo-Saxon roots. This is why English often has a multitude of near-synonyms.

Anglo-Saxon/Germanic roots	Latin/French roots
stench	odour
buy	purchase
weep	cry
wise	prudent
weird	strange
begin	commence
pick	select

Play with making sentences using the words in the left-hand column ('She was so wise it made me weep' / 'The man had a weird stench' / 'Go on, buy anything you like, take your pick…') and then translate them into words in the right-hand column ('She was so prudent it made me cry' / 'The man had a strange odour' / 'Go on, purchase anything you like, make your selection'). You will find that the first set of sentences has a much earthier feel than the second, and that the second sounds rather more courtly and perhaps a little more abstract.

To be a writer, you do not need to have a complete scholarly understanding of the development of the language in which you are working; but you do need to have a sensitivity to the depth and the nuance of the words that you are using, and to the way that words *feel*.

Keri Hulme, *The Bone People*

'I think the shape of words brings a response from the reader – a tiny, subconscious, unacknowledged but definite response. "OK" studs a sentence. "Okay" is a more mellow flowing word when read silently. "Bluegreen" is a meld, conveying a colour neither blue nor green but both: "blue-green" is a two-colour mix.'

Although I have been stressing reading out loud, the feel of words when spoken and when read on the page is different. When spoken, there is no difference between 'OK' and 'okay'; but when written the difference is considerable: the first feels more abrupt and less flowing, the second more casual. Good writing works both on the page and also for the voice. You will need to think about both.

Workshop: the written and the spoken voice

This workshop may be useful to think through the relationship between written 'voice' and your spoken voice. It is a good exercise to do with others, so that you can compare notes.

1 Setting up

Firstly, get hold of a recording device: most computers should be able to record you. If not, an old tape recorder will do the trick.

Now select two pages of your work-in-progress to read out loud.

Finally, choose one topic from the following list of clichés:

- my greatest love
- a memorable holiday
- my dream job
- the worst day of my life.

If these topics seem too appallingly clichéd, feel free to come up with another.

2 Recording from the page

Now record yourself reading the two pages of your novel. Read straight through, without any additional commentary or introduction. You want to be reading *only* the words on the page. If you stumble, don't worry. Just keep on going. The recording can be rough at the edges.

When you have done this, take a short break so you can shake off the 'mood' of the novel.

3 Recording from the voice

Now record yourself talking for around 5–10 minutes about one of the topics listed above. If it helps and you are working with somebody else, they can interview you about the topic, but make sure that your interviewer doesn't interject too much: the aim is for you to speak as much as possible for these 5 minutes or so.

Now take another break.

4 Exploring the spoken voice

Sit down with both recordings and listen to them all the way through. Ask yourself the following questions. You may need to stop the recordings from time to time, to go back and listen, or to make notes.

- How does your spoken 'voice' differ from your written 'voice'? How are they similar?
- Are the kinds of words that you use different? Are the written words, for example, more 'highbrow' than the spoken words?
- Which recording feels more straightforward in terms of logic and clarity?
- Are there any problems with the 'written' voice? Could they be addressed by taking on qualities from your spoken voice?

5 Exploring the written 'voice'

This final part of the exercise may be a bit more arduous, so feel free to skip it if you like. But if the earlier stages have provoked your interest, then sit down and roughly transcribe the second recording. This should take about an hour.

Now place your written and spoken prose side by side. Ask yourself the following questions:

- How do they *look different* on the page?
- Is there a difference in sentence length?
- Are there any differences between the two pieces in terms of their formality or their vocabulary?

At the end of this exercise you should have a sense of how your spoken and written voices differ. If the differences are very wide, then ask yourself what aspects of the written voice require attention, and whether there are any aspects of the spoken voice that might be introduced into your writing to help solve these problems.

Where to next?

This concludes the third part of this book on redrafting. Eventually, if you redraft with sufficient care and attention, you will end up with a completed manuscript. But that point may still be quite a way off, so the next section of this book is about how you can keep sane while fashioning and refashioning your manuscript.

PART FOUR
Keeping sane

15

Introduction: how, when and where to work

This next part of the book is all about how to keep sane. Writing a novel is a demanding job. It is not, perhaps, the most demanding job in the world, but it is nevertheless difficult. So in this section of the book we will be looking at how to deal with difficulties, distractions, writers' block and other gremlins.

Difficulty is not something that you should avoid, or before which you should take fright. Arguably, to do anything well will involve a degree of difficulty. But it also makes sense not to multiply difficulties beyond what is absolutely necessary, and to find ways of responding intelligently to any difficulties that arise along the way.

This introductory chapter looks at how you can set up a solid basis for your working life, and how you can find the time and space to carry out the substantial work that you will need to do to complete your novel.

Advice on advice

 Richard Burton, *The Anatomy of Melancholy*

'Who cannot give good counsel? 'Tis cheap, it costs them nothing.'

One thing that you will find if you are early on in your life as a novelist is that novelists love giving advice. There will be quite a lot of advice in this part of the book. But, as I suggested at the very beginning, it makes sense to evaluate this advice carefully to see whether it will work for you. I have heard hundreds of novelists talking about their work over the years, and almost all of them have been liberal with handing out advice. Some novelists tell you that you must get up at five every morning. Then, they will say, you should go for a swim, preferably in the nude, after which you should walk the dog (if you don't have a dog, you should perhaps buy one now). On your return home, you should sit down and write by hand (using special ink imported from an artisanal ink supplier based in Tbilisi) for four hours, without interruption, before breakfasting on kippers and jackfruit.

However, when writers say 'You should do this…', what they are in fact saying is, 'This is what works for me.' And because novels are all very different from one another and novelists are all very different from one other, what works for them may not work for you. This, of course, also applies to *all* the advice in this book. If it works – that is, if it helps you craft the best novel of which you are capable – then make use of it. If it doesn't, then ignore it.

 ## Snapshot: navigating advice

This exercise is designed to cure you of being overawed by the advice given by writers. Spend an hour or so looking through interviews with writers. There are many book-length published collections of interviews that you might be able to track down, or else you can have a look online (the *Paris Review* website (www.parisreview.org) has some excellent interviews with top-notch writers. There are a couple of articles called 'Ten rules for writing fiction' on the *Guardian* newspaper's website (www.theguardian.com/uk) that may be useful here as well).

Skim through the interviews, and for each writer extract two or three pieces of advice. Now your job is simply to try to pair up pieces of completely contradictory advice. Who disagrees with whom? And why? If you want to have some fun, include the advice in this book in the exercise and find as many writers as possible who disagree with what I am saying here.

What you should find is that the advice writers give will depend on many things, in particular the writer's *personality*, and also on the *kind of book* that they are writing.

This chapter is about finding out what kind of approach to your work will suit you. There are several things to take into account here: the different aspects of the job, your own character, quirks and peculiarities, the tools available, and practical issues such as cost and time.

No perfect conditions

Most writers I know have some sneaking fantasy of the *ideal conditions* for writing. This is fine: there is nothing wrong with daydreaming. It is one of the things that writers do. But it is worth remembering that these are, in the end, only fantasies. There are, of course, better and worse places to write, and it makes sense to find the best *possible* conditions. However, if you sit around waiting for the *perfect* conditions, you'll never get started. However well you set up your writing space and your schedule, however good you are at driving away friends, family and pets so that you can work in peace, there will always be problems and difficulties. Even if you end up in that mountainside hut, with only the mountain goats, and the twittering sparrows in the eaves for company, you may find that instead of writing you become dispirited and lonely, or you go quietly mad, or you become fixated on how distracting the sparrows are. I have known writers who have retired to the wilds to write, and failed to write a single world. I have known people who have managed to turn out astonishing novels while juggling three jobs, two small children and endless obligations. Your conditions for writing do not need to be perfect. They need to be *good enough*. This is not to say that you shouldn't retreat to the wilds – some writers work well in such conditions (I do). But don't feel that you have to.

Focus point

There are no perfect conditions for writing.

Why is this important? Because it is easy to put off writing endlessly until you get into just the right conditions to get started. 'I'd write a novel,' you say to yourself, 'but I can't start writing my novel until...' If you get into this habit, given that the world never fully conforms to our wishes, you may never start writing at all.

What should I write with? The writer's toolkit

Let's begin, then, with the question of technology. Whatever kind of writer you are – whether you work using fiendishly clever pieces of software, or whether you prefer a pencil and a notepad – you are reliant upon technology. According to my dictionary, 'technology' means 'the application of knowledge for practical purposes'. Paper, pencils, computers and typewriters are all technologies. In fact, many people would argue that, by this definition, *writing itself is a kind of technology*: it depends upon a body of knowledge and it is used for practical purposes like recording stories and poems. So the first thing to say here is that there's no need to dismiss technology or to say, as some writers do, that you disapprove of technology. Instead, the question is what *kinds* of technologies suit you as a writer.

Key idea

All writers depend upon technologies – from pencils and paper to complex computers – to do their work. What technologies you favour will depend on how you yourself work best.

THE OLD-FASHIONED WAY

One of the good things about writing novels is that the start-up costs are negligible. All you need is a pen or pencil, plentiful quantities of paper to write on, bread and water to keep you alive (perhaps with the occasional lemon to keep scurvy at bay), and that's enough to get going with the writing. Pens and paper are still cheap and widely available. The table below gives some advantages of working with pen and paper.

Pen and paper	
Pros	**Cons**
• Cheap and portable.	• Harder to make backups.
• Available almost everywhere.	• Eventually somebody will need to type up your written scripts.
• Do not require electricity.	
• Some writers feel that writing with a pen is more 'physical' and 'real' than with a computer.	• There may be issues with handwriting (if your writing is poor, will you be able to read it later?).
• Easy to eliminate distractions.	• If you touch-type, you will find that writing by hand is slower.
• Continue to work well after the apocalypse.	

Some writers claim that writing drafts by hand gives them a physical connection with their work that they cannot get any other way. All writing is a process that involves some kind of physical activity; but the feeling of working with pen and paper can set up a steady rhythm of work that some writers find particularly valuable.

THE MECHANICAL WAY

 # Agatha Christie, *An Autobiography*

'All I needed was a steady table and a typewriter.'

Thanks to the rise of the computer, typewriters are harder to get hold of than in the past, although you may be able to find one cheap in a second-hand store. There's something undeniably satisfying about banging out words on a typewriter. I wrote my early short stories on a typewriter. I used to enjoy the rhythm and the feel, the clatter of the keys.

Typewriters	
Pros	**Cons**
• You can pick up an old typewriter fairly cheaply.	• Again, backups can be a problem.
• If you touch-type, it is quicker than writing by hand.	• It is increasingly hard to get ribbons, etc. for typewriters.
• If it was good enough for Hemingway…	• Typewriters may sound fabulous, but they might annoy the neighbours.
• No electricity is needed (if it is a manual typewriter).	
• Paper lasts a long time.	

WORD PROCESSORS AND OTHER TOOLS

Most writers, these days, find that, at least at some point in the writing process, they are using word processors or other similar tools. Microsoft Word is ubiquitous, and many publishers will request manuscripts in .doc or .docx format. But Microsoft's offerings are not the only tools available. There are other word processors out there, including the free Open Office (www.openoffice.org) and Libre Office (www.libreoffice.org) suites. These days, I write using *Scrivener* (www.literatureandlatte.com), a wonderful writing tool that allows a degree of flexibility that I find suits my writing style. I can move chapters and sections around with ease, combine bits of text or split them, and generally do whatever I like to fashion and refashion my text. Tools and technologies change fast, and if you are reading a copy of this book that is a few years old, things may have moved on. But remember that it is possible to get so intoxicated by trying out new tools that you never actually get down to writing. Try to find a tool that works and, for this one novel at least, stick with it. A few are listed in the Resources section at the end of this book.

One disadvantage of electronic tools over, say, typewriters or writing by hand, is that some writers find that, because it is so easy to edit as they go along, they tend to be less committed, and to think less hard, about early drafts. If you *know* that you can change what you are writing without any trouble, it is sometimes all too tempting to just leave a note in the text saying '[fill something in here]' and move on. But this is a habit that can mean that you often fail to make clear decisions about the direction of your work, and this is something that can store up problems for later.

Word processors and similar tools	
Pros	**Cons**
• Widely available.	• Some writers don't like the 'feel' of words on a screen.
• You don't have to 'type up' a final manuscript to send to a publisher.	• The ability to edit easily means that drafting and editing are harder to separate.
• Publishers increasingly want .doc files sent to them.	• You are dependent upon electricity.
• Easy to edit, go back, change and alter text.	• Greater risk of repetitive strain injury (RSI).

Of course, with the growth of mobile technology, writers increasingly work on tablets, smartphones and so on. While some novelists are purists and insist that you must write in one way or another, the truth is that the tools any one novelist uses will always be particular to them and idiosyncratic. The trick is to find a toolkit that works for you.

YOUR PHYSICAL WELL-BEING

One other thing to think about is the question of your physical well-being. You might find it easy enough to type a text message on your smartphone; but a whole novel might cause problems. And there is some evidence that typing a large amount on touch-screens is not very good for you. Be careful: things like RSI, or repetitive strain injury, can blight a writer's life.

Find a way of writing that is physically comfortable for you. Think about good lighting, having a comfortable posture where strain is at a minimum and – most importantly of all – taking regular breaks. You can experiment with posture: Hemingway claimed that he wrote standing up, nude, his toes nestling in the pelt of a lesser kudu that he had shot himself. There is also a long tradition of writers dictating their books. You can now do this automatically with voice-recognition software.

Focus point

Writing is demanding physical activity. To avoid repetitive strain energy, make sure that you look after your posture, minimize strain and take regular breaks.

Snapshot: writing is a physical act

For this snapshot, simply note down a few details about how and where you work. In particular, note the following:

- What tools do you use?
- Which environment do you usually write in? At a table? Standing up? In bed? On the bus?
- Do you experience any physical discomfort while writing? If so, where do you experience the physical discomfort?
- Is your writing space well lit?
- Is it cluttered or tidy? (You may prefer to write in clutter, or you may like a clean desk.)
- What is your posture? Do you feel any degree of strain?
- Do you take regular breaks?

In the light of this, think about how you can improve your level of comfort when it comes to writing. In particular, you should think about:

- posture
- taking regular breaks (many people find that brief breaks of a couple of minutes every quarter of an hour, and longer breaks of 10 minutes every hour help them maintain concentration and minimize strain).

Think about how you can rearrange your writing space to make writing easier.

A NOTE ON BACKING UP

Whatever you use to write, you will need to make copies of your work so that in case of fire, flood, electrical failure, gnawing animals or the coming of the apocalypse, you do not lose your hard-won work. This applies just as much to writers who write by hand as it does to writers who use computers.

Think about how you can have a clear and efficient backup routine. When I started writing, I made notes by hand in one of those old-style notebooks with carbon paper that you could put between the leaves, so that every page had two copies. When I finished a few pages, I tore out the copies, bundled them up, and posted one to a different address, so that effectively I had one copy still on me, and one copy posted elsewhere.

If you write by hand, make sure that you regularly photocopy your handwritten pages, and store a copy in a safe place. The same goes for if you write using a typewriter.

Focus point

Whatever you use to write with, it pays to make *multiple* copies of your work.

If you are using electronic tools, then there are two different ways of backing up. You can back up *onsite*, meaning you keep copies in the same place that you write. You might, for example, back up to an external hard drive. Or you can back up *offsite*, meaning that copies of your files are stored on a server somewhere else. This means that, if your house is burgled or if it burns down, then you still have a copy of your novel available.

It makes sense to back up *both* onsite *and* offsite. If you are writing by computer, then tools that can back up *automatically* are useful, so that you do not have to remember to back up. Many tools will back up 'in the background' – in other words, without interrupting your working – at regular intervals, meaning that if your computer crashes, you can salvage a recent copy. The Resources section, again, has some suggestions for tools that you can use. Years ago I lost a month's intensive work because I was relying on manually backing up. At the end of each day of writing, I would think about backing up and then think, 'No, I'm tired. I'll do it tomorrow…' The days turned to weeks, and the weeks passed, and the words accumulated, until one morning I switched on my computer and got an error message.

I never got those words back.

Key idea

If you write by computer, then you need a backup system. The best backup system will:
- back up automatically and at regular intervals
- have both *onsite* backups (for example, to a hard disk in your household) and offsite *backups* (for example, to a server elsewhere).

DOES IT *MATTER* WHAT TOOLS I USE?

Many writers are evangelical about the particular tools they use, and they will tell you that, if you are serious about writing, you *must* use what they use. Again, take this with a pinch of salt. What matters are the following questions:

1 **Are you writing in a way that is comfortable?**
2 **Are you writing in a way that is sustainable?**
    a When you get to the end of your project, will you have a properly formatted manuscript to send to your publisher or to prepare for publication yourself?
    b Do you have a way of making copies of your work, in case of fire, flood or apocalypse?

Other than this, it doesn't really matter how you get those words down, as long as – eventually, at least – you end up with a manuscript that is in a fit state to send to the publisher, or else to start thinking about how you can publish yourself.

When should I write? Finding the time

I have never sat down and calculated the number of hours it takes to write a novel. I would find it very hard to do so, in part because the writing of a novel involves so many things – talking to people, sitting and thinking and staring out of the window, researching, editing, putting words on the page, heading out to the library – that it is hard to keep track. But I do know this: the time it takes to write a novel should be measured more in months and years than in hours.

Even if it is hard to gauge precisely *how long it* takes to write a novel, at the same time it is clear that, however long it takes, it takes a very long time. Finding time to write can be difficult. If you decide to write only when you feel like it, or only when you *happen to have the time*, then you will very likely not write very much at all. Among all the many commitments that we all have – jobs, family obligations, obligations to friends, dogs that need walking, and the various bits of paperwork that seem a necessary part of contemporary life – it is very easy to find that the time you have to write dwindles to almost nothing.

There are two questions here. The first is the question of *what kind of routine* suits you as a writer. The second is how you might practically go about *establishing* this routine.

WHAT ROUTINE SUITS YOU BEST?

Whatever routine you come up with, however structured or unstructured your writing time, producing a book requires a certain degree of commitment and discipline. I find that, early on in a project, I have to actively make time to work on the book. But other times, when I'm in the thick of things, the book I'm working on *creates its own discipline*: it is no longer a set of ideas in my head, but a set of objective issues out there on the page that I need to address. So, early on into a project, I have to structure my time to find space for the novel. Later on, the problem is reversed: the demands of the novel are such that I have to structure my time to find space for anything else.

Key idea

The rhythm of your work may vary over the lifespan of your novel, depending on whether you are researching, drafting, revising or preparing your manuscript for submission to publishers.

Finding out what suits you best as a novelist may take several novels. Often, I research around the other things I do in my life (I also teach creative writing, so I have a day job to fit in). I might take two years doing initial research on a novel, reading in the evenings, looking up scholarly publications, sending emails to people, making notes. I might also travel for more intensive research. Then, in phase two, when I come to draft the novel, I like to write in bursts of intense activity. I go away on my own for a fortnight or longer, forget about everything else, and write. When I do this, I am appallingly antisocial. I work for up to 15 hours a day. I wander around muttering to myself. I look strange and wild-eyed. I don't bother shaving. I stare into space. I wear odd hats. It's not something anybody else should have to witness. After this, I can work on revisions, often by setting a routine to revise a chapter, or a certain number of words, a day. Revising is a more systematic, workaday kind of process. It does not require any fancy headwear. Finally, when completing the manuscript and preparing for publication, I set aside a day or two to really give the book my full concentration.

Focus point

Novelists evolve their own patterns of work through long experience. Whatever pattern you eventually evolve, it can be useful to start out by setting up a more formal routine.

ESTABLISHING A ROUTINE

The first thing, if you are serious about establishing a routine, might be to find out when you work best, and settle on a time. *When* you decide to write is entirely up to you. You may be the kind of person who is at their best at five in the morning every day, when the house is quiet and even the birds in the trees outside have not yet woken up. You may, on the other hand, prefer to sit down and write after you have got the business of the day out of the way. You may like to write steadily, a few hundred words a day; or you may like to write in larger chunks. It might be that two mornings a week suits you better than every day.

There are two ways of setting routines for writing. One is, if you are writing a first draft, to set yourself a word count to complete every day or week. Different writers work at different speeds; but between one and two thousand words a day is usually manageable. Another approach is to set aside a certain amount of time and to make sure that you dedicate this to writing, however many words you write. After all, 'writing' doesn't just mean putting words on the page. It might also involve daydreaming, staring into space, scribbling notes, doodling…

Focus point

If you want to set a routine for writing, think about whether you want to commit yourself to a certain amount of *time*, or else to a particular *word count*. Either way, don't be *too* ambitious. It is important to have a routine that you can sustain.

Once you have decided on *when*, it makes sense to let other people know. You need to take your routine seriously; but you also need to make sure that other people take your routine seriously. Just because you are staring into space, it doesn't mean that you are available for a quick chat. Treat your writing with all the seriousness you would treat any other job. And just as you wouldn't agree to go and meet up with a friend when you should be at work (you *wouldn't*, would you…?), you also shouldn't agree to interrupt your writing routine for the same thing. It can be immensely liberating to set aside at least a few hours every week dedicated *only* to writing.

If you do settle on a time to write and you manage to communicate this to everybody else, you will find that all kinds of things start to intrude upon it. It can be useful to let other people know that they shouldn't disturb you when you are writing. Explain to them that writing is work like any other job. If you are going to get the novel written, you will need the co-operation of other people around you. We'll look at the question of distraction – and how you can deal with it – in the following chapter.

Snapshot: finding your own routine.

Different routines work for different writers. Here are a series of decisions to think about while developing a routine:

- Set a word limit *or* set a minimum time that you want to spend writing.
- Decide whether you are going to have a *daily* or a *weekly* routine.
- If a daily routine, decide when you are going to work: morning, daytime, evening, or the dead of night.
- Think about what else to build into your routine (for example, some writers like to build walking into their routines) to help support your writing.

When you have thought through these questions, then if you've got a daily routine, commit yourself to it *for a single week.* If you have a weekly routine (for example, you will write every Friday from 9 a.m. to 12 p.m., and from 2 p.m. to 5 p.m.), then commit yourself to it *for a single month.*

At the end of this period, evaluate how you have done. Was your routine easy to sustain? What difficulties did you have? How do you need to adjust your routine to make it work better for you?

Finding a space to write

It is worth experimenting with the question of *where* you write best. I know writers who prefer to write in coffee shops or cafés, who like to write in places with a hum and buzz of human life going on in the background. Other people like to write in places that are isolated, out of sight of all other human beings. I know writers who prefer to write in sheds, writers who find train journeys beneficial for getting drafts on paper, writers who write at the kitchen table, and writers who hire writing studios or functional office-like rooms.

There are no rules about where is the best place to write. The following exercise may help you think about some of the factors involved.

Snapshot: finding a place to write

Where you decide to write will depend in large part upon your own particular approach to writing. The following questions should help you think through some of the issues:

- Do you need access to resources (books/Internet, etc.)?
- Do you need your own space, or are you happy to share it?
- Do you work well at home, or away from home?
- Do you want a *dedicated* space, or a space that has other functions as well?

Knowing when to stop

Sanmao, *Stories of the Sahara*

'Writing is important. But sometimes putting down the pen and not writing is actually more important.'

If you have a big project to get finished, it can be easy to find yourself so totally immersed in your work that you don't find room for anything else. It is good sometimes to stop writing. Hemingway liked to fish and hunt and engage in manly pursuits like that. Other writers like to play music, or go for walks. When it all gets too much, I go into the kitchen and bake things.

Leaving space around your writing and knowing when to stop is not just about remembering that there are more things that matter in the world than good writing. It is also about recognizing that good writing *feeds off* other activities. If you stop writing for a while and do something else, often when you come back to your desk, ideas fall into place, problems solve themselves, and blockages in the writing process are eased.

Not only this but, if you are in the writing game for the long term, then you need to cultivate a life that supports your writing. For most of us, that life will necessarily involve a lot more than sitting on our own and putting words on the page. Put the pen down. Go outside. Meet up with friends. Make sure that you nourish your life in other ways. Then, when you sit down to write, you will have something to write about.

Where to next?

Even if you have successfully set up the practical conditions for writing, you may find that once you start you hit all kinds of difficulties. You may find yourself distracted, or bored, or lonely, or frustrated, or simply unable to write, and suffering from that mysterious ailment sometimes known as 'writer's block'. The next chapter looks at how you can deal with these problems.

16

Distractions, writer's block and other gremlins

Writing novels is never a straightforward process. There will be times when it feels as if the work is going very well, and there will be times when you succumb to frustration, irritation, exasperation and even (perhaps) despair. This is all completely normal, but it is good to be prepared and to know how to deal with these problems and glitches.

We'll start this chapter by looking at that terrible and mysterious curse known as 'writer's block', before going on to look at more specific problems and difficulties in the writing process, and also at some advice about how you might best deal with these problems as they arise.

Focus point

Writing a novel is a large undertaking. You should not expect the whole process to go smoothly from start to finish.

Writer's block

Imagine that you have been under the weather for a few weeks. You are not sure what is wrong, but you know that something is not right. You are off your food. You find it difficult to sleep at night, and when you do manage to get a bit of sleep, you have restless and unsettled dreams. You feel as if your whole body is aching. And, above all, you find yourself caught in some strange general malaise where you just don't feel right. So you decide that you must be sick and, like any sensible person, you make an appointment with the doctor.

You arrive at the doctor's surgery and wait to be called. Eventually you see the doctor, who examines you carefully. Then she leans back in her chair, takes her spectacles off, and looks very serious indeed. She puts on that special face doctors have when they pass on bad news. 'Well,' she says. 'I'm afraid I know what is wrong.'

'Yes?' you say.
'You are ill,' she says.
'Ill? What kind of ill?'
'Oh, you know,' she says. 'Just ill. Anyway, time up!'
'You can't tell me anything else?' you ask.
She shrugs. 'I'm sorry, I have other patients waiting…'
You stand up and prepare to leave. She gives you a sympathetic smile. 'Get well soon!' she says.

In such a situation, the doctor has told you almost nothing about your condition, and absolutely nothing about the causes of that condition or how it might be cured, if it can be cured. Diagnoses of writer's block are like this: they correctly identify that there is a problem, but they don't throw any light on *what* the problem is, nor on what might be done about it. It is not that saying somebody has writer's block is incorrect. It is just not very helpful. Just as 'illness' covers all kinds of problems with very different causes and very different cures, so does 'writer's block'.

Key idea

Writer's block is not a single, mysterious condition that affects writers. It is a general term for a wide range of smaller and more specific problems that may crop up in the writing process.

Dealing with problems in the writing process

Philip Pullman

'All writing is difficult. The most you can hope for is a day when it goes reasonably easily. Plumbers don't get plumber's block, and doctors don't get doctor's block; why should writers be the only profession that gives a special name to the difficulty of working, and then expects sympathy for it?'

If you are having problems in the writing process, try getting beyond the idea of having 'writer's block' to look more closely at what is preventing you from writing and why. This involves a much more careful and forensic breaking-down of what specific problems you are having. It is only on the basis of a more careful diagnosis of what isn't working well that it is possible to come up with a cure. As Philip Pullman points out, although writing is difficult, it is not unusual in being difficult. Lots of things are difficult. Raising guinea pigs is probably pretty difficult. However, Pullman's rather crotchety lack of sympathy doesn't help you with diagnosing the problems you may be having; so take a look at this list of possible ailments:

- Impatience
- Self-doubt
- Perfectionism
- Lack of research or preparation
- Indecision
- Distraction (either mental or external)
- Exhaustion/tiredness.

Snapshot: diagnosing your ailments

The purpose of this exercise is to diagnose what is getting in the way of your writing. Fill in the table below to see what the main things that stand in the way of your writing are. Just tick the boxes according to how frequently you experience these things. If you want to add a note, then do so. So, for example, I might note under number 6 that my cat is often a major distraction, at least around his teatime.

Although this diagnostic chart is rough and ready, it should give a broad picture of the things that are getting in your way. The following sections are designed to address some of these problems.

Difficulty	Rarely/never	Sometimes	Often
Impatience			
Self-doubt			
Perfectionism			
Lack of research or preparation			
Indecision			
Distraction			
Exhaustion/tiredness			

Impatience

Some time ago I heard a talk by the wonderful writer Alan Garner. In the questions after the talk, when he was asked about writer's block, he said that, although he didn't really believe in writer's block, he did believe in writer's *impatience*.

Impatience can happen on different levels. You can be impatient to get started, you can be impatient to get finished, you can be impatient to get to the next chapter, you can (and almost certainly will!) be impatient to hear back from publishers. Impatience may be a commendable desire to get on with things – that itchy sense of work needing to be done – but it may be something rather more complex and counterproductive. Often, you can tell which kind of impatience it is by seeing what happens when you sit down to actually write. If, once you are writing, the impatience goes away, then it is not really a problem: the impatience was not with the writing but with the thing that was stopping you writing. But if the impatience remains, then you have a problem on your hands.

 Orhan Pamuk

'A novelist is essentially a person who covers distance through his patience, slowly, like an ant. A novelist impresses us not by his demonic and romantic vision, but by his patience.'

Focus point

Impatience is not always bad: if you are impatient about *not* writing, this can spur you to get back to work. But impatience within the writing process itself is usually counterproductive.

There are a number of reasons why you might be feeling impatient with your writing, and, depending on what is making you impatient, you may need to deal with the problem in different ways. Impatience is about wanting specific outcomes (completing the chapter, getting a contract, winning the Nobel Prize in Literature) and wanting them now. Here are some of the reasons you might find yourself suffering from impatience.

1 You just need to give yourself writing time

Alan Garner's point is that writing takes as long as it takes: there are few short cuts. As a writer, you are not fully in control of your own mind, or of the story that you are telling. Of course, you give shape to your story, this being part of the craft of being a writer; but also your story will take shape of its own accord. It is well known in studies of creativity that often brilliant ideas emerge not in the heat of intense thought but later, while you are doing something else. Ideas cannot be forced like toothpaste out of a tube. You need both the ability to make an intense effort and the ability to switch off. Knowing which of these to do when can be tricky. Nevertheless, if you are *really* stuck, leaving the writing for a while can be very useful. While you are doing something else, you may find that things fall into place.

Hilary Mantel

'If you get stuck, get away from your desk.'

Remember: you will not solve all the problems with your book overnight. You will solve them piecemeal, one by one, over long periods of time, both through applying effort and through being able to put everything to one side and let the ideas stew away in your mind of their own accord.

2 You are trying to do too much at once

Another thing that can lead to impatience is thinking about your work on too large a scale: wanting to solve all the problems at once. There are at least two kinds of trying to do too much at once. One is when you forget that writing involves many different processes, processes that are not necessarily compatible with one another. Research is not quite the same as sketching out a structure for your novel; neither of these is the same as drafting a section; and drafting is not the same thing as editing a passage you have already drafted.

Ask yourself at any one time: *What is it that I am actually doing?* If you are drafting, then stick with drafting. If you are editing, then stick with editing. Of course, there may be times when these various processes are a bit more entangled than this; but being aware that writing a novel involves many different processes with many different rhythms will allow you to separate out some of these processes.

 Key idea

You cannot work on all aspects of your novel at once. If you are drafting, stick with drafting. If you are redrafting, stick with redrafting. If you are researching, stick with researching.

3 You have unrealistic expectations

The other version of doing too much at once is having unrealistic expectations about how much you can achieve in the time available. The writers I know all write at different paces. You need to find your own pace. It is easy to be intimidated by those who write faster ('How productive they are!' you think enviously) or by those who write more slowly ('What care they take!' you glower). Get a sense of how much it is realistic for you to do in the time you have available, and don't try to push yourself too far beyond this. It might be that you can write 600 words in an afternoon. It might be that you can write 6,000. As long as the final book is good, then who among your readers will care?

Self-doubt

I had a friend who told me the following story, a story he swears is true. A long time ago now he was in a bookstore in New York, browsing in the poetry section, when the poet Allen Ginsberg came along. Ginsberg, it seems, had been lurking among the bookshelves waiting for somebody to pick up a copy of one of his books, which is precisely what my friend did. So this friend of mine looked up from his Allen Ginsberg book to see the great beatnik poet standing before him, peering through his thick-rimmed glasses. The conversation went something like this:

'I'm Allen Ginsberg!'
'Yes, I know.'
'You are reading my book.'
'Yes.'
'Do you like it?'
(Smiling politely and reassuringly) 'Yes I do. Very much.'
'But do you think it is good?'
'Good?'
'Good poetry? Do you think I am a good poet?'
'Yes, of course. You are a very good poet.'
'Really? You are not just saying that…?'

Whether true or not, I like this story because it is a reminder that writers are probably all, to one extent or another, assailed by self-doubt. In fact, I would say that writers *should be* capable of self-doubt. Writers, of all people, should know that the human mind is a wily, unruly, disordered kind of thing, and that no mind should be fully trusted, not even their own. And a degree of self-doubt is perhaps an important part of your toolkit as a writer. From one point of view, self-doubt can be seen as a form of curiosity. It is thinking 'What if the thing that I have written doesn't work as well as it should?' or 'What if this chapter could be better?'

As with impatience, so with self-doubt: it pays to be aware of whether this is just a part of your mind trying to get to grips with the thing that you are working on, or whether it is something that is actually getting in the way of your work. I'll call the first constructive self-doubt and the second destructive self-doubt.

DEALING WITH DESTRUCTIVE SELF-DOUBT

Destructive self-doubt goes like this. You are happily writing your novel. Then you look at it one day and come across a sentence that doesn't even make grammatical sense. You sigh and read on. The next sentence is even worse. And what's more, your characters seem stupid and phoney. Gritting your teeth, you press on and, as you do, the terrible truth dawns upon you: this is the worst book ever written. You are a fool, an idiot, a moron, a halfwit. You should probably be taken out and shot for even thinking you could write a novel. There is nothing – absolutely nothing – of value in the pages that you have accumulated. So you take the pile of paper, and you put it in the waste-paper bin. Then you go and get a box of matches and strike a match, to drop into the waste-paper basket and to save the world from your idiocy (and to save yourself from the shame of being so unspeakably, utterly, bad at writing).

Well, my advice is this: stop right there! Blow out the match. Take the papers out of the bin. Put them in a folder. Switch off the computer. Go for a walk. Whatever you do, do not destroy the pages over which you have been labouring. Just put them to one side and go and do something else. Then, when the balance of your mind has returned, come back to your work, and ask yourself two simple questions:

1 **What aspects of my novel work?**

2 **What aspects of my novel don't work?**

Write a list, if it helps, on a piece of paper divided into two. On one side, just jot down what you think is successful and persuasive and pleasing about what you have written; and on the other side, write down what you think doesn't work so well.

Focus point

Your work in progress is probably neither as bad as you think it is in moments of despair, nor as much a work of genius as you think it is in moments of overblown self-confidence. The reality is almost certainly somewhere in the middle.

The most important thing to remember in terms of the writing process is that you don't have to get it right first time. You are not a brain surgeon. A slip of the pen, a badly phrased sentence or a few dud pages can be easily dealt with in the way that a slip of the scalpel, a badly performed operation or a few dud days in the operating theatre cannot. Keep that despair and doubt in check, don't destroy your work (even the most dubious pieces of work can contain a phrase or a throwaway line that can develop into something later), and don't expect to get everything right first time.

Perfectionism

Closely related to self-doubt, I think, is perfectionism. Perfectionism is the notion that, in whatever endeavour we are engaged, not only is there such a thing as perfection, but we should attain it.

I am aware that opinions differ in this respect, but – the hyperbole of reviewers and blurb writers aside – I am not sure that there is such a thing as a perfect novel. This is not because I think that somehow there is the possibility that one day somebody might write a perfect novel but that this perfection has not yet been attained; it is rather that I don't see what it would mean to call a novel perfect. To judge a novel as 'perfect', we would have to ask for whom this novel was perfect, and according to which criteria. Given that the criteria for what actually makes a novel a novel are rather baggy and vague, it is hard to see how we could judge a novel to be perfect.

 Key idea

There is no such thing as a 'perfect novel', because there is no universally agreed set of criteria on the basis of which we might judge a novel to be perfect.

Having said this, of course I find that some novels are mind-blowingly good. But being mind-blowingly good is not the same as being perfect; and for every single novel that I find mind-blowingly good, I could probably name six or seven friends who were indifferent or positively antagonistic towards this very same novel.

There are some novelists who are such perfectionists that they never send out their work. This kind of perfectionism is closely allied with self-doubt, in that it holds up the novel to an impossible standard, and then sees it largely in terms of its shortcomings. This is a shame, as it can deprive the world of many, many mind-blowingly good novels. Reread Part Three of this book on redrafting if you want to see what you can improve about your book. Turn to Part Five to look at how you can turn your manuscript into something publishable. But forget about perfection.

DEALING WITH PERFECTIONISM

We need a bit more forensic attention to diagnose problems with perfectionism. Once again, the question is simple: *How is perfectionism stopping you from writing?*

Often, the problem may be self-doubt: you lack confidence, so you hold your work to impossible standards. But sometimes the problem lies elsewhere. Perfectionism can be a problem with *lack of momentum*. It might be that your anxieties over every last comma are so profound that you simply do not progress with the kind of momentum that you need to get the project finished. If this is the case, it is worth reminding yourself that a novel may go through many more stages before it is completed and in the hands of the reading public.

Another problem with perfectionism is that the extreme obsession with literary hygiene that can go with this perfectionism can cause you to overlook the fact that much of what is interesting and good in writing comes out of the sheer mess of the writing process. We are not as in control of all this as we think we are. The determination to impose order upon writing can stop the writing ordering *itself*.

Finally, I prefer to think of novels not in terms of perfection, but in terms of filling particular niches in the ecology of literature and stories as a whole. Look at those gibbons swinging through the treetops. How expert they are! How exquisitely attuned they are to their environment! How mind-blowingly skilled! But many gibbons end up with broken bones, due to falls from heights: like the best novels, they are supremely attuned to their environment; but they are not perfect.

Lack of research or preparation

Another thing that often gets in the way of the writing process is that a story is not yet ready to emerge. If you find that your characters are just wandering around not really doing much, if all possible options seem open to them, if the story just doesn't seem to have anything impelling it forwards, it may be necessary to go back to deepen and enrich your sense of what your story is, where it is happening, and who your characters are.

DEALING WITH LACK OF RESEARCH OR PREPARATION

If you suspect that this may be a problem, give yourself some time off actually writing any of your novel. Instead, go back to researching, planning and making notes for a while. Leave the actual text alone. Perhaps even go back to some of the earlier exercises in this book to see whether they can help to round out your writing. Then come back to the text to get a fresh view.

Indecision

Some kinds of indecision are rooted in lack of preparation. You have two ideas and don't know which to follow because you haven't resolved more fundamental questions about your novel. But there is another kind of indecision in which you have a number of equally good options. You don't know whether you want your character to move to New York or Paris, perhaps; or else you are not sure whether you want the end of your book to end with devastating tragedy, or with a glimmer of the light of hope, or with a joke. So how do you deal with this kind of indecision?

DEALING WITH INDECISION

If you suffer from indecision, the first thing to recognize is that there is no absolutely right decision out there in the universe, waiting for you to stumble upon it. We have already explored this in the section on ideas: if you are faced with two ideas that feel equally good, it may be that they *are* equally good.

There are, of course, *better* and *worse* decisions; but if two decisions seem equally good, you can proceed by going with one or the other and seeing what comes of it. At worst, you will end up somewhere that you don't really want to end up, and if this happens you can go back and try the other path.

 ## Focus point

Instead of thinking about 'right' and 'wrong' decisions in your writing, think about following your decisions – whatever they are – through to their logical conclusions.

Distraction

The penultimate gremlin in this chapter is that persistent demon: distraction. I have never met a writer who has been free of distraction. Perhaps writers *need* to be distracted, because they need to be interested in the world. But there are many times, particularly in an age of always-on connectivity, when distraction becomes a problem.

Broadly speaking, distraction can be said to come in more or less two kinds. The first are those distractions that are visited upon us from outside. Back in 1797, when Coleridge was interrupted from his opium-fuelled vision of the court of Kubla Khan by a 'person on business from Porlock', he found that he simply couldn't get back into the poem, and one of his great masterworks remained tantalizingly unfinished.

While there is no such thing as a distraction-free environment, distraction is not just about your environment but also about your habits of mind. You can put yourself in a distraction-rich environment, or in a relatively distraction-poor environment. But if your mind is determined to be distracted, it can be distracted by anything!

DEALING WITH DISTRACTION

When it comes to your environment, what you need to do is limit rather than eliminate distractions.

The Internet is a particularly serious distraction. There are some excellent tools out there that can help minimize these distractions by temporarily blocking the Internet. Or if you don't need to do any research online (and checking social network accounts is, usually, *not* research) then you can turn the Internet off at the router. A few tools are suggested in the Resources section at the end of this book.

Snapshot: dealing with distraction

Try the following things as a way of dealing with distraction:

- Find a time to write when distractions are fewer. Often, writers prefer to write in the early mornings, when phone calls are few, the children (if they have children) are still dozings, and there are not too many demands.
- Turn off anything that bleeps, flashes, rings or summons. Switch off that mobile. Unplug the telephone from the wall (if you still have such an archaic device).
- Go the whole hog. Jonathan Franzen, while writing his novel *The Corrections*, wrote on a typewriter while wearing earplugs, earmuffs and a blindfold.

Exhaustion/tiredness

Writing can be hard work. So another problem can simply be that you are too tired to continue. Sometimes you just need a break, whether this is a short break to recover your strength and go on writing, or a longer period of stepping away from your desk and attending to the other aspects of living in the world.

DEALING WITH EXHAUSTION AND TIREDNESS

Getting up, making a cup of tea or coffee, stretching your legs, going for a quick walk, checking in with the cat – all of these can be a way of just refreshing yourself so that you can return to your work with fuller concentration. It doesn't sound particularly glamorous or sexy but, to keep up the momentum when it comes to your novel, it can be worth paying attention to eating well, exercising well and getting a good night's sleep. Oh, and, even though I've just said that making a cup of coffee can help, go easy on the caffeine.

Honoré de Balzac

'Many people claim coffee inspires them, but, as everybody knows, coffee only makes boring people even more boring.'

Giving yourself a helping hand

This is quite a long list of problems and things that get in the way. There may also be a number of things that you can do that – while they are themselves unrelated to writing – actively help you with sustaining yourself as you write. When you are in the middle of a writing project, you may find that you become too involved and you start to neglect things that would actually help the writing process.

Write down at least five things that you find help give you an overall sense of well-being, and that will help you to return to your writing with renewed energy. These might be physical activities (swimming, walking, cycling, yoga), ways of relaxing and unwinding (going to the cinema, playing music, visiting friends) or anything you like. What is important is that these things have *no direct connection with writing*. Write them down as a list.

Now make sure that you actively timetable in to do at least two of these things every week.

Workshop: making friends with your own head

The novelist Russell Hoban once talked about writing as a process of 'making friends with your own head'. This exercise is a way of getting to know your own quirks and gremlins a bit better, so that you can deal with them more effectively. In other words, if you are finding that you are regularly 'blocked' as a writer, it can be useful to pay more attention to the things that get in the way of your writing, so that you can find more carefully honed strategies for dealing with these problems. For this workshop, you will need a small notebook – use a notebook on paper, rather than an electronic version.

Week 1

In the first week, you will be looking more closely at the problems that get in the way of your writing. Keep the notebook beside you as you write, and at the end of each writing session, before you finish, jot down a few notes on the following.

What problem did you face? Was it: impatience; self-doubt; perfectionism; lack of research or preparation; indecision; distraction (either mental or external); or exhaustion/tiredness?

How did this problem manifest itself? What did you end up doing instead of writing? What happened during your writing session?

See the example below:

Problem	Manifestation
Tuesday morning: distraction	Spent 40 minutes on social media looking at videos of cats and pandas.
Wednesday afternoon: self-doubt	Grumpiness, frustration, inability to concentrate.
Thursday morning: impatience	Became frustrated. Left desk. Found myself 40 minutes later sitting outside eating ice cream.

Keep these records for every writing session this week. It can be useful to pair up with another writer, so that you can compare notes as you go along. At the end of the week, you should be able to see a pattern emerging. Now, either on your own or with a friend, go back over your notes and try to establish what your current *three* major causes for writer's block are. Write down the problems and some thoughts about how you could address these problems in the coming week. The table below gives an example:

Problem (diagnosis)	Strategy (treatment)
Addiction to social media (distraction).	Download and use SelfControl or some other similar tool.
Frustrated that my writing is not good enough, so not making progress (perfectionism).	Finish the draft of chapter x, regardless of whether I think it is good or not.
Always too tired in the mornings to write (exhaustion).	Cut down on caffeine, and make sure I get a good night's sleep.

What you are doing here is, week by week, diagnosing the problems with your writing, and then deciding on a treatment.

Week 2 (and subsequent weeks)

In the second week, while continuing to note down problems as they arise in your notebook, start putting into effect the various strategies you have come up with for dealing with the problems that were troubling you the week before. At the end of the second week, review your chart from the week before, with its diagnoses and suggested treatment. Mark those treatments that have worked for you and those that haven't. Perhaps, for example, writing blindfold is simply not for you. Of course, if in the *middle* of the week it becomes absolutely clear that the measures you have put in place to prevent writer's block are themselves becoming a problem, you don't need to wait until the end of the week to abandon them.

In the light of this, you should have a better idea of the problems that you face individually as a writer and some of the strategies that work, or that do not work, in addressing these problems.

Now you can, once again, go over your notebook from week two, select three more problems (they may be different problems this week, particularly if some of the strategies you came up with the week before worked!) and come up with another three concrete strategies for dealing with them.

If you can keep this exercise going for up to a month, perhaps more, then you may be able to get a clearer idea of the things that stop you writing, and the things that help you with writing.

Where to next?

Novelists are, at heart, social animals: after all, they are in the business of communication. If this chapter is about the more solitary aspects of dealing with the problems and difficulties of writing, the next chapter is about how you can go elsewhere for all kinds of help and support.

17

Finding support

In this chapter we are going to look at the ways in which you can find support while writing your novel. This chapter is mainly about support you might need *during* the writing process. The later chapters on publishing later have plenty of extra advice about support that may be of use to you once your book is finished and ready for publication.

Focus point

Although writing a novel may feel a solitary business, you are not alone: there are all kinds of places where you can go to find support.

A note on solitude

Sara Maitland, *How to Be Alone*

'You have an inchoate, inarticulate, groping feeling that there is something else, something more, something that may be scary but may also be beautiful. You know that other people, across the centuries and from a wide range of cultures and countries, have found this something and they have usually found it alone, in solitude.'

Writing can be a solitary job. And this, perhaps, is part of the appeal of writing. We live in a world in which perpetual and frenetic engagement with others is often taken to be the norm. We are encouraged to connect, to network, to interact. Many of us are interconnected in a way that is unprecedented in human history. We are wired up 24 hours a day to virtual social networks. We have connections that span the globe: instant messaging, email, telephone, social media, blogs… The flood has become a deluge. In this whirlwind of interaction, solitude can sometimes seem a bit… well, a bit odd. The neighbour who lives alone, the person who goes to the cinema in the afternoon without anybody else, the solitary diner – these people are all potentially objects of suspicion. What are they up to? Why don't they have any friends? What crime have they committed? Hermits these days are few and far between. Who, after all, would want to be a hermit, unless it was in a cave with 24-hour Internet access?

Most writers, however, are hermits of a sort and have some kind of desire for solitude. If, as a writer, you crave solitude to write, then you should take this seriously.

Key idea

Solitude is not just freedom from distraction: many writers find that it is also a precondition for being able to write at all.

Although much of writing is indeed a solitary business, there will be times when you find that you need the support of others. This chapter is about finding that support.

What support do I have already?

Before launching into exploring the various kinds of support available to you, try the following exercise to explore the support you already have. There might be organizations that you turn to for help. There might be people who support you. It may be that certain habits help support your writing, or there are certain places in which you write that support your writing. You may also be a member of an online or offline writers' group.

Snapshot: sources of support

Think about what sources of support you already have for your writing. Support can come in various forms. Note down the support you have under the following three headings:

1 Moral/personal support
2 Practical/material support
3 Supporting activities.

Moral/personal support can range from having connections with fellow writers, to having people around you who believe that writing novels is worthwhile, to having access to communities where you can get good feedback. Practical/material support might involve financial support (if you have a rich benefactor, then this is material support!), the various practical set-ups that help you with writing, places where you write, or people who offer practical and material help. Supporting activities are the things that you are doing already that help support your practice as a writer.

Look over this list and ask yourself where you are lacking support. What kind of support do you not have at the moment but you feel that you need? Don't worry yet about how to go about finding that support. That is what the rest of this chapter is for. Write down three realistic things that you think would be helpful to supporting your writing (one for each category if you like, but otherwise, just three things that seem as if they would help).

It may be that certain kinds of support blur between various categories. For example, I have friends who are fellow writers who offer both practical and moral support, who are willing not only to hear me out when I talk about how hard I am finding the novel that I am currently working on, but who will also help me find ways of practically developing my work further. And there are some things that I do as a writer – for example, I like blogging about what I am up to – that put me in touch with people who sometimes offer me both practical and moral support. So don't worry too much about the classifications here. What is important is just to get a general idea of the broad basis of support that you have.

Support from non-writers

Many of the people you are surrounded by may not be writers themselves. In fact, if you are a writer, then the last thing that you might want to do is to be surrounded by other writers all the time. Spending time with non-writers can be good to remind you that, although it matters, writing is not the *only* thing that matters in the world. And your non-writer friends may be able to give you all kinds of practical and moral support that you need to keep on writing.

If people are going to be in a position to help support you with your writing, they need to know what you are up to. This is why it makes sense to tell people that you are writing a novel. Only if people know will they be in a position to help out, and also to make allowances for the various strange forms of behaviour that you may find yourself exhibiting as a novelist.

Sometimes others may take a while to get round to the idea that you are serious about your novel. When I started to take writing seriously, I designated a 'writing day' set aside for writing, thinking or wandering around daydreaming – all of which are essential activities. Some of my friends didn't quite understand what I was up to, even though I told them I was writing a novel, and so they would call me on my writing day and invite me out for coffee, 'as I wasn't doing anything'. It took a little while, but in the end I realized that I needed to take my writing day as seriously as I would a day at work, and that I needed to see it as similarly non-negotiable. At first, I felt awkward about turning people down like this, particularly if they would sometimes bump into me later in the day, sitting in a café with a notebook and staring out of the window as if I was doing nothing at all. But eventually they got used to it, and so did I: and the relief of actually taking my writing seriously was enormous.

 Focus point

If you set aside time for writing, see this as non-negotiable and treat it with the same importance that you would treat a job or any other work that you took seriously.

Generally speaking, my non-writer friends have always been very supportive. They have kept me sane, mopped my fevered artist's brow when I have become overwrought, taken me out for a coffee or a glass of beer, asked how I am doing, commiserated with me as I have complained about publishers or the difficulty of finding time to write, told me that I should by no means give up writing whatever else I do, and generally given me enormous amounts of support, encouragement and help.

Connecting with other writers through informal networks

Another way of finding support is through connections with other writers. These can be informal (for example, you have a friend who is also working on a novel who you like to meet up with over coffee to chat) or formal (for example, membership of a writers' group).

If you spend long enough in the writing world, you will soon build up informal networks of connections with other writers. It can be good to maintain these connections: it gives a sense that what you are doing is not so strange, unusual or extraordinary, it puts you in touch with other people who can read your work or help you out, and it allows you to find out and explore other approaches to the whole business of writing. Sometimes these connections can lead to interesting openings or opportunities. But the main thing is that they are connections with other human beings who are trying to do something not entirely at odds with what you are trying to do. And so, if you find that your workmates or family or other friends don't really understand why you are labouring long hours over your novel, then it can be good to have these links to other writers who may be able to understand rather better.

Formal approaches: writers' groups

Alongside these informal connections, there are also more formal writers' groups. Most towns will have several writers' groups, catering to different kinds of writers. You may have to look around to find one that suits. If you can't find one that suits, you may want to set up one of your own.

Writers' groups may offer friendship, advice and encouragement; but they may also offer bracing criticism, some much-needed perspective, and vigorous feedback. They may be groups to which members bring along their work to be discussed, or they may be groups for actually writing. Some groups are very well established, for example the Tindal Street Fiction Group in Birmingham (UK), which at the time of writing has a long and distinguished history of 30 years and has given rise to a large number of highly successful writers.

What kind of writers' group you want to be involved in depends very much on the kind of writer you are and what kind of support you are looking for. Some writers may be looking for an environment in which they can intensively develop and redevelop their work. Some may hunger for bracing criticism and rigorous feedback. Other writers may have other places where they can find this, and may seek other things out of a writers' group: a sense of comradeship, perhaps; or a range of connections with other writers who live locally or who share the same interests. It may take a while asking around about local writers' groups before you find a place where you feel happy.

Setting up a writers' group

If there is no local writers' group, then you might think of setting up your own. The following snapshot is a way of thinking through how you might go about this.

Snapshot: a template for a writers' group

Think how you might be able to use or adapt the following template to set up a writers' group:

- Agree to meet regularly, but not too often. Once a month is usually sufficient.
- Think about how to establish a stable membership, which helps build trust. Writers' groups often depend upon having a high level of trust between members.
- Groups differ in size. My suggestion is a group of six to 16 members. Below six, and it is a little hard to get enough momentum going. Over 16, and it becomes hard to keep track of everyone.

- Choose a venue for meetings that is quiet, easy to get to and – most of all – free. Your library may be able to help, and many cafés and bars are happy to host groups like this. Or you can meet in people's homes.
- One format that often works is that two or three members are nominated each session to bring their work for discussion. If they bring up to 2,000 words each, this should be plenty to talk about. The job of the other members is to give feedback.
- Feedback is generally deeper and better if the work is circulated in advance.
- Some groups work on the basis that the writer remains silent while their work is being talked about. This can be tough at first; but it is often a good way of giving space for genuine discussion of the work.
- Keep sessions to a maximum of three hours, so the spirits don't flag!

This is only a suggestion for how you could proceed with running a writers' group. There are many other models that you can use.

There are, however, some potential disadvantages of writers' groups. One potential problem is that, if the only amount anybody is ever reading is 2,000 words, then this is not a forum in which you may be able to get feedback on the overall structure of your novel. Feedback in writers' groups can tend to home in on small details and leave the big picture untouched. Then there is the question of whether you feel inclined to share your work in this way: some writers like their writing to be intensely private and solitary until they eventually get round to sending it to their agent or their publisher. Finally, there are some writers who simply don't much like other people (and other people don't like them). If this is you, then you are better off not in a writers' group.

Writers' groups online

There are also many writers' groups and communities online. These, once again, can vary. Some can have hundreds of thousands of members. Others may be 'closed' and limited to just a handful of members. A couple of the larger communities are listed in the Resources section at the end of this book.

An external eye: who to share your work with, and when

With this proliferation of writers' groups and communities, it is possible as a writer to feel a moral obligation to get involved, as if the only way of being a writer is to be endlessly sharing drafts with writers' groups, with friends or online. But this may simply be another example of our contemporary mania for interaction: if you don't want to share your work in this way, or if you are not ready, then that is fine. To know *whether* you are ready, the following questions may be useful to reflect upon.

Novels take time to grow into sturdy trees, and they all start life as tender little shoots. If you plant them out too early, you can sometimes risk them being taken by the frost. For myself, first drafts remain entirely private. I do not show anybody any of a first draft. They are entirely my own affair. If anybody asks to look, I will refuse. I want the space to work things out for myself. I want to push the project as far as I can on its own. Generally speaking, I'll do another couple of drafts as well before I show anybody. I like my novels to become a bit more robust, to put down roots. I worry that, if I show my work to others too early, it will wither and die, or too much advice will push it in the wrong direction. Only after a few drafts will I pass my novel to a couple of trusted friends for their thoughts and their comments.

This raises the question of what the 'right person' might be. In my own experience, the right person is a good *reader*. They may or may not be a writer themselves. That really doesn't matter. But they will be able to read thoughtfully, critically and sympathetically. A good reader is not necessarily a reader who likes your work. A good reader is a reader who is sympathetic to what you are trying to do, and whose feedback can help you do it more successfully.

- Are they willing to read your work?
- Are they able to focus on the writing and not on the writer?
- Are they capable of raising questions both at the small scale ('What does this word mean?') and at the large scale ('Do you need Chapters 1, 2 and 3 at all?')?

The term sometimes used for this 'external eye' upon your novel is 'beta reader'. This term derives from software development in which 'beta testers' will trial software that is not yet released, but that may contain all kinds of bugs and glitches. The purpose of using beta readers is so that these bugs can be ironed out.

 ## Key idea

The term 'beta reader' is a term for readers who read your work to iron out problems before it goes on general release. It is a term that is generally applied to self-publishing rather than to third-party publishing.

Thoughts on feedback

You cannot tell how effective your writing is until you have some sense of how readers will respond to your work. Trying your work out on a sympathetic but critical audience can help you see what needs changing, what works well, which jokes work, and so on.

 ## Julia Bell, *The Creative Writing Coursebook*

'I suppose it's like standing on the edge of a high diving board just before you jump off: a mixture of nerves, vertigo, exhilaration. You so want the work to be good, but by submitting it to criticism you are accepting that there is still something not right about it.'

Giving good feedback on work is an art. My agent can sum up what's wrong with a whole novel in a single paragraph, leading to another two months of rewriting. This kind of skill comes from long experience.

 ## Snapshot: how to give good feedback

The following suggestions and pointers will help you become better at giving feedback to your fellow writers, and will be useful to give to people who are reading *your* work.

- Feedback should be on the work itself. It is not a pretext for talking about the writer, about the ills of society, or about anything else.
- Good feedback is not about subjective likes and dislikes. Whether you like or don't like a piece of work is less useful to the writer than observations about what works and what doesn't.

- Feedback is always from a particular angle. It is never wholly subjective nor wholly objective. There is room for genuine differences of opinion.
- Be specific and investigative. Don't say, 'The beginning doesn't work.' Say, 'If you start with the third paragraph, then put the material from the opening paragraphs later, this would work better...'
- Be constructive: the job of feedback is to make the writing as good as it can possibly be.
- The best feedback comes out of a basic sympathy with what the author is trying to do.
- Remember, there may be several solutions to the same problem.

Dealing with criticism

There is a paradox to seeking criticism: *as a writer* you want the strongest, most vigorous criticism possible, so that you can improve your work; but *as a human being* you just want your reader to say, 'I liked it.'

The first question to think about if you receive critical feedback is this: given that I have not successfully communicated what I want or need to communicate, how can I express these things differently so that I can communicate them better? It may be that you have simply chosen the wrong audience. But it may be that the criticism points to the fact that – however great your idea, however carefully you have thought it through, and however long you have spent working on the novel – you have not communicated as well as you could have done. Sometimes, however, criticism might go a bit deeper, and you realize that there is something up with the ideas underpinning your novel. So you may need to wind back a little further and think about how to clarify or hone your ideas.

Either way, when you get critical feedback, it makes sense not to question *yourself*, but instead to question *the work*. We'll look a bit more closely at some of this in the section on dealing with third-party publishers.

Organizations that support writers

Before the close of this chapter, I should say something about organizations that support writers. Your local region may have a writing development agency that offers mentorship, support and opportunities. Have a look at what is available in your local region (there's a list for the UK in the Resources section).

There are also national bodies that help support writers. Again, these are listed in the Resources: whatever kind of writer you are – whether you are self-published or third-party published, whatever your genre, however you want to work, there will be an organization out there that will be able to help you.

What is important to remember, in other words, is that as a novelist, even if much of your work is solitary, you are not alone. You are part of a broad community of people who write. But how you decide to engage with this community is up to you.

Writing classes and further study

Most towns will also have more formal writing classes that you can join. Many universities also offer MA and PhD programmes in creative writing. The first thing to say about these is that, although if the teaching is good they may help your development as a writer, it is not essential to do one of these courses. If you just want to work on a novel and want more rigorous and systematic advice, support and help, then an MA programme might be useful but a PhD might be overkill. PhD programmes often involve all kinds of other features which are not strictly related to getting your novel written.

 Focus point

If life in academia appeals to you, and you are thinking you might like to teach in universities later on, then a PhD qualification may be useful (although it need not be in creative writing); but simply in terms of getting the novel written, it may be more than you need.

Local adult education classes can often be useful as well, although the level of these courses will vary a good deal. As a novelist, you are in for the long haul, so sometimes the format of these courses may not suit you. But have a look around – get in touch with those who tutor on these courses to ask about what they do and to see if what they do will be of use to you.

Mentorships, consultancies, etc.

Another way you can get help and support is through exploring possibilities for mentoring schemes, or employing the services of a literary consultancy to get more robust and sustained feedback on your novel. These schemes differ wildly. Some mentoring schemes are excellent, are underpinned by public funds (and so are often available at no cost), and can be of considerable benefit. Similarly, some consultancy services are very good. *The Writers' Compass*, run by NAWE or the National Association of Writers in Education (www.nawe.co.uk), offers a huge amount of information about training, workshops, mentoring and coaching, and other things that may be of use, and at the time of writing is probably the best first port of call to find out about opportunities such as these.

Getting away from it all

Another thing that can help is getting away on a writing course, residential retreat or residency. Writers' retreats and residencies are increasingly popular. Some of them offer free board and lodgings (or even a small stipend) as well as time to write in relative peace and quiet. Others, for example the writing courses run by the Arvon Foundation (www.arvon.org), will cost you – but they will give you an experience of working alongside other writers, with intensive feedback from professional writers, and they often offer grants and other forms of financial support.

Workshop: cultivating your support networks

This workshop is about exploring how you can cultivate networks that will support you as a writer. Because the kind of support you want and need will differ, you shouldn't feel the obligation to work through systematically. You will be the best judge of what will be useful, and what will be less useful.

First, go back to the earlier exercise ('Snapshot: sources of support') that looks at the sources of support you already have in place, and any notes you made about support you need. This will be your starting point for thinking about how to develop more robust support networks.

1 Finding out what you need

Now go through the following list and rank each item from 1 to 5 according to how useful you think it might be, where '5' is 'very useful' and '1' is 'not very useful'.

   a Membership of an online writers' group

   b Membership of a face-to-face writers' group

   c Setting up your own writers' group

   d Finding some beta readers

   e Going on a writing retreat or residency

   f Joining a writers' organization

   g Finding support from non-writers

2 Researching your options

Taking the most important of these first, research how you can develop these networks. You may want to do some of the following:

- Contact your local writing development agency (see Resources).
- Search for an online writers' group that might suit you.
- Go to your local library and find out about local writing groups and organizations.
- Contact your local university to see whether they offer creative writing courses: you may not want to do a course, but they may have mailing lists for events and activities.
- Contact friends who write to see whether they want to be in a writing group
- Explore possibilities for residencies and retreats (use *The Writers' Compass* as a starting point if you are in the UK).
- Research writers' organizations and professional bodies that you might be able to join.

Make notes on anything that you think is worth following up. Make use of the appendices for this book as a starting point for your explorations.

3 Making a plan of action

When you have done this, you can start to make a plan of action. It can take time to put these kinds of networks in place, so it might help to think in terms of weeks or months rather than days. Try to reduce your notes from part 2 of this exercise into a to-do list of *at least three* concrete actions that you can undertake to start to develop your support networks. After a month (put a date in your diary), you might want to evaluate your progress and see how you are doing with building up these broader networks and mechanisms of support.

Where to next?

In this part of the book we've covered a lot of information about the practicalities of getting your novel drafted, and how to keep sane while doing so. If all this has gone well, then you will eventually have a novel on your hands. The next part of this book is all about publishing, and what you need to know to make the transition from unpublished to published novelist.

PART FIVE

Publishing

18

Introduction: the 'why' and 'how' of publishing

Let us say that your novel is finished, and it is as good as it can possibly be. The prose is sparkling, the story compelling, the feedback from your various readers is excellent. You feel that *now,* after months and perhaps years of painstaking work, you are ready to release it into the world. So now you can turn your attention to the question of publication.

Key idea

'Publication' is the process of preparing and issuing your work so that it can be read by the public.

Publication is the holy grail of aspiring novelists. It may seem like a distant goal but, in reality, publication is not particularly exceptional. Thousands of books are published each day. And, if your novel is good enough, there is no reason why your book should not be one of them (of course, very many *bad* books are published each day as well, but you'll want to make sure that yours is one of the good ones).

Publishing is something that you can do yourself (self-publishing) or something that you can contract out to others to do on your behalf (third-party publishing). There are advantages and disadvantages to each of these approaches, but both are equally forms of publishing.

Key idea

There are two broad options open to you when you are thinking about publishing your work. Either *you* can become publisher of your own work (*self*-publishing) or *somebody else* can publish your work (*third-party* publishing).

Of course, publication is not obligatory. You are free to write as many novels as you like and never publish any of them, or leave them to posterity in a shoebox under the stairs. There may be reasons why you *don't* want to publish your novel. You may feel it is not ready. You may think that it is not good enough and that you want to write another. You may simply not be very interested: the challenge was in the writing of the thing, and publication is not your concern. If you don't want to publish your novel, that's fine. But if you've gone to all the effort of writing it, do at least *consider* publishing it: you might be depriving readers of something wonderful and new and surprising.

In this section of the book we will be looking at how you can take the final draft of your book and nurse it through the process of publication, so that eventually you can see your book, whether it is printed on paper or is a digital edition, in the hands of those mythical and mysterious beasts, the public.

This section consists of five chapters. The present chapter explores some general questions about what publication involves. In the next chapter we'll look at how to prepare your manuscript for publication, then in Chapter 20 we'll look at questions of copyright, ethics and law – questions that you need to know about if you are putting your words in the public domain. Chapter 21 is about how you might go it alone and join the self-publishing revolution. Finally, Chapter 22 looks at the third-party publishing world.

Is my work ready?

One crucial question to ask, however you are planning on going about publishing your work, is whether your book is *ready* for publication. The question of readiness is often even more of an issue if you are self-publishing because, when you publish your own work, there is nothing standing between you and the public.

The following checklist gives a few things that you would do well to bear in mind if you are considering whether your work is ready for publication.

Snapshot: is your work ready?

Answer the questions in the following checklist. If you answer 'no' to any of these questions, it may be that your work is not quite ready for publication. If you answer 'yes' to all the questions, you *may* be in a position to think about publishing your work – but proceed with caution!

Question	YES	NO
Is your work finished?		
Are there any parts that you think don't work?		
Are there any sections with which you are uneasy?		
Has the book been redrafted at least three times?		
Have you read through the entire manuscript as a novel?		
Have you proofread the manuscript?		
Have you got feedback on your work from at least two other critical readers?		
Have you addressed, to your satisfaction, the feedback of your readers?		

Let's look at these questions, briefly, in turn.

IS YOUR WORK FINISHED?

In the world of fiction, generally speaking you should never think about sending out an unfinished manuscript to a third-party publishing house. As with all rules, there are exceptions: if you are a celebrity, and if your name alone will help you sell books, you may be able to get a contract on the basis of a couple of sample chapters. But, for most of us, publishers want books to be finished before they will consider them. Some writers ask why they should have to finish their books if they don't have evidence of commitment from a publisher. Publishers can justifiably respond by asking why they should consider publishing a book if they don't have evidence of commitment from a writer. If you believe in your book, you will finish it. (If you are self-publishing, this is obviously also true. Nobody wants to read half a novel.)

ARE THERE ANY PARTS THAT DON'T WORK?

If you have identified problems in your work, make sure that you solve them before you start thinking about publication. If they feel insoluble, seek advice from friends, fellow writers or beta readers, and ask *how* you might solve them. It is your job to make the book as good as it can possibly be.

ARE THERE ANY SECTIONS YOU ARE UNEASY WITH?

This is slightly more subtle than simply asking about what does and doesn't work. You may not have identified any particular problems with your novel; but there may be sections that cause you a nagging unease. It may be that you have a feeling that Chapter 7 *isn't quite right*. You may find yourself a little troubled by a certain character. You may find yourself, when you are thinking about the book, continually snagging on a part of the plot that, while not wholly implausible, doesn't quite convince. One of the most useful skills a writer can have is the ability to recognize this nagging unease, and take appropriate steps to address it.

HAVE YOU REDRAFTED AT LEAST THREE TIMES?

Most novelists will redraft more than three times. But as a rule of thumb (which means you can ignore it if you think it doesn't apply), you should have *at the very least* three redrafts. If it helps, you can follow the pattern of this book and think of one as a redraft for structure, one as a redraft for logic, and one as a redraft for language.

HAVE YOU READ THE ENTIRE MANUSCRIPT *AS A NOVEL?*

It might seem blindingly obvious that what you have written is a novel. But reading for craft and reading to redraft are different from reading your book *as a novel*. Most of your readers will read the book neither as an exquisite piece of craftsmanship nor with an eye to correcting problems, but simply as a novel. It is worth having a go at reading the book straight through, relatively quickly, without making any notes, corrections or notes in the margin, and seeing how it stands up to this kind of reading.

HAVE YOU PROOFREAD?

Yu dont want two put you're potential publisher off because youve maid stupid mistakes and haven't red the manuscript threw. Chapter 21 explores how to prepare your work for publication. If you are sending your work to third-party publishers, there will almost certainly be a few small errors in your manuscript: but they should be very, very few.

HAVE YOU GOT FEEDBACK ON YOUR WORK FROM AT LEAST TWO OTHER CRITICAL READERS?

You are not necessarily the best judge of your work. Before trying your novel out on the wider world, it makes sense to test it out on an audience. Just as you wouldn't launch a passenger jet without a few test flights and some rigorous checks, you shouldn't expect the public to take a chance on your novel if you haven't tried it out.

HAVE YOU ADDRESSED, TO YOUR SATISFACTION, THE FEEDBACK OF YOUR READERS?

There is no point in getting feedback if you do not actually respond to it. So the final question is whether you have fully addressed your readers' feedback. This doesn't mean agreeing with them, but it does mean being able to *respond to* all the points that they raise, at least to your own satisfaction.

If the answer to all these questions is 'yes', then you may be ready to think about moving on to the next stage.

Focus point

Your work does not have to be perfect. It just has to be *as ready as it is ever going to be*.

How should I publish my work?

If you feel that your work is as ready as it is ever going to be, then you can start to think about how you should publish your work. There are all kinds of ways you can do this. You could just run off multiple copies on the photocopier and hand these out to friends. You could bundle the whole thing up as a PDF and stick it on your website or blog. These are both forms of publication. And these are perfectly noble and honourable ways of going about making your work available to the general public. Or you might want to serialize your novel in blog form, or publish it as a free homemade magazine, issuing the novel chapter by chapter and making it available in your local coffee shop. On the other hand, you may want to go with a third-party publishing house, whether it is one of the large mainstream publishers or a small independent. Or, failing that, you may want to go it alone and self-publish your work, either as an ebook or as a paper-based book, or both.

If there are two major options – third-party publishing and self-publishing – then there are advantages and disadvantages to each. The way you decide to go may depend on the kind of book you are writing, the audience you have in mind, the profile that you already have as a writer, and the question of what you want to get out of publishing your book.

Focus point

There is no single 'right' way to publish a book: the way you publish will depend upon the book itself, your intended audience, yourself, and what you want out of publishing.

Let's break down some of the questions that you might want to ask about how to go about publishing.

WHAT KIND OF BOOK IS IT?

What genre does your book fit into? This is an important question for commercial publishers who want to know where it will sit on the shelves of bricks-and-mortar bookstores. But it is also an important question for self-publishers, who want to know how to pitch their book. One thing that can be useful is the following exercise, thinking about the 'family resemblances' between books.

Ludwig Wittgenstein, *Philosophical Investigations*

'I can think of no better expression to characterize these similarities than "family resemblances"; for the various resemblances between members of a family: build, features, colour of eyes, gait, temperament, etc. etc. overlap and criss-cross in the same way.'

Snapshot: family resemblances

Think of the ten books that most resemble yours. They may all resemble your book in different ways (and not resemble one another that much at all), so think about those ten books as books with which your own novel shares some kind of family resemblance (see the quote from Wittgenstein above).

Write down the titles of these ten books. Now ask yourself how these books are published.

- Are they self-published or third-party published?
- If the books are third-party published, are they published with relatively small or independent publishers, with mainstream publishers, or with publishers that are in one way or another 'niche'?
- If the books are self-published, how are they published? As ebooks, or as ebooks and on paper? What platforms are they available on, and how were they made available? You may need to do some research online to find out the answers to these questions.
- Finally, what does this say about your own book and how you might think of publishing it?

WHAT IS YOUR AUDIENCE?

When thinking about publication, also think about your audience. Do you have a sense of who you are writing for? Do you have a ready-made audience? If you are a blogger and already have a substantial number of readers, or your novel is related to a particular theme or community of interest, then you may have a pre-made audience. If you can have a better sense of who your audience is, then you can have a sense of how to reach them.

Focus point

If you already have a readership or some kind of profile as a writer (for example, you write a popular blog), then take this this ready-made audience into account when you are exploring how to publish your work.

WHAT IS YOUR PROFILE AS A WRITER?

Do you already have a profile as a writer? Are you part of a community? Is this community offline or online? Have you established a reputation as a particular *kind* of writer? Do you have a reputation for something outside writing fiction that may give you an audience for your fiction?

WHAT DO YOU WANT TO GET OUT OF PUBLISHING YOUR BOOK?

If you are getting to the end of the writing process, it can be useful to step back and ask yourself what you are hoping to get out of publishing your book. There are all kinds of reasons why you might want to put your book into the world. You might think that it has an important message or story that people need to hear. You might think that it is simply *better* than many of the novels out there (and you might be right). You might have a particular audience in mind. Or you might be thinking about publishing your book for more personal reasons. You may simply long for the day when you hold a copy of a book – *your* book – in your hand. You may want to develop a career as a writer, or in the writing world.

If you want readers, but couldn't care less about money, and if you have a blog with a good following, you might want to give your book away as a download from your blog. You could notch up a few thousand readers fairly easily. If the idea of being a plucky outsider appeals to you, or if you want total creative freedom, self-publishing may be the way forward. If you long to be a part of the cultural mainstream, and you want the pleasure of working with professionals with long experience in the publishing industry, then look at third-party publishing. While it pays to be modest in your expectations – some income and quiet renown in certain circles are more likely than millions of pounds and everlasting fame and glory – having a sense of what you want out of the publishing process is a good way to focus your decision-making process.

> ## Snapshot: what do you want?
>
> Write down a list of five or six of the things that you want to get out of publishing your book. Be as honest and frank as you can (even if you know that this wish-list is unreasonable). Now look at this list and rank the items in order of importance. What does this tell you about the best approach to publishing your book?

How not to publish: vanity publishers, sharks and scoundrels

One way that you should *not* publish is by going with a vanity press. Vanity publishing is so called because it serves nothing but the vanity of the authors involved. And, to be frank, for those who have been caught within these scams, it can be pretty bruising for your vanity as well.

So what is vanity publishing? It works like this. I set up a publishing house and advertise for submissions. You send me your manuscript. I send you back a letter saying how wonderful your book is (even if it is terrible) and offer you what I call a 'co-publishing' deal, or something like that.

Focus point

Vanity presses never advertise themselves as vanity presses.

What this 'deal' usually involves is you paying a sum – let's say £4,000 – for publishing the book, while I promise to promote your book and get it into bookshops and so on.

What actually happens is that you pay me £4,000. In return, I produce a book at your expense. As I have already made a profit, I do not need to work to actually sell the book (which I know may not be sellable), so I simply move on to find another author. That is my business model.

Vanity publishers insist that they are providing a service, turning manuscripts that would otherwise not be published into finished books of which their owners can be proud. But there are four problems here:

1 **Quality control:** vanity publishers are universally upbeat about your manuscript when you send it to them, however poor it may be.

2 **Honesty:** vanity publishers masquerade as mainstream publishers and, in doing so, they misrepresent themselves.

3 **Cost:** these days there are so many ways that you can go about publishing your book yourself – via self-publishing and print-on-demand – that there should be no need at all to resort to vanity publishing.

4 **Reputation:** if you publish with a vanity press, this harms your reputation as a writer.

With the rise of the Internet and of ebooks, as well as the slow decay in the traditional book-publishing market, there has recently been an explosion of different publishing models, and a proliferation of companies trying out new approaches to putting out novels. This all makes things rather murkier than they were in the past when it was relatively easy to distinguish vanity publishers from mainstream publishers. But the general principle is this: any publisher should be making an investment in the work that they publish. If you self-publish, *you* are the publisher, and it is *your* investment. If you publish with a third party, then the third-party publisher should make this investment. But you should not be investing *on behalf of* a third party so that they can publish your book at a profit.

Focus point

You should *never* pay a publisher to publish your novel.

If you are not sure about a publisher's reputation, then make sure that you do your research before you send your work out to them. Once the publisher has started to express an interest, you also need to make sure that you read the contract they send very carefully: in this way you will know exactly what you are agreeing to. There is more about contracts in the chapter on third-party publishing.

The confidence trick

Alice Munro

'In writing, I've always had a lot of confidence, mixed with a dread that this confidence is entirely misplaced.'

Whichever way you decide to publish your work, it takes a degree of confidence to put your words out there in the public realm. Whether you are contacting more traditional mainstream publishing houses or whether you are making your work available by self-publishing, confidence matters. In fact, confidence can make the difference between your work being well received and not being well received.

What I mean by this is that you need to be able to stand fully behind your work if you want it to succeed. This does not mean claiming that you are the greatest genius since Virginia Woolf or Vladimir Nabokov, or claiming that your debut novel will outsell Stephen King. It means having a degree of substantial and justified confidence that *you have done your job well*.

If you are contacting third-party publishers, they want a sense that you are standing behind your work. They do not want you to tell them that your work is a work of genius. But they *do* want a sense that you as a writer know what you are doing, that you are presenting your work in a professional fashion, and that you take your own work seriously. Similarly, if you are publishing your own work, then this also requires a measured belief in the worth of what you are doing. If you are uncertain or unconfident in your work, your readers will pick up on your uncertainty, and they will read your book less charitably.

How can you have sufficient confidence in your work? The first way is by being sure that your novel is as good as it can possibly be when you present it to your public or your publisher. The second is by recognizing that in putting your novel into the world, you are doing something impressive, but at the same time something utterly mundane, something that hundreds of thousands of people have done before you. If they could do it, why not you? But the final thing to remember is that often confidence comes through actually doing something: do not wait until you have the confidence to take the plunge. If the novel is ready, put it out there, and see what happens.

Where to next?

Now that we have covered some aspects of the publication process, it is time to look more closely at what you need to do to prepare your work for publication, whether you are self-publishing or whether you want to go with a third-party publisher. Whichever route you decide to take, you will need to make sure that your manuscript is in a form ready to take it to the next stage.

19

Preparing your work for publication

You may think that when you have redrafted your novel for the *n*th time, it is as close to perfection as it is ever going to get. You have sweated over every last comma, you have polished and repolished until you can polish the manuscript no more. But there is still much more to do before your book sees the light of day. A book is a complex artefact. In the process leading up to the publication of your novel, you will need to be familiar with the way that books are structured and with the processes that turn a manuscript into a finished book. This is all the more the case if you are self-publishing your work, in which situation you will have to take responsibility for *all* stages of the process.

However you decide to go about publishing your work, the process leading up to publication is much the same:

- Your book will need to be properly and professionally edited.
- Your book will need to be proofread.
- The cover will need to be designed.
- There will need to be a blurb for the book.
- You may want to secure endorsements from well-known writers (if you can get them) to encourage people to buy your book.
- You will need to think about how your book is going to be distributed, marketed and sold.

This chapter will look at this process of publication, whether you are self-publishing or publishing with a third party.

Developmental editing

If you are publishing with a third-party publisher, once your book is accepted, you will be appointed an editor. Your editor's job is to begin to fashion your raw material into a novel that is ready to hit the bookshelves. This is sometimes called 'developmental editing' (it is also called 'substantive editing', or simply 'editing'). This is the point at which an editor may work with you to refashion, sometimes significantly, aspects of your project. Developmental editors may make all kinds of suggestions about your work, such as recommending that you:

- cut out or substantially revise subplots

- remove unnecessary characters

- bring one or more characters more into focus

- remove whole chapters and sections that do not work

- rearrange the order of chapters in the manuscript

- fill in or address plot holes

- rewrite parts of the book to deepen and enrich the story

- rework your dialogue

- adjust the text for pacing (which might involve merging or splitting chapters, cutting chunks, adding new material, etc.).

In other words, this stage of the editorial process may involve large-scale revisions of your work. This can be an illuminating, if sometimes difficult, process; but a good editor who really appreciates what you are trying to do is *the best possible friend your book can have*. Note that last sentence carefully. The editor does not aim to be *your* friend. They may end up being so, but that is beside the point. Their task is to be the friend, the champion, and the advocate of your *novel*. And if this involves a certain amount of kicking and screaming along the way, a good editor will recognize that this cannot be helped.

Of course, there are *bad* editors: editors who try to push your book in the wrong direction, who don't really appreciate your book, or who are simply uninterested. But if you have a good and wise editor then, even if their advice is difficult and painful at times, you should cherish them. Even if editing is a difficult process, remember that your editor is not the enemy. You both want the same thing: you both want your book to be as persuasive as possible when it eventually comes into the hands of your readers.

 ## Focus point

Editors may sometimes make suggestions for substantial changes. When working with third-party editors, many of whom are seasoned professionals, you should take their advice seriously, while also remembering that there is usually room for discussion and negotiation.

If you are self-publishing, you won't have the benefit of a professional developmental editor. If this is the case, you need to make sure that you have an equivalent level of feedback on your book from disinterested and skilled third parties. You may have intelligent and thoughtful beta readers who can help you refashion your manuscript, you may have friends with whom you can exchange drafts, or you may have polished your novel until it is gleaming at a writers' group.

Key idea

However you get the editorial attention you need, you should always be sure that, when the book is about to go into the world, you can *fully* stand behind it.

Copy-editing

The next step in the process will be copy-editing. The borderline between developmental editing and copy-editing is sometimes not entirely clear. But if developmental editing involves asking the big questions about your work, copy-editing is about the fine-tuning of your manuscript.

As with developmental editing, many of the things that we have already looked at in the section on redrafting your manuscript will happen *again* at the copy-editing stage. The difference is that it is a disinterested outsider who is doing the work. And this difference makes all the difference. You as a writer have all kinds of knowledge about your fictional world that readers will not have, so it is impossible for you to see the book objectively, independent of this knowledge. Your editor may, by this stage, be over-involved as well. The copy-editor's job is to see what the book looks like as a whole, from the perspective of somebody who is uninvolved and who has none of their own interests at stake in the book.

As Carol Fisher Saller says in her book *The Subversive Copy Editor*, a good copy-editor's role is to work *with* the writer *in the interests* of the reader.

Carol Fisher Saller, *The Subversive Copy Editor*

'What I am suggesting is that [as a copy-editor] your first loyalty be to the audience of the work you're editing: that is, the reader.'

The copy-editor, in other words, is concerned with making sure that your book works for the reader, making sure that readers do not dismiss it due to glaring errors, needless complexities or other quirks. The last thing you want is for your book to go out there into the world, and for your readers and reviewers all to point out that there is a terrible, terrible mistake on the first page. It is embarrassing and it undermines all the careful, painstaking work that you have done elsewhere.

It may well be (and usually should be) the case that your developmental editor is not the same as your copy-editor. For my first novel, I worked closely with two developmental editors at the publishing house. We batted the manuscript back and forth for several months, culminating in an epic editorial session during which we monopolized the corner of a local coffee house, spreading papers everywhere and going through line by line. It was only after all this was done, when the developmental editors were satisfied with the book, that the book went out to the copy-editor to troubleshoot it for further problems. This was a much more hands-off process. My copy-editor mentioned that she had enjoyed the book, and this was nice to hear. But her enjoyment was also beside the point. Her job was simply to iron out blunders, inconsistencies and moments of clumsiness or ambiguity.

If you are self-publishing, you will need a copy-editor. We will look at this in more depth in the self-publishing chapter.

Typesetting

Once your book has passed out of the hands of the copy-editor, it will then be typeset. If you are self-publishing, this may be the most technically difficult and most challenging part of the entire process. Typesetting turns your manuscript (it is a bit anachronistic to call it a 'manuscript', which literally means 'written by hand', but most people still use the term) into a *proof* copy. The manuscript is a working copy for you as a writer, and for your editors, to fashion into shape. Only once you are ready to go public should you think about turning this working copy into a typeset proof that is almost ready to enter the world at large.

There are some good self-publishing guides out there that give in-depth advice on typesetting: I've mentioned a few in the Resources section at the end of this book. But some of the things that you will need to think about when typesetting your novel are:

- book format and page size
- margin size
- division of the text into chapters, sections and parts
- typography (font choice, size, design and layout on the page)
- illustrations and diagrams
- front matter and back matter.

If you are self-publishing and you are *only* producing an ebook, then some of these won't apply, as e-readers allow the reader to adjust the typography and layout of your book to suit their own tastes. If you are *not* self-publishing, much of this will be dealt with by your publisher; but it can still be useful to know, because the more you can be aware of and understand the process your book is going through, the better you will be able to work with your publisher.

If you are typesetting yourself, remember that good design is design that doesn't get in the way of your reader's experience of the text (there are exceptions to this: you may *want* it to get in the way, which is fine – but be aware that this is what you are doing if you are doing it). Good design is often *invisible*. Bad design shouts from the rooftops, 'Look at me!'

Typesetting for the page and for ebook are different processes. The discussion below relates mainly to typesetting for the page. There is some material on typesetting for ebooks in the next chapter on self-publishing, as well as more detail on the nuts and bolts of what you need to know about typesetting if you are going it alone.

BOOK FORMAT AND PAGE SIZE

If you are producing a printed book, you will need to think about how big the published book going to be. There are standard sizes of books, and so you will need to do research. The decision about format will affect the way people make use of your book. In the UK there are standard book sizes that look like this:

A format	178 mm × 111 mm	Standard paperback size, often associated with mass-market paperbacks
B format	198 mm × 126 mm	Slightly larger paperback size, often associated with more 'highbrow' literary fiction
C format	216 mm × 138 mm	Large-sized paperback, often used for academic books, etc.

Although these are standard sizes, different publishers may vary in the formats that they prefer. If you self-publish with a print-on-demand publisher, you may find that you are using slightly different page sizes from these. Do not worry too much about any of this, but it is worth being aware of the differences and what the format of a book suggests to its readers about the kind of book it is.

MARGIN SIZE

Do you want luxurious, large margins, or do you want to fit more words to a page? Think about what effect margin size will have on the number of pages. Look at comparable books to see how they manage margin size. Remember that when it comes to book design, *simplicity* and *consistency* are the most important things. This applies to margins, to typography, and to how you handle all other aspects of the typesetting process.

DIVISION INTO CHAPTERS, SECTIONS AND PARTS

Your text may be divided into chapters, sections and parts. There may be a prologue and an epilogue (although you should think about whether you *really* need these). You will need to think about how you manage this division of the text. It is usual to begin new chapters on a new page.

LAYING OUT ILLUSTRATIONS, DIAGRAMS, ETC.

Just because you are writing fiction, it doesn't mean that you are barred from using illustrations. But if you do want them, you need to think about how these will be laid out on the page. If you are third-party publishing, you may want to talk to the publisher about how they can handle illustrations. My first novel contained a map that I drew myself. My second novel contained a piece of music that I had to typeset myself using professional music-writing software.

TYPOGRAPHY

You will need to think about what typefaces you will use. Do not go for anything fancy. Go for a simple, elegant, serif font. A serif font is a font that has those little kicks and hooks at the ends of letters, as in the diagram below.

SERIF FONTS	SANS-SERIF FONTS
This is a serif font.	This is a sans-serif font.

Almost *all* published fiction is typeset exclusively in serif fonts. There are some exceptions but, if you are making an exception, you need to have a very good reason for doing so. 'I like this sans-serif font better' is not a good reason.

Good book design is all about simplicity, clarity, consistency and attention to detail. You will need to think about legibility, about the 'feel' that a particular typeface gives your book, about the length of printed lines (an average of around 12 words per line is considered about optimum), and about how the typeset text looks on the page. Typography is an incredibly skilled art. If you want to go it alone, then you will need to do your research and develop a deeper understanding of typefaces and book design.

Key idea

'Typography', from the Greek for 'form' and 'writing', is about how text is designed and laid out on the page.

Try the following exercise to get you thinking about aspects of typography.

Snapshot: thinking about typography

Select several novels in print form. For this exercise, you are not looking at content, but instead you are looking at how the words are laid out on the page.

Have a look inside the books and compare the text. Which one is most attractively laid out? Which one is least attractively laid out? Can you find any clues about what the font might be (sometimes – although relatively rarely – this is mentioned on the copyright page at the front of the book)?

Take a page of each of the novels and estimate the number of words per line in the main text. How does this correlate with readability?

Look at how section headings, chapter headings, page numbers and running headers and footers (the text at the top and bottom of every page) are laid out. Where are the page numbers? Are they at the top or the bottom? Are they in the middle or at the outside edges?

FRONT MATTER AND BACK MATTER

Front matter refers to all the material at the beginning of your book before the story itself starts. This includes things like: copyright page; title page; dedication; tables of contents; and so on. If you are self-publishing, carefully study the front matter of the books in your possession to see how you want to handle this. *Back matter* includes the stuff at the end such as an index (what? in a novel? – well, you never know…), or perhaps an acknowledgements page or an author's note.

Snapshot: the anatomy of a copyright page

Pull a few novels down from your shelves and look at the copyright pages that appear at the beginning. You will see that these pages are more varied than you might imagine. Read through several, to get a sense of which components are *always* present.

Generally, a simple copyright page for a UK book will look something like this, with the relevant details put in between the square brackets.

> First published in [YEAR] by [PUBLISHER]
>
> This edition published in [YEAR] by [PUBLISHER]
>
> [PUBLISHER'S ADDRESS]
>
> All rights reserved
>
> Copyright © [AUTHOR NAME] [YEAR OF PUBLICATION OF THIS EDITION]
>
> The right of [AUTHOR NAME] to be identified as author of this work has been asserted in accordance with Section 77 of the Copyright, Designs and Patents Act, 1988.
>
> Printed in [PLACE] by [PRINTER]
>
> [ISBN]

If you are planning on self-publishing, you can use the guide above – and also research the copyright pages in the books that you have on your shelves – to draft your own copyright page.

Disclaimers

Sometimes copyright pages will include disclaimers as well, to say that your book is a work of fiction, and should be taken as such. A disclaimer often reads something like this: 'All characters appearing in this work are fictitious. Any resemblance to real persons, living or dead, is purely coincidental.' Remember, however, that just putting a disclaimer in will not necessarily protect you from libel.

Some writers like to play with disclaimers. I don't recommend that you do this, but the following quotations give two examples.

Dorothy L. Sayers, *The Three Red Herrings*

'If I have accidentally given any real person's name to a nasty character, please convey my apologies to that person, and assure him or her that it was entirely unintentional. Even bad characters have to be called something.'

Dave Eggers, *A Heartbreaking Work of Staggering Genius*

'Any resemblance to persons living or dead should be plainly apparent to them and those who know them, especially if the author has been kind enough to have provided their real names and, in some cases, their phone numbers.'

Proofreading

After your book has been typeset, then you will have a copy of what is known as a proof. Most third-party publishers these days send out proofs as PDF files, although in the past they would be bundled up and sent in the post. A proof copy should look exactly as your final book will look. It will be laid out exactly as the published book will look on the page and all of the typography, design and layout decisions will have now been made. The reason why PDF files have become the standard for this is that page layout and design can be fixed. If you open a PDF on any device, if the producer of the PDF has done everything properly, it should look exactly the same.

Proofs are exciting because, when you have a proof copy, you know that your book is *almost there*. But don't get too excited just yet: there is a lot of work still to be done. The text will be there in its final form, laid out just as it will be laid out in the published version of the book; but you are not yet ready to go to press. You now need a further stage of editorial attention. You need to *proofread*.

There is often a lot of confusion about the difference between proofreading and copy-editing, but the distinction is actually quite simple.

Key idea

Copy-editing is about making sure that the content of your book is absolutely right *before* the book is typeset. Proofreading is about correcting final errors *after* typesetting.

Because typesetting is a complex, skilled and expensive process, by the time you get to the proof stage, it is simply too late to make major edits to your book. If you are being published by a third-party publisher, who has had to pay a professional typesetter to lay out your book, then if you make too many significant changes at this stage, your contract may require you to pay the costs of sending the book *back* to the typesetter. So, by the time you have the proofs in your hand, you should expect your book to more or less stand or fall as it is. This means that proofs are not just exciting: they are also rather terrifying.

PROFESSIONAL PROOFREADERS

If you are published by a third-party publisher, they will pass your book on to a professional proofreader who will go through it to pick up any errors. But they will also send you a copy of the proofs to go through yourself. If you are self-publishing, I would advise you to employ a proofreader for your work, because writers are too involved, and are therefore not the best proofreaders of their own work. This doesn't mean that you shouldn't *also* proofread your own work, only that you shouldn't be the *only* person proofreading it.

Focus point

All books, whether self-published or published by third-party publishers, require *professional* proofreading. In the UK, the Society for Editors and Proofreaders, SfEP (www.sfep.org.uk), will be able to provide you with a list of experienced proofreaders.

One reason why proofreading is difficult is that novels are designed to provoke our interest, to draw us into the story that is being told: but the moment you allow yourself to be drawn in, then you are no longer *proof*reading, you are just *reading*. Only if you step back from the story and refuse to get involved can you focus your attention on picking up errors.

WHAT TO LOOK FOR

A professional proofreader probably will not check facts or worry about the timescale of your story (as a good copy-editor might). Proofreaders are not concerned about the story at all, about whether your book is good or bad, about whether the characters are convincing or not. Instead, what they care about is *detail*. They care about the text being accurate, clear, consistent and error-free. These are the following kinds of problems that you will need to be on the lookout for at the proof stage:

- spelling and punctuation (in particular, look out for apostrophe errors)
- other typos
- grammatical errors such as problems with changing verb tenses
- small stylistic problems
- misused or commonly confused words (for example 'affect' and 'effect')
- typographic and layout errors
- inconsistent spacing between words.

A novel is a complex thing. Let us say that you have written a substantial novel that is 100,000 words long, or around 400 pages (I've chosen this sum for the sake of the easy maths). This gives you plenty of scope for errors to creep in. Even the most fastidious writer will make mistakes, and further errors may have crept into your book *during* the editorial process. Nobody is perfect. So let us say that we generously allow ourselves a margin of imperfection of 0.1 per cent. That sounds reasonable. In most areas of life, this would seem pretty good. However, when it comes to your novel, this would equate to 100 errors. In other words, your reader would come across an error *every four pages*. This might be enough for them to put the book down and give up.

This is why *all novels need to be proofread*. Even if you have a 0.1 per cent margin of error, if these errors have stuck around for so long that if they have slipped your notice when you sent the manuscript off to your publisher, or slipped your copy-editor's notice, then they must be tenacious. You are going to have to work hard to root them out.

 Focus point

Small errors of spacing, typography, punctuation and spelling may seem trivial individually, but they mount up very quickly across a large book. Your margin of error, if you want your book to be taken seriously, is very small.

PROOFREADING TIPS

I am assuming that your book is going to be professionally proofread by somebody else (even if you happen to be a professional proofreader, you should not rely only on yourself when it comes to your own book). But your publisher will certainly expect you to read the proofs as well, if you have a third-party publisher. And if you are publishing your own work, you should expect it of yourself. This is not a *substitute for* professional proofreading, but a *supplement to* professional proofreading. Here's some advice on how to go about working through your proofs.

- Print out the proof copy: it is easier to read proofs on the printed page than on the screen.
- Use a non-transparent ruler to go through line by line.
- Proofreading involves an enormous amount of concentration. Make sure that your environment is clutter-free. Do not listen to music or have any other distractions in the background.
- Take regular breaks. Five minutes every 20 minutes will help enormously. For proofreading, you need sustained and unbroken attention. If you do not schedule breaks, then your mind will decide when to insert its own breaks, but it won't tell you that this is what is doing. This will mean you'll miss things.
- If you find yourself getting drawn into the story too much, read *backwards*: if you read from the bottom of the page to the top, you can pick up typos and spelling errors that you might otherwise miss. Reading backwards stops you from getting involved in the story, allowing you to focus on technical errors and glitches.

You may need several 'passes' through your manuscript to pick up the errors.

PROOFREADING VOODOO

Professional proofreaders use a number of standard marks to make absolutely clear the changes that are needed. In the UK, the standard marks are referred to as BSI (British Standard Institution) 5261C. These can be found fairly easily with a quick web search. To the uninitiated, they can seem like strange and mystical voodoo; and, as a *writer*, you do not necessarily have to learn these marks. Nevertheless, it can be useful to know how to understand them if you come across them. Printing out a copy for reference may be useful.

Cover design

The advice that you should never judge a book by its cover is, generally speaking, bad advice. Covers can tell you a lot about books, even if they cannot tell you *everything*. Although covers are not infallible guides to the contents of a book, they are specifically designed to give an indication of what your book is like, and to appeal to a particular audience. So while you should not *definitively* judge a book by its cover, a cover is a good way of getting at least some sense of what a book is about. Ideally, *all* aspects of a book's design should reflect the content.

Richard Hendel, *On Book Design*

'The author's words are the heart of book design.'

If you are to be published by a third-party publisher, you may find that you have little choice about cover design. The publisher may send you one or two options to choose between, or send you the cover for your approval; but if you do not approve, they may simply go ahead anyway. This can be frustrating for writers, and it is always worth arguing the case if you think that the cover designs suggested by your publisher are *really* bad, but often there is not a great deal that you can do about it.

Cover design depends upon budget. If a publisher has a decent budget, they may be able to pay the designer enough to get them to actually *read the book* and come up with some design ideas. If they are running to tighter margins, they may contact the designer with a few ideas, but not expect the designer actually to look at the book itself.

Key idea

Remember that, from a publisher's point of view, the cover design does not just have to relate to the contents of your book. It also has to place the book within a particular part of the market.

Self-published novelists will need to think quite hard about designing a cover for their book. To pay a designer costs money; but if you do not have fairly substantial design skills yourself, you are not going to do your book justice. Think about commissioning a cover design if you are at all unsure about whether you are up to the task. If you want to do it yourself, then keep things simple: part of the art of good design lies in simplicity.

Snapshot: judging books by their covers

Go to the library and pick up a pile of books at random. Do not look at the back covers or inside the book. Just look at the front covers. Lay them out on the table in front of you.

For each book, write a few sentences about the following questions. Be as precise as possible.

- What kind of book is it?
- What is the intended readership?
- What other books is it like?
- What is the *mood* of the book?

Now take a short break. After the break, return to the books, and to your comments, and explore the books more fully: read the back covers, read the contents, and so on. How accurate are your judgements about the books based only on the covers?

Endorsements, reviews and blurbs

Even a small bookshop may have more books in it than you could ever hope to read. Attention and time are limited resources. Books need to be presented in a way that will persuade readers to pick up *this* book rather than *another* book. Alongside good cover design, another way that readers can tell if this is the kind of book that they want to read is through endorsements and review extracts on the cover, and through the blurb that is usually found on the back of the book. We'll look at these in turn.

ENDORSEMENTS

Endorsements are favourable comments written about your book by well-known people: often writers who are higher up the food chain than you are yourself. If you are self-publishing and you know any established writers, you can always ask them to read your book and, if they like it, to give you an endorsement. Endorsements are done purely out of goodwill, as a leg-up to other writers. Do remember that no writer is *obliged* to give you an endorsement, and that asking them to do so involves asking them to invest a considerable amount of time in reading your book. There's always a danger that they might not even *like* your book. The expectation is that an endorser will say something *favourable* about the book that they are endorsing; so if you have asked somebody to endorse your book and they turn you down – or if they get back to you and say that on this occasion they would prefer not to – then it probably means that the book is not their kind of thing. Thank them and move on.

Third-party publishers will often seek endorsements themselves, using their networks of connections. But they may also ask you for ideas about who might be good to endorse your work. If you have got to the stage of a signing a contract with a third-party publisher, you might want to start thinking about who could endorse your work. Be ambitious, but not too ambitious. Don't just go through the list of recent Nobel Prize in Literature winners and copy out all the names. Think about people who may have an interest in the subject-matter of your book, people whose books you admire and with whom you, as a writer, feel a kinship, or people you know.

Some people think that endorsements are a bit of a scam. They are certainly less objective than reviews. But if an endorser is well chosen, their endorsement can say quite a lot about a book and can help the reader get a sense of whether this is the book for them.

REVIEWS

If this is the first edition of the book, and if you are published through a third-party publisher, then your publisher may send out uncorrected proof copies of the book to reviewers, so that the book can be published with choice quotes from these pre-reviews. If your book goes into subsequent editions, then it will carry reviews of the first edition. If you self-publish, particularly if you use print-on-demand, you can add review copy to books fairly easily.

Reviews are different from endorsements in that they are solicited without the expectation that they will necessarily be favourable. In other words, as a reviewer, I should be free to say (within the limits of the law and human decency) whatever I like. Good reviews can help sway the reader who is wondering whether or not to buy your book. Even a mixed review can have quotes that you can extract and use in publicity and marketing material, as well as on the cover. However, you should be careful to quote faithfully. Sometimes you see reviews with sections cut out, marked by ellipses: '…' It is fine to condense review quotes or to quote selectively, but do not do violence to the sense of the review, because this is dishonest and this dishonesty will, in the long run, do you no favours.

Here's an example. Let's say that on the cover of my book I have the following quote: 'Buckingham's novel is… the work of a wayward genius.' If the original quote is 'Buckingham's novel is not only a compelling and fascinating tale, but also the work of a wayward genius', then it is fine to abridge the quote (although you might choose not to). But if the original reads, 'Buckingham's novel is a total mess, although one cannot help suspecting that the author is so in the grip of delusion that he himself believes it to be the work of a wayward genius', then the abridgement is simply an attempt to deceive and should be avoided.

Snapshot: unabridging reviews

This is a relatively quick and fun exercise. Take some recent novels and look at the reviews on their cover pages. Notice whether there are any reviews that are abridged. Then see whether you can track down the original review and find out what the publisher has left out. This should be particularly straightforward with newspaper reviews because many newspaper archives are available online.

Why do you think the publishers abridged the reviews? Do the unabridged originals give you a different idea of the book?

BLURBS

Sometimes people refer to endorsements as 'blurbs'. Others use the term 'endorsement' for the things that other people say about your book, and 'blurb' for the chunk of text that the publisher puts on the cover of a book to give the reader a sense of what kind of book it is. This is the sense in which I'm going to be using the word 'blurb' here.

Even if you are published by a third-party publisher, you may be asked to provide a blurb for your own book, or to work with the publisher to produce one. The point of a blurb is to give a reader a sense of what kind of book this is, to provoke their curiosity and to draw them in so that they are tempted to buy themselves a copy. A good blurb manages to give a feel of your novel without giving away too much of the plot or appearing too smug and self-satisfied. Writing blurbs is quite an art.

 Focus point

A blurb should:

- convey the feeling or the atmosphere of the book
- intrigue the reader sufficiently to persuade them to pick up the book
- not give away too many plot details
- allow the reader to get to know what kind and genre of book this is
- if a work of fiction, introduce the main protagonists and any major antagonists.

Two things in particular to avoid in blurbs are:

1 evaluative statements ('this is a powerful and astonishing tale')
2 too many rhetorical questions ('Will Patsy marry the man of her dreams? Will One-Legged Len regain his position as CEO? Will this endless multiplication of rhetorical questions become tiresome?')

It is easy in blurbs to go over the top and just gush about how wonderful your book is. But a blurb should not be evaluative. Readers are wise enough to know that almost *all* writers think that their own books are wonderful – just as almost all parents think that their newly born children are wonderful. However, just saying, 'This thing I have created is wonderful' is not going to convince anybody.

Workshop: thinking about the publishing world

In this chapter we have looked at the question of preparing your work for publishing. You can now think of getting your book ready for a journey out into the big, wide world. It is time, that is to say, for your book to leave home.

While for most of this chapter we have been looking at what your novel needs to be ready to venture out into the world, in this workshop I want to raise the question of what you need to know about the world into which it is about to step. In other words, this workshop is about getting to know the publishing world more fully.

1 Getting a sense of the publishing world

Either by using the books pages in newspapers or else by using industry journals such as *The Bookseller* and *Publishers' Weekly* (we looked at these in Chapter 3 – your local library may have copies), have a look at recent discussions about what is going on in the book world. You might also want to use blogs such as Futurebook (www.futurebook.net), which is run by the *Bookseller*. Browse through articles for an hour or so, making note of any that are of interest.

- Now identify *three* major issues that are being discussed.
- When you have done that, research the different viewpoints that there are upon these issues.
- In the light of your research, think about what impact they may have upon you as a writer (make notes if it helps).

2 Thinking about the market

The market for books is always changing, and is highly subject to the uncertain whims and winds of fashion. But this uncertain world is the world that you will be entering once you have launched your book. Again, an hour or so browsing through articles might be time well spent. Try to explore the following questions:

1 What notable successes in third-party publishing have there been in the past year? Drawing upon what people in the writing industry are saying, why do you think these books have been successful?

2 What notable successes in self-publishing have there been in the past year? Again, why do you think they have been successful?

3 Thinking about your book in relation to the market

In the light of these explorations, how do you think your book stands in relation to the market? The following questions might be worth exploring:

- Does your project suit a self-publishing model or a third-party publishing model better?
- How might you be able to best present your book to make sure it succeeds in the market?
- Has your reading of current trends and fashions given you any ideas about how and where you could publish the book?
- What else might you need to do to make sure that your book can survive and thrive in the current market?
- Has your reading given you any ideas about connections to follow up, people to contact, or *concrete action* that you can take to explore possibilities for publication?

Where to next?

Before moving on to explore self-publishing and third-party publishing, you will need to think about questions of ethics, law and copyright. If you are putting words out into the public domain, you are subject to all kinds of legal demands and constraints – and it pays to know what these are. This is the subject of the next chapter.

20

Copyright, ethics and the law

When you publish something, you put your words into the public sphere; and because the public sphere is not a complete free-for-all but is instead a place bound by laws and restrictions, you need to know where you stand. Writers often like to depict themselves as advocates of unfettered freedom, but when you start to look at question of ethics, responsibility and legality, this view of the unfettered artist becomes rather more difficult to sustain and the situation becomes a bit more complex.

This chapter is about all of these complexities. It is about the question of *who owns what* (that is to say, copyright). It is about the question of *what you can and can't do* (that is to say, law), and it is about *what you ought and ought not to do* (that is to say, ethics). It is important to point out here that this chapter cannot offer legal advice. If you want this, you'll need to talk to a lawyer. Laws differ in different parts of the world, and are always subject to change and interpretation. This chapter is no more than a snapshot of some of the things that are worth keeping in mind. In short: if you follow the advice here to the letter and still end up in court, I can't accept responsibility. And if you follow this advice to the letter and end up in prison, don't expect me to come and deliver you a cake to make you feel better. I'll sympathize, of course, but I have books to write and can't really spare the time.

Copyright for writers

 Key idea

According to the *Oxford English Dictionary*, copyright is 'the exclusive and assignable legal right, given to the originator for a fixed number of years, to print, publish, perform, film, or record literary, artistic, or musical material'.

To understand copyright, it can be useful to break this definition down:

- **Exclusive**: if *I* own the copyright, you don't.
- **Assignable**: if *I* own the copyright, I can *give* it to you (after which *you* exclusively own it).
- **Legal right**: this right is protected by law.
- **Given to the originator**: if I create something, then I own the copyright.
- **For a fixed number of years**: copyright eventually *expires*.
- **To print, publish, perform, film or record literary, artistic, or musical material**: copyright is for works that are considered to be *creative* and *unique*. This is interpreted widely: a newspaper article is subject to copyright; computer code is subject to copyright; a mime is subject to copyright.

WHAT IS THE PURPOSE OF COPYRIGHT?

 Article 27 (2) of the Universal Declaration of Human Rights

'Everyone has the right to the protection of the moral and material interests resulting from any scientific, literary or artistic production of which he is the author.'

The purpose of copyright is ultimately very simple: it is a system that ensures that creators of works can be properly credited and recompensed for their work. This enables them (in an ideal world at least) to gain enough of an income to go on producing. In UK law, there are two basic principles of copyright:

1 Copyright belongs to the artist unless the work is created in the course of the artist's employment, in which case copyright may (but does not necessarily) belong to the employer.

2 Copyright in the UK generally lasts for 70 years from the end of the year the artist died (***post mortem auctoris***, sometimes written simply as *pma*).

What this means, at least in the UK, is that:

- You automatically own the copyright of your work without having to 'claim' it. It is an automatic right enshrined in law, although you can give the copyright away and transfer it to somebody else.

- You should assume that any works within the 70 years' period are the copyright of their original creators or their estates.
- It is your responsibility to establish the copyright situation of any resources that you use in your own work.
- As long as your work is original and exhibits a degree of 'skill, labour or judgement', then the moment your work is produced (not published, simply written), you own the copyright to that work.

Focus point

Copyright is an *automatic right*. You own the copyright of something by virtue of creating it yourself.

Copyright subdivides into two different kinds of rights: what can be called 'commercial' rights, or the rights to exploit a work for financial gain; and what are called 'moral' rights. You may have seen at the beginning of books the phrase, 'The Author asserts his/her moral right to be identified as the Author of the work in relation to all such rights as are granted by the Author to the Publisher under the terms and conditions of this Agreement.' Moral rights cover:

- the right to claim authorship
- the right to object to any treatment of the work 'prejudicial to personal honour or reputation'.

If, in other words, an unscrupulous publisher decides that they want to remove your name from the cover of your novel, and if you have retained moral rights, you can ask them to desist, thanks to your right to claim authorship.

Copyright and your own work

Copyright will affect you as a writer in two different ways. It will affect you as a creator of your own works, and it will affect you as somebody who makes use of the works of others.

When it comes to your own work, because – as we have already seen – copyright is an automatic right, in the UK at least there is no need to jump through any hoops to claim copyright. In the United States, although copyright is an automatic right, you can also *register* copyright. This has some benefits – chiefly that it allows you to go to court in the case of copyright infringement, since it provides an unambiguous public record of copyright in the work.

If you do not need, under most circumstances, to *claim* copyright, what you will need to do when you publish your work is to *assert* your copyright. This is to let others know that the work is in copyright and who the copyright owner is. According to the UK Copyright Service, notice of copyright should be apparent to the reader when they start reading your work, which is why in novels it is usually on the information page at the very start. To give notice of copyright is very simple. You can use the copyright symbol © or the word 'copyright' followed by the year of publication and your name, as follows:

© 2015 A. N. Author

GRANTING RIGHTS TO OTHERS

If you automatically own the rights to your work, when you publish with a third-party publisher, what you are doing is granting the limited right to somebody else to publish it in a particular context, language and format. What you *should not* be doing is granting the copyright itself.

There are cases in which writers will be offered a one-off fee in return for reassigning the copyright of their work (remember, copyright is *assignable*). In a few limited cases, this is acceptable: for example, if you are writing entries for an encyclopaedia, or academic journal articles, this is often usual practice. But, as a general principle, this should *never* be the case for fictional works. So, if a publisher asks you to grant them copyright outright, just say a polite 'no' and find yourself another publisher.

 Focus point

No reputable fiction publisher will ask you to assign your copyright to them. Instead they will ask you to grant limited rights to publish the work in a particular format, language and context.

What you grant publishers, instead of ownership of copyright, is a limited licence to reproduce your work, *under certain conditions*. Granting rights to others in this fashion can be one way in which you can make use of your copyright for financial gain (or at least for fame). Rights are what is known as 'divisible', so you can split up the rights that you grant in all kinds of ways. I could sell the right to make action figures from my first novel to one person, the film rights to another, the right to make a radio serialization to another, and the right to translate the book into Icelandic to yet another person.

CONTRACTS AND GRANT OF RIGHTS

If you publish your book with a traditional publisher, there will be a section of the contract that will read something like 'Grant of Rights'. Here the contract sets out the specific rights that you have agreed to grant the publisher. In this section you will find the core rights, which are rights to the publication of the work in various paper formats – and increasingly in ebook format – in a particular territory. If the contract here says something like 'all rights', you should argue to make it more specific, for example, that you grant the publisher the right to publish the book within a particular language and country or set of countries (this is what is meant by 'territory'), in a clearly defined range of formats.

Your contract will probably also have a section marked 'subsidiary rights'. These might include:

- rights to the publication of extracts in journals, magazines, etc.
- rights to audio-book editions
- rights to publication of book-club editions
- rights relating to dramatic performances
- rights to film or TV adaptations
- rights to video game / action-figure tie-ins.

The rights you grant will depend, in part, on what kind of deal you can get. If you are going to be published with a publishing house that has a large foreign rights department, they will probably ask to handle translation rights. If so, it might make sense to agree to this, because they will have contacts that you don't. But if your publisher is small and is not going to actively try to exploit these rights, then you might be better holding on to them yourself.

Focus point

When granting rights to publishers, as a rule of thumb make sure that you are only granting rights that the publisher is actively going to try to exploit.

Snapshot: reading contracts

This might be a good time to think more about contracts. This exercise is of direct relevance if you are publishing with a third-party publisher. If you have an agent, they may deal with much of this. But if you are third-party publishing without an agent, the following approach may help with reading and negotiating your contract. If you are wondering whether to self-publish or third-party publish, then this exercise might be a good way of thinking through some of the issues. Do a web search for some sample fiction contracts, download them, and work through the exercise accordingly.

1 Download a good guide to contracts. Reading contracts is a complex business, but there are excellent free guides available. Try the 'Guide to Publishing Contracts' on the Society of Authors (www.societyofauthors.org) web page.

2 Work through your contract with the guide by your side. Contracts will usually have precisely numbered paragraphs. Note down any paragraphs that you do not understand. Check these against the contracts guide to see whether you can find out what the agreement is. If you are still unclear, you may need to consult with another writer, or ask the publisher to clarify the clause.

3 Note in particular:

- what rights are being offered
- on what basis they are being offered (royalties, advances, etc. – see the next chapter)

- what obligations you are undertaking as the author
- what obligations the publisher is undertaking.

4 Mark any clauses with which you are unhappy or with which you disagree. You may need to do some research to see whether the terms are reasonable and get into dialogue with the publishers about these clauses.

5 Make a list of queries, questions for further research, and action points to take back to your potential publisher.

Copyright and the work of others

The second question is that of how you go about using *other people's* work. Just as you don't want other people to use your copyrighted materials without permission, so you shouldn't want to use the work of others without appropriate permission.

What this means in practice is that if you quote from or directly use somebody else's work in your novel, you need to make sure that you have the appropriate permissions to make use of this work. If you quote from a song, or if you use the image of a painting in your book, you need to clear this with the copyright owner. The bottom line is this: when it comes to copyright, you need to make sure that you are clear on the copyright situation of *everything* that you use within your book. If you have not done so already, it is sensible to run through your manuscript to check for possible problems.

Snapshot: copyright and your work

Once you have a copy of your book in draft form, go through a copy of your manuscript and mark any points at which you are using somebody else's work. These might include:

- quotations
- song lyrics
- poems
- extracts from other books
- musical scores
- pieces of dialogue from film or TV shows
- images.

Make a list of these. These are problems that you will need to address later. We'll come back to them in the final workshop exercise.

You might think that you can get away with quoting just a few lines of a song; but it pays to err on the side of caution. If you *do* quote song lyrics or poems, then things can get expensive, as the novelist Blake Morrison found when his editor told him that he had to clear the rights for a few lines in one of his novels. For two lines of Bob Marley's 'I Shot the Sheriff', he paid £1,000. For one line of 'When I'm Sixty-four' (technically 'When I'm Sixty-four' is also one line from 'When I'm Sixty-four', but as it is the title as well, I'm allowed to quote it here!), he paid £735. In fact, for a handful of lyrics, he ended up with a bill of close to £4,500. Fortunately, his publisher paid half, but still, this is more than anybody would want to pay.

It is not always this expensive. Sometimes I have written to publishers or authors to ask permission to quote from work, and I have received charming replies saying, 'Yes, certainly, we'd love you to use the work, and we'll let you do it for free.' Sometimes I have ended up paying tiny fees (£2.50 was a recent fee for an image I am using in a forthcoming book) just to cover administrative costs.

After his bruising experience, Morrison decided that in future books he would simply make up songs and bands, and get round the problem that way.

Blake Morrison

'Don't ever quote lines from pop songs.'

Remember that *you can negotiate* these costs. If you ask for permission to quote something, and you get a response asking for a fee, it is worth writing back to say, very politely, that you can either offer a lower fee, or that as a writer with a rather modest income, you'd very much appreciate it if they reconsidered and were willing to let you use the copyright material for no fee at all. If the rights holders say no, then you have the choice of either paying up or simply cutting out the quote. However, if you ask for permission and it is refused, or you cannot negotiate a fee, *never* simply go ahead and use the material anyway.

Do also remember that – as rights are divisible – it may be that the rights holder will give you the right to reproduce the work only in a particular language or territory. This can get complicated if there are later overseas editions or translations of your work. Again, don't let all this put you off, but it is good to be aware of this. And if you can be aware of it at the beginning of the writing process, then this is all the better.

PUBLIC DOMAIN MATERIALS

Not all work will be *in* copyright. If work is out of copyright, then it is considered to be in the 'public domain' and thus free to use. You may be able to use scans of images or books that are out of the 70 years *pma* limit; similarly, old postcards where the rights holder is untraceable can sometimes be reasonably considered to be in the public domain (although this is a complex area). However, beware of complications. For example, a work of literature might be out of copyright, but a particular edited *edition* of the work may be in copyright. Finally, something may be out of copyright in one region but *in* copyright in another region.

Key idea

Material in the public domain is material the copyright of which has expired, making it free to use and reuse.

You may be able to find what are called 'royalty free' materials to use in your work. This doesn't mean that they are free. It means that you pay a one-off fee rather than being licensed on a royalty basis. Royalty payments depend on the number of copies made of a particular work. But if the image was royalty-free, then once you had paid for permission to use it *in a particular work*, you could make as many copies of that one work as you liked. If you wanted to use the image in *another* work, then you would pay again. Often, royalty-free materials are available for a relatively low cost, so it is worth exploring this avenue, particularly if you are looking at self-publishing and thinking about cover design. There is a list of places where you can find royalty-free materials in the resources section at the end of this book.

Copyleft and new models of copyright

The rise of the Internet has led to a lot of heated debates around copyright. The ease of copying has led to a whole range of phenomena – from creative mash-ups of copyrighted work to outright piracy – that have stretched copyright law almost to breaking point. Partly as a result of this, there have been some interesting developments in copyright, in particular the notion of 'copyleft'.

'Copyleft' was born in the collaborative world of free software development ('free as in "free speech"', as founder of the Free Software Foundation, Richard Stallman, put it, 'not as in "free beer"'), but it has spread beyond the world of software to encompass all kinds of cultural creations.

 Key idea

'Copyleft' is the term given to copyright agreements that aim to enshrine in law principles such as: freedom to use, freedom to share and freedom to make derivative works.

Copyleft agreements generally have a clause in which all derivative works should be issued under the same licence. This means that if you freely use copylefted materials, then other people can use your own copylefted materials in a similar fashion. One of the most well-known approaches to this is the creative commons campaign (www.creativecommons.org – although not all CC licences are technically speaking 'copyleft'). Creative commons licences are designed to have both human-readable and legalese forms, so that they are not only understandable by those of us who are not lawyers, but also properly and fully worked out to have full legal standing.

Copyleft may have implications for you, both as a creator of new work and as somebody who seeks to use the work of others in various ways. It is a challenging idea for novelists, because it goes against the grain of the notion of the individual creative novelist. Although the notion of copyleft may not affect you as a writer, be aware that this is a growing area of copyright law.

Dealing with copyright infringement

You may also find yourself confronting issues around the infringement of the copyright of your own work. Blatant theft of work, in the sense of writers claiming that they have written work that is written by others, is relatively uncommon. But there are all kinds of other cases where the copyright situation is more murky. Have a look at the following situations:

1 Somebody puts up a low-budget YouTube video of an unauthorized amateur theatre adaptation of your novel.

2 You find a pirated version of your self-published novel available online as a PDF via an Internet search.

3 You find a pirated version of your novel (published by a third-party publisher) available as a downloadable free ebook.

In case number 1, you *could* call your lawyer and ask the theatre company to immediately desist. And *technically* this might well be copyright infringement, as you haven't granted rights for a stage version. However, this might not be the best move. After all, if your novel has not had a great deal of exposure, then this might help your book sales. You might be delighted that people are doing such wonderful, creative things with your work. Perhaps getting into dialogue with the theatre company might be better, and seeing whether you can negotiate a mutually beneficial arrangement.

In cases 2 and 3, you might want to intervene. If you are published by a mainstream publisher, a simple email to the publisher should suffice, and they can chase it up. If you are self-published, on the other hand, chasing up piracy can be difficult and time-consuming. Your first port of call would be to contact the website owner with a formal request for them to desist. But it can be a struggle as an individual to get your work removed, and you need to balance a concern with protecting your work with a concern with protecting your time. If you are a member of a writers' union such as the Writers' Guild (www.writersguild.org.uk) or the Society of Authors (www.societyofauthors.org), they may be able to advise you on pursuing legal action.

Snapshot: getting up to date on copyright

Take an hour for this exercise. Select at least two of the following sources:

The Bookseller (www.thebookseller.com)

Publishers' Weekly (www.publishersweekly.com)

The Authors' Licensing and Collecting Society (www.alcs.co.uk)

The Society of Authors (www.societyofauthors.org).

Read through any recent discussions or updates relating to copyright, and how it affects writers. Make a note of anything that you think will affect you as a writer.

Trademarks

Another intellectual property issue you need to consider is that of use of trademarks. If you are writing a novel set in the contemporary world, you will almost inevitably come across this problem. What if your character goes into a bar and orders a soft drink? Can you use a brand-name product? Or do you have to invent a drink called something like Kooky Kola? Thankfully, you don't need to resort to the latter course of action. As long as you are not calling into question the good name of the product in question, you are entitled to refer to it. But if your story involves your character's teeth falling out because of over-indulging in [*insert name of famous brand-name drink here*], then the company's legal department may have something to say.

 ## Focus point

You should not use trademarks in way that is directly disparaging, that is potentially libellous, or that could lead to confusion as to who owns the trademark.

This means that you should not use trademarks in the title of your book, as this could not only mean that *anything* in your book could be associated with the trademark, but also that it could be considered an attempt to pass your work off as somehow associated with that trademark.

Libel

Another legal issue that you may face is that of libel law. Libel law protects not only individuals but also companies and organizations against *defamation* – in other words, against claims or imputations against them that are: a) untrue (or not demonstrably true), derogatory or offensive; and b) harmful to their reputation or standing.

 ## Key idea

In the UK, claiming that your work is fiction is no defence against libel.

Even basing your characters closely on living individuals can be considered libellous if it can be argued that readers could reasonably make the connection with the individual in question. Acceptable defences against libel are as follows:

- **justification:** what you say is demonstrably true
- **fair comment:** what you say is in the public interest
- **privilege:** what you say is published 'on an occasion of privilege', which essentially applies to journalistic reporting.

UK libel law is particularly strict, and so it makes sense to be very careful in this respect. All novels – even the most fantastical – are based on a novelist's experiences.

And readers will expect to make connections between your writings and your biography, even if these connections seem to you to be spurious. So be careful, in writing your characters, to make sure that you are not simply drawing direct from life.

Other legal issues

These are at least some of the major legal questions that you need to be aware of when you write your novel. It pays to be aware of the broader legal situation in the country in which you are publishing. Some places may have other laws about what can and cannot be said for all kinds of reasons. When does an explicit sex scene become obscenity? When, if you are writing a thriller, does your meticulously researched account of how to make bombs become 'incitement to terrorism'? If you are published by a mainstream publisher, then they will almost certainly take a fairly strong line on making sure that the books they publish are not at risk of legal challenge. If you are self-publishing, you should explore any issues and, if necessary, seek legal advice, *before* you publish your work.

Ethics

Questions of what you can and can't write about are legal questions. But beyond that there are questions of what you ought and ought not to write – in other words, *ethical* questions. This is a complex area. I know some writers who claim that writers have only one ethical commitment, and that is to tell the truth. This is unconvincing, in part because there are many different truths that you could write about, and so this still leaves open the question of *why you are telling this particular truth*.

You will be held to account ethically for what you have written. And often you will be held to account for things that surprise you: the things that people are troubled by in your work may not be the things that you *think* they will be troubled by. When you write a novel, it is as a part of a social world, and the novel that you write will have an impact upon that world. It will affect your personal relationships, it will affect the way you are seen by others, it will perhaps even affect the way the other people respond to one another. Here are some questions that may crop up:

- Questions about the justice of how you represent or misrepresent historical characters, individuals or collectives
- Questions about the possible implications of putting your stories in the public domain
- Questions about whether the information you have in your novel may be harmful
- Questions about the possible political implications of what you write
- Questions about what you should *leave out* of a story that is based on historical fact.

None of these questions should *stop* you writing your novel. But you should be able to satisfy yourself that you have thought through these issues. And if you keep alive to these ethical questions *while* writing your novel, you may end up writing a richer, more ethically complex novel, and you may be more prepared for the questions that crop up once it is published.

Workshop: thinking through copyright, law and ethics

This final workshop is a way of going through your work and making sure that you are clear about the various issues involved. It is probably best to leave this workshop until your book is completed, at least in draft form.

1 Copyright

Go back to the snapshot above, and look at the copyright issues in your work. For each item do the following:

- Establish who the rights holder (if anybody) is for the material you are wanting to use.
- If the work is neither in the public domain nor out of copyright, find out who to contact about the rights to use the material.

Later, when you know how your novel is to be published, you can write to these people and organizations to negotiate permission to use the material. You may want to wait until you have a contract or have decided how to self-publish, as the agreements may depend on how and where your work is to be published.

The following table might be a useful template for you to make sure that you have picked up on every issue, and that you have recorded the action taken to resolve any problems, and the outcome of this action.

Page	Material used	Copyright status	Action taken	Outcome

2 Legal issues

Now go through your manuscript. Write down a list of any areas where you need to give attention to legal issues in your writing. In particular, pay attention to:

- use of trademarked names
- potentially libellous material
- other passages that may be open to legal challenge.

When you have done this, *do your research* into where you stand on these legal issues. After this, *make any changes* to your manuscript that you need to protect yourself from legal challenge.

3 Ethical issues

Finally, have a think through the ethical questions that could be raised for you personally by publishing your novel. Write down a list of any questions that you think are important to address, and that you think other people may ask. For example, you might ask:

- Is this a true representation of this era, time or place?
- Am I misrepresenting this particular group of people?
- Is there anything that makes me uneasy about this book being in the public sphere?
- Is there anything in my novel that I think will be actively or potentially harmful?

You may find that you don't have *answers* to these questions. That is fine: this is not about tidying everything up so that your novel is safe and uncontentious. It is about really thinking through the complex ethical issues that are there in any good novel, so that you are sure that you can stand behind your work, and so that you may be ready for any questions that are put to you, or issues that arise, after your novel's publication.

Where to next?

In this chapter we have seen that putting a novel out into the world is not a trivial thing. There are all kinds of legal and ethical implications to putting words in the public domain, and you owe it to yourself to think through these implications. However, now that all these issues have been cleared away, it is possible to think about moving towards publication, whether through publishing yourself or through third-party publishing. This is the subject of the next two chapters.

21

Self-publishing

Self-publishing has seen an extraordinary boom over the last few years. There are two reasons for this. The first is the rapid rise of the ebook. The second is the growth in print-on-demand publishing. These two developments, taken together, have put quality self-publishing and distribution within the reach of ordinary mortals. If you are independent-spirited and entrepreneurial, and relish the thought of going it alone, self-publishing can be a good option. This chapter explores the nuts and bolts of how you go about it.

Ebooks and print-on-demand

Now that ebook readers are so widespread and affordable as to be mainstream, ebook publishing has spiralled. Ebook platforms are arguably a very good thing for writers. With an ebook reader connected to the Internet, it is possible for users to purchase books at the touch of a button, and to have the book delivered instantly.

As a reader, I read both on the page and also in ebook format. At the time of writing this, it is hard to tell whether this is a transitional stage and one day I will find myself reading only in electronic format, or whether this mixed environment of ebooks and paper-based books (sometimes called *p*books) is going to continue; but one thing is clear: the rise of ebooks has made the book market much more volatile and much more interesting.

 Key idea

While third-party publishers still dominate the market for paper books, self-published books have already cornered a huge share of the ebook market.

Alongside the rise of the ebook, one factor has fuelled the boom in self-publishing, and that is the rise in print-on-demand services. These services allow books to be printed according to the demand of readers rather than as a huge batch of books printed in advance in the hope that these books will sell. Most third-party publishers still think largely in terms of print runs. When they sign a contract on a book, they will attempt to estimate sales figures for the book and they will settle on a first-edition print run. They will decide to publish, say, 10,000 copies of the book, and they will offer an advance. Then they will have to shift 10,000 copies. This business model makes sense for a large company. But if you are an individual, then to print even 1,000 copies of your book up front and try to sell them will be something of a challenge (and a risk). If, however, you can have a way of only printing books as and when they are needed, then the risk is lower. This is what Internet print-on-demand technologies have given writers: the ability to design and upload their books, making it available both in ebook and printed versions with no up-front printing costs. Print-on-demand has become a powerful force in publishing, allowing self-published writers to compete with third-party published writers, whether on paper or in electronic format.

What it takes

 Steven Berkoff

'I think self-publishing brings back a sense of self-worth.'

If you simply write your books and they are published by third-party publishers, then there are many things that you don't have to get too involved in. If your publisher is big enough, there will be marketing people – or even whole departments – to deal with marketing your novel. There will be editors who will work with you on editing your book. There will be salespeople to deal with getting your book into bookstores. There will be rights departments to negotiate with Hollywood when they come calling. There will, in short, be armies of publishing professionals who are there to support your book's journey out into the world. Even if you are with a small literary publisher (some small publishers are run by enthusiasts from their kitchens), you will have somebody else putting a lot of work into getting your book into shape and out into the world. But if you are self-publishing, you will have to do most, or all, of this yourself.

Self-publishing, in other words, requires a huge amount of commitment. You need to be meticulous and uncompromising. You need to have an entrepreneurial spirit, because you will need to promote your book yourself. You need to be willing to take time away from the writing process to think about typesetting or online marketing campaigns. And you also need to have at least *some* money to invest in your project up front.
We will look at costs below, but as a rough guide, if you are self-publishing a novel to professional standard, then the cost should not be any less than you might be willing to spend on going on holiday for a week. All publishers invest financially in books that they believe in: and if you are publishing your own work, you should do the same.

If all this sounds rather daunting, then I should add that self-publishing *well* can also be hugely rewarding.

Stigma and snobbishness

Let's get one thing out of the way first. Is there a stigma associated with self-publishing? And will being self-published harm your chances of being taken seriously as a writer? These questions have no simple 'yes/no' answers. Certainly, the boundaries between self-publishing and third-party publishing are becoming a lot more porous. To the extent that there is a self-publishing revolution under way, it is not happening through the big publishers being overthrown once and for all by tides of indie and self-published authors. Instead, it is happening because of a rapid growth of good self-published books available to readers.

Focus point

The more good self-published books there are in the world, the less readers will ask whether this or that book is self-published. Instead, they will ask: *Is this book any good*?

If you are going to self-publish your own work, be aware that there is still a lingering stigma associated with self-publishing. This should not make you doubt your decision to self-publish, but it might help you be prepared for some of the responses you may get to your book. If readers are sniffy and snobbish about self-publishing, when it comes down to it their snobbishness is *their* affair. Ultimately, if your book is good, there is nothing ignoble about taking the self-publishing route – and there may in fact be many benefits.

Snapshot: exploring self-publishing success

If you are thinking about self-publishing, it can be useful to explore some success stories. The following exercise is about this research.

- See whether you can find out the names of the authors behind some of the major success stories in self-publishing in the last year or two.
- Select two or three authors from this list, and search online for interviews with these authors, or articles about their success.
- What advice can you get from studying the success of these authors? What does their experience tell you about how you might approach the world of self-publishing?

The advantages and disadvantages of self-publishing

Hugh Howey

'Traditional publishing is much too restrictive. I don't want to pump out the same book over and over. I want to challenge myself and produce the work that I feel is missing from the marketplace.'

Self-publishing and third-party publishing are simply alternative *routes* to getting your words out there into the public domain. And, as different routes, they each have their own advantages and disadvantages. The following table gives some of the advantages of self-publishing.

Some advantages of self-publishing	
Control	You have creative control over every aspect of the publication process.
Insight into the publishing process	There is a significant learning curve, but if you self-publish you will learn a lot about how books are produced and sold.
Higher percentages	You will typically earn a far higher percentage of the cover price in royalties.
Faster payments	Usually you will be paid for book sales monthly.
Rapid turnaround from manuscript to publication	If you are in a hurry to publish your book, and have the time to put into it, the process can be much quicker when self-publishing.
Retention of rights	You retain all rights to your work, rather than licensing them to somebody else.
Ease of producing new editions	If you want to put out a second edition, or make editorial changes after publication, you can (but this is no excuse not to get things right first time!).

There are, however, downsides to self-publishing. The following table gives some disadvantages.

Some disadvantages of self-publishing	
Reputation and image	There is still some stigma attached to self-publishing. Your book needs to be very good to overcome this prejudice.
Bookstore sales	You will find it hard to get your books sold in high-street bookstores.
Investment	Any publisher has to invest financially in new projects. You are no different. There will be up-front costs involved in preparing your book for publication.
Time and effort	Self-publishing requires a huge time commitment. You may need to learn a whole range of new skills. On the other hand, once you've done it once, it gets easier.
Reviews, etc.	You will find it harder to get reviews for self-published work.
Marketing	You will be responsible for all the marketing of your book yourself.
Editorial care	A good third-party publisher will make your book better: you will need to find ways of doing this yourself.

How should I self-publish: paper book, ebook, or both?

The next question is *how* you want to self-publish. Effectively, you have two choices: ebook or paper edition. Some self-published books (and some third-party published books) will be published using only one of these formats; and you are at liberty to choose only one or another of these approaches. There is no compulsion to put out your book in either format: you are your own boss. As with all decisions, there are advantages and disadvantages to both.

PAPER BOOKS

I know self-published writers who have effectively set up their own publishing houses. They have negotiated with printers, decided on a print run, and then – once the boxes full of books are delivered – they have attempted to get their books into bookstores or found other ways of selling them off to the public. However, for present purposes, I am going to assume that, if you are self-publishing paper editions of your books, you are going to be thinking about print-on-demand. The advantages of print-on-demand are:

- very few up-front costs
- good distribution networks
- no storage costs.

Relatively few up-front costs

If you publish your book using print-on-demand, you do not have to pay up front for a whole print run. The cost for the production of each book is factored into the cover price and passed on directly to the buyer. There will still be some up-front costs such as:

- editorial and proofreading costs
- cover design costs
- costs of marketing and promotion.

Nevertheless, if you use print-on-demand, in general your initial investment will be relatively low.

Good distribution networks

Print-on-demand publishers such as IngramSpark (www.ingramspark.com), Lulu (www.lulu.com) and Amazon CreateSpace (www.createspace.com) will not only deal with printing your book but also with distributing it to buyers, not just nationally but also internationally. You are not responsible for sending your books out to those people who buy it. You just wait to see the sales figures pile up.

No storage costs

Your storage costs will also be non-existent. If you produce a print run of 1,000 books, you not only have to deal with distributing these books but you also have to find a place to put them while you are trying to sell them off. A thousand books can take up more space than you'd think.

There are, however, disadvantages to print-on-demand. The first is that at present, you are unlikely to get your books into high-street bookstores (although things are changing fast: before long, it may be possible to go into a bookstore, search for a print-on-demand book, and get it produced for you on the spot).

The other disadvantage is that for many print-on-demand services, production standards are not *quite* up to scratch: print-on-demand books – however meticulous the author is in producing them – are often not at quite the same level as third-party published books in terms of production values. Again, this is changing, but if you are going to go with print-on-demand, you need to do your research.

Choosing your service

The current major players in both print and digital self-publishing are listed below.

Major print-on-demand services	
Amazon CreateSpace	www.createspace.com
Lulu	www.lulu.com
IngramSpark	www.ingramspark.com

Major ebook services	
Amazon Kindle Direct Publishing	kdp.amazon.com
Lulu	www.lulu.com
Smashwords	www.smashwords.com
IngramSpark	www.ingramspark.com

All of these services offer the ability to upload your final files, to upload cover designs, to set prices, and to distribute your books in various territories and formats. This is a rapidly changing market, and so if this book is even a couple of years old, there may be new players in the market and new options for you. Do your research first of all, make sure that you are happy with the deal that is being offered, and make your choices wisely.

Preparing your manuscript for publication

The process of moving from your final edited manuscript to having a published book on your hands is a complex one. Here is an overview of what you will need to do. This list follows the outline in the previous chapter, but is tailored for self-publishing.

EDITORIAL WORK

First of all, you will need to make sure that your work is professionally edited. As a self-published author, you may think that you can do this yourself; but if you do, you would be wrong. It is absolutely essential that you get your book professionally edited if you want to stand out from the crowd.

We saw in the last chapter that there was a difference between *substantive* or *developmental* editing, on the one hand, and *copy*-editing on the other. Briefly, *developmental* editing is about developing your novel so that it works as a story. *Copy*-editing is about ironing out any remaining problems before the manuscript is typeset.

As a self-published writer, you may not have a developmental editor, so you will need good beta readers: people who can closely read your drafts and give you high-quality feedback. The quality of the feedback you get will depend very much on the skills and experience of your beta readers, so do select carefully for the job. You may also want to employ a professional manuscript appraisal service at this stage.

While whether you decide that your work needs *developmental* editing or not is largely up to you, and depends in part on how much feedback you have already received over the course of writing and redrafting your novel, *copy*-editing is absolutely essential.

Focus point

Consider employing a professional copy-editor to read your work. In the UK, you can find a list through the Society for Editors and Proofreaders, SfEP: http://www.sfep.org.uk

TYPESETTING FOR THE PAGE

Typesetting your manuscript is another hurdle that you will have to navigate alone if you are self-publishing. As I mentioned in the previous chapter, the approach here is completely different depending on whether you are publishing a paper edition or an ebook. We'll look at these in turn.

When typesetting books for the printed page, most professional designers will use desktop publishing (DTP) software. Two common pieces of software are Adobe InDesign, which has more or less become the industry standard, and QuarkXPress (often referred to just as 'Quark'). You *can* typeset a book in word-processing software such as Microsoft Word, but the typography will not be as high quality. On the other hand, there can be a bit of a steep learning curve to Quark and InDesign. If you are in this for the long haul, and if you are the kind of writer who likes getting to grips with software and has a fine attention to detail, then eventually you might be better off buying some DTP software so that you can learn how to typeset your own books. But this will take time, money and effort. You are free also, of course, to commission somebody else to typeset your book for you; but once again, this will cost.

Key idea

While you can use a word processor to typeset your book, the results will be better if you use desktop publishing software.

If you decide to use a word processor, you can get by (and many self-published authors get by very well) if you are sufficiently meticulous and careful. There are many guides online to typesetting in Word. And if you are using a print-on-demand service, then the website of the service you use will almost certainly give you very detailed information about layout, format and how to submit files for publication.

Focus point

To prepare the entire manuscript for publication, you will usually need to produce two PDF (Portable Document Format) files: one for the typeset content of the book and one for the cover.

TYPESETTING FOR EBOOKS

If typesetting your book for ebook publication, you will need to take a very different approach. While type on the printed page is fixed, when users view your book on an ereader, they can change typefaces, font sizes, margin widths and all the other typographic details. Remember, too, that an ereader doesn't really have pages *at all*, at least not in the way that a book does. The text just rolls onwards. It may be broken up into sections and chapters, but it doesn't have pages.

Key idea

The page is not a natural division in an ebook.

Not only this, but readers will be viewing your ebook on all kinds of different devices. In this sense, ebook formatting has the same problems as website formatting: just as visitors to a website may be viewing it on a computer with a large screen or a tiny mobile phone screen – or anything in between – as well as on a range of web browsers, so it is with your ebook. You do not *know* whether the reader is going to be looking at it on a smartphone, on a large plasma screen, or projected on to the wall of their house.

When typesetting ebooks, you effectively have two options. You can either use a word processor (or your favourite writing tool) or you can do it all by hand. The first route may be more familiar, but it may create formatting problems for your readers. Word processors and similar kinds of software work on a principle known as WYSIWYG (pronounced 'wizzy-wig'), or 'what you see is what you get'. In other words, what you see on the screen is – very roughly – what the eventual output is going to look like. But WYSIWYG doesn't work so well if the design can be viewed on all kinds of devices at all kinds of size. Here we'll look very briefly at each approach.

Ebook formatting by word processor

Some services such as Lulu and Smashwords (www.smashwords.com) have detailed descriptions of how to edit a Word document so that it can be uploaded and successfully converted into an ebook format. And some pieces of writing software such as Scrivener (www.literatureandlatte.com) can do a passable job of converting your text into an ebook. However, this approach is not failsafe. If you are publishing with Amazon's Kindle Direct Publishing, or KDP (kdp.amazon.com), note their warning that using Word documents may lead to formatting problems.

What you need to do here is first choose what service you are going to use, and then read the instructions very thoroughly and decide how to proceed.

Focus point

Although you can format an ebook using a word processor, you are much better off doing it by hand.

Ebook formatting by hand

If you really want to produce a clean ebook file that will look beautiful on *every* device on which it is viewed, then you can do things by hand. I made an analogy above with websites that can be viewed on multiple devices, but this is more than an analogy, because most ebook files are based on HTML – which is the standard way of writing and laying out web pages as well. HTML is what is called a *markup* language. What this means is that, rather than using WYSIWYG formatting like this,

Some words are in *italics* and some are in **bold**.

you have a plain text file to which you add *tags*. These tags act as instructions that can be interpreted by the ereader. So the marked-up plain text instruction to produce the line above would look like this:

```
Some words are in <em>italics</em> and some are in
<strong>bold</strong>.
```

The beauty of this is that these instructions can be translated into nicely formatted text on *whatever* device your reader is using, and however they have their reader set up. There are some very good guides out there to how to use HTML to format your files ready for publication in ebook format. The process usually involves the following stages:

1 Strip out all the word-processor formatting from your text by pasting it into a plain text or programmers' editor (for example Notepad++ or jEdit).
2 Put back all the formatting you need using HTML codes.
3 Save in HTML format.
4 Convert the saved files to ebook format such as .mobi or .epub.

While this may seem like a complex process, it is fairly mechanical and fairly straightforward to learn. It may take a couple of days of patient work, but you will be glad that you did it. Covering these stages in depth is a little beyond the scope of this book; however, the Resources and Further Reading sections suggest some useful guides for ebook formatting that you can get hold of free online.

PROOFREADING

Once you have final proofs, you will need to proofread them for errors. If you are publishing for ebook and in paper format, you will ideally need to proofread *both* versions. Not all commercial publishers do this, and it leads to some unfortunate errors in ebook editions. If you are self-publishing in both formats, you can probably get away with getting professional proofreading help on the paper version of the manuscript, and then working very carefully through the ebook version (or, ideally, the marked-up HTML files) to replicate the corrections there.

COVER DESIGN, ENDORSEMENTS AND BLURBS

Again, if you are a designer, then you *can* do this yourself; but do think about getting a professional cover design produced for your book. Some self-publishing services will offer you an automatic cover designer. This can save on these costs, but invariably these automatic cover designers don't look as good as professionally designed covers. Particularly when it comes to paper editions, the cover of your book matters a great deal. You do not want to put potential readers off by shoddy cover design; and if your words have been carefully honed and crafted, you do not want them presented to the public in a slapdash wrapping.

If you decide to commission a cover designer, make sure that you ask to see some of their other work so that you know that you are happy that they are going to do a good-quality job. Remember that a good cover – particularly for ebooks – should look good both at full size and when shrunk down to a thumbnail.

 Focus point

Remember that your cover should include not just your name and the title of the book. It might also carry some glowing endorsements from other writers, as well as a well-written (and proofread) blurb on the back.

Snapshot: understanding the process

Select one of the major players from the lists above – either for ebook publishing, or for print-on-demand publishing.

Go to the website of the service, and either download, or read online, their guidelines for publishing.

As you go along, note down:

- any skills that you need to develop
- anything that you don't understand and that requires further research
- the major stages involved in publishing via that platform.

It may be that at the end of this exploration, you decide that the service in question is not for you and that you want to try publishing elsewhere. Remember that you can take the process step by step: you don't need to understand everything at the outset and you don't need to do everything at once.

What will it cost?

To get an idea of what it might cost to self-publish, you need to distinguish firstly between *essential* and *non-essential* costs. Essential costs are things that you simply *have* to get done professionally if you want your book to pass muster. The things that are marked non-essential are things that you can get away with doing yourself, if you have the time and patience and are good at attention to detail.

Note that some things are calculated by word (copy-editing and proofreading), while other things are calculated by page (typesetting), so you may need a calculator handy.

Snapshot: how much will it cost?

Use the table below to estimate the cost of self-publishing your book.

Task	Essential, recommended or non-essential	Estimated cost for a good-quality job	Your estimate
Developmental editing	Non-essential. You can enlist beta-readers, your fellow writers, etc.	Depends on length, but upwards of £400	
Copy-editing	Essential. You shouldn't skimp on copy-editing.	£15 per 1,000 words	
Typesetting for print	Non-essential. If you have the skills, you can do this yourself.	Usually calculated by page. £1.00–2.50 a page.	
Typesetting for ebook	Non-essential. This is a ticklish but fairly straightforward process (and easier than for print).	£150	
Cover design	Recommended. Unless you are a designer or have an eye for design, leave well alone.	£300	

Proofreading	Essential. You need a proofreader.	£7.50 per 1,000 words	
Total estimated cost			

If this all seems eye-wateringly expensive, then there may be ways you can save. If you have a tame proofreader or copy-editor (and if they are professionals with track records), you may be able to barter with them: they can proofread your book while you are building them a treehouse or fixing their car.

Going to print or pixel

Now you are ready to launch your book into the world, whether as an ebook, as a paper edition, or both. For paper editions, I am assuming that you are going to be using a print-on-demand service; if you decide not to, and to source your own printer and produce a limited print run, then that is fine as well – almost everything that has gone before in this chapter will be of use to you, but from now onwards you will be on your own.

Generally, for *paper* editions, you will want to choose one print-on-demand publisher and stick with them. A paperback is a paperback, so you don't need to use more than one service. If you are producing an *ebook*, however, you will want to distribute it in several formats and in several places. You will at the very least want to use a .mobi format that is readable by Kindles and an .epub format that is readable by other ebook readers.

Almost all the large online ebook publishers will have comprehensive help files to assist you with getting your work published on their platforms. You should read these help files closely so that you know exactly what their requirements are. If you are publishing in ebook format, you will also need to think about DRM, or Digital Rights Management.

 Key idea

Digital Rights Management (DRM) is a collective name for technologies that are used to protect copyright by means of restricting copying, redistribution or access to digital resources such as ebooks and music.

This may seem to be a good thing for you as a writer. But the jury is very much out on this, in part because DRM doesn't necessarily work very well, and in part because it is unpopular with readers. If you are having to decide one way or the other, familiarize yourself with the debates online, and then make your choice.

Prices

Another thing to think about when self-publishing is *how to price* your book. This is a complex area, in particular if you are looking at ebooks, and it pays to do your research. People will have different expectations when it comes to self-published and third-party-published books, so do your research to see how similar books are priced. Remember that you have more freedom when self-publishing to change the price of your book, in particular when it comes to ebook editions. At the time of launching your book in ebook format, you may want to offer a reduced price (or even give it away for free) to garner some initial reviews, before you revert to the usual selling price.

ISBNs

All published books should have an ISBN to identify them. An ISBN, or International Standard Book Number, is a 13-digit code (until 2007 it was ten digits) that uniquely identifies your book. If you publish both an ebook and a paper edition, they must have separate ISBNs. ISBNs are attached to the specific *edition* of a book. If you publish in both paperback and hardback, you will also have two ISBNs, not one. The ISBN system in the UK is administered by Nielsen UK ISBN agency. You can find out more here: www.isbn.nielsenbook.co.uk. ISBNs are usually sold in batches of ten, and at the time of writing a batch costs £132.00. Some self-publishing services will assign you an ISBN as a part of the package you sign up for, or else you can buy your own.

Case study: Satya Robyn

If you are thinking about setting out on the path of self-publishing, it may all feel rather daunting. In such cases, it can be useful to hear from people who have successfully navigated the winding pathways you are about to tread. The following story, from a novelist who has been successful both in self-publishing and third-party publishing, may help you to get a sense of the pleasures and challenges of going it alone.

> 'I never set out to be a self-published writer but, at the moment, I'm very happy to be one. Here's my story. I finished my first novel when I was in my late twenties and managed to find an agent very quickly. While they tried to place my book with a publisher I wrote my second novel, and by the time we parted ways (when my agent went on maternity leave) I had three unpublished novels. A small publisher took on all three novels (they preferred their authors not to have agents) and published them over the next couple of years. I had moderate success with these books, and one of them was placed on promotion in a major bookshop, but I didn't earn much money. We also parted ways and by this time I had a fourth novel. I started looking for a new agent, but I was beginning to feel impatient and disillusioned by the world of

traditional publishing. I'd already successfully self-published a collection of poetry and a self-help book, so I thought I'd take things into my own hands.

'Self-publishing gives me complete control over cover design, my blurb, and other aspects of packaging the book. With the help of my husband, I released the book on Kindle and made it free for a few days through the Amazon KDP Select feature. Several hundred thousand free downloads later, Amazon started recommending my book to people. As more people bought it and gave it positive reviews, Amazon suggested it to even more people. So far I have sold more than 30,000 copies of this book.

'It's been a different story with my fifth novel. Amazon knows who bought my last book but I don't, and so I can't get in touch with them directly. Putting the book on to a free promotion didn't have the same effect as last time either, as these days many more authors are using this technique.

'The moral of the story? Except for a few writers in the upper echelons, there is no guarantee that your latest book will be read, regardless of how successful your last one was. Having a publisher with a huge marketing budget might have helped, but regardless of your attempts to control things, books have a life of their own. All you can do as a writer is to keep writing, to keep making the best decisions you can for your books and your career, and to hand the rest over for the universe to decide. For me, the most important part of being a writer has always been the process of writing. If readers receive something from my books, that makes me very happy, but it can't be the only thing to sustain me. I'm going to keep writing.'

From self-publishing to third-party publishing

There is one particular story that is often told in the press, and that is the story of the self-published author who is 'picked up' by a third-party publisher, whose talent is spotted, and who is eventually 'properly' published. This kind of story always makes me a bit uneasy. I'm perfectly happy with self-published authors entering into contracts with third-party publishers if they wish to. And I am perfectly happy with authors who have always published with third-party publishers deciding to go it alone and to self-publish their next work. This movement between self-publishing and third-party publishing is increasingly common. But what makes me uneasy about these stories is the assumption that the role of self-publishing is simply to act as a giant 'slush-pile' (see the next chapter) for third-party publishers to trawl. If you are self-publishing because it may be a *route into* third-party publishing, you are self-publishing for the wrong reasons. Self-publish because you believe in your work. Self-publish because you believe that self-publishing is worth doing. Self-publish because you relish the freedom that comes along with publishing in this fashion. But if you see self-publishing merely as a step on to the 'higher' stage of third-party publishing, you are missing out on all that is good and wonderful about self-publishing.

Workshop: researching self-publishing

This workshop is designed as a simple way to help you navigate through the complexities of self-publishing. By the end of the workshop, you should have an idea about the self-publishing service that will work best for you.

1 Exploring the options

Do a web search to see what services are currently available for self-publishing. You might also look at the website of ALLi, the Alliance of Independent Authors (www. selfpublishingadvice.org) which is good for keeping up to date with trends. Alongside larger services such as Lulu, CreateSpace and Smashwords, you may find some smaller, more niche providers. Write a list of five or six self-publishing services that seem interesting. Now evaluate them according to the following criteria:

- **Ease of use:** how straightforward is it to use the publishing platform? Mark this 1–5, where '1' is 'easy' and '5' is 'complex'.
- **Cost:** how much will it cost you? You may also want to note what is factored into this cost.
- **Quality of end result** (you may need to do some hunting around to find out about this): how good are the final books, whether in print or ebook format? Mark this 1–5, where '1' is 'poor' and '5' is 'very good'.
- **Distribution:** how and where are the books distributed?
- **Format:** do they publish paper books, ebooks or both?
- **Reputation:** how good a reputation does the company have? Again, mark this 1–5, where '1' is 'poor' and '5' is 'very good'.

Name of service	Ease of use (1–5)	Quality	Distribution (1–5)	Format	Reputation (1–5)

2 Narrowing down your options

In the light of these findings, narrow down your options so that you have either:

- one ebook publisher and one print-on-demand publisher, *or*
- one publisher that you are happy with for both ebooks and print-on-demand.

At this stage, if you haven't already, you should *buy books* in both ebook and hard-copy format (if you are intending to publish both ways). This is so that you can be sure that the quality is up to scratch. If you buy the books and the quality is not good enough, you may need to find another provider.

3 Moving ahead

Finally, you are ready to start moving into the practicalities of self-publishing. Make a few notes on the following questions, so that you have a sense of the road ahead.

- What do you need to learn? What do you need to learn (for example, perhaps you need to learn some basic HTML) to publish with this provider?

- What is your timescale? Can you set a reasonable timescale for publishing taking this route? If this is the first time you have self-published, it may take a little longer as you get used to how things work.

- What other services do you need? You may need to employ copy-editors, proofreaders and cover designers. It can be best to find your own rather than using built-in tools or 'add-on' services from your service provider.

- What will it cost? Now that you have decided on a service to investigate, how does this affect the costings that you worked out earlier? Try going through the costings again to see what the cost might be of self-publishing by this route.

By now, you should have an outline of what you need to do to get your work out into the public domain. It will take a lot of time and careful work before you can launch your book, but if you have finished your novel and worked through the exercises in this chapter, you are well on the way to being a self-published author. Good luck!

Where to next?

If in this chapter we have explored the possibilities of self-publishing, the next chapter is about third-party publishing, and how you go about finding somebody else to publish your novel.

22

Third-party publishing

Some people refer to what I am calling 'third-party' publishing as 'traditional' publishing; but I'm not sure that this is quite right. There are long traditions both of self-publishing and of writers getting their work published by third parties: neither is more or less traditional than the other. And although for a while third-party publishing has been very much the most dominant model of publishing, this is currently changing. So 'third-party publishing' is a more neutral, and more accurate, term for the process of finding somebody else to put your work out into the world.

In this chapter we will look at the ins and outs of third-party publishing. We will look at what publishers do, how to get in touch with them, what they like and don't like, and how to manage the business of contracts. We will also look at the role of agents.

Anne Lamott, *Bird by Bird*

'I still encourage anyone who feels at all compelled to write to do so. I just try to warn people who hope to get published that publication is not all it is cracked up to be. But writing is.'

Agents: do you need them? What do and don't they do?

When setting out, novelists often ask, 'Do I need an agent?' There is no straightforward answer to this question. It can be hard to secure contracts *both* with agents *and* with publishers; and opinions differ on which is harder for a first-time novelist.

Key idea

The role of an agent is to be an *intermediary* between the writer and a third party.

If there *is* no third party, then there is no need to have an agent. If your self-published novel generates interest in film rights, on the other hand, you *might* need an agent. So even if you are self-publishing, this section might be useful to you. An agent can certainly help you secure a publishing deal, but having an agent is not itself a guarantee that you will find a publisher. Conversely, not having an agent in no way bars you from your book being published by a third-party publisher, although it may be harder to get your book placed with one of the large, mainstream publishing houses. The broad difference between agents and publishers is that agents are concerned with taking on *writers*, while publishers may be interested in taking on *books*, or series of books. An agent may help you nurture your career across several books and several genres of publishing in a way that publishers will not.

WHAT IS AN AGENT?

An agent is somebody employed by a writer to represent their work to publishers. So an agent's job is to act as an intermediary between the writer and the commercial world of writing.

Focus point

Authors employ agents – rather than the other way round.

A contract with an agent will usually mean that you commit yourself to working exclusively with this agent, and to channelling all your work via your agent. Your agent will attempt to sell the rights to this work to publishers and in return you will pay the agent a percentage of your *earnings*. This is usually around 10–20 per cent (15 per cent is usual).

Because your agent is generally representing your work *as a whole*, what an agent usually wants to have on their books are writers with some chance of longevity: 10–15 per cent of one book contract may not be very much, but over time, and with several books under your belt, the returns will be better. So if you are only ever going to write one book, it may not be worth an agent's while to champion you – unless that book is a hit. But if an agent knows that you are the kind of writer who is going to keep on writing and keep on producing books, then you are far less of a gamble.

Some agents will be very engaged with the writers on their lists. Others will be a bit more cool and distanced. Some work for large literary agencies that employ a large number of agents and have hundreds of authors on their books. Others are staunchly independent. Here are some advantages and disadvantages of having an agent.

ADVANTAGES OF HAVING AN AGENT

If your agent is a good one, then there can be a great many advantages to having an agent. Here are just a few.

Getting your work placed

Many major publishers say that they are not willing to consider submissions from writers without agents. In these cases, if you do not have an agent, you may find it hard to get your foot on the ladder with these publishers. That is not to say that it is impossible: if you have personal connections, if an editor knows and likes your work, or if your book is particularly suited to a list, you can still get in touch with a polite query to say that, although you understand that this is an unagented submission, in this case you think that they might be interested. You may strike it lucky. But, in general, an agent will give you more options for placing your book.

Knowing the industry

One of the things an agent can also do – if they are good at their job – is have the kind of overview of the writing industry that you yourself might lack. They may be able to see opportunities for publishing your work that you might miss. If they are established, then they will have long-standing connections with editors and publishers whom they trust, and who trust them.

Giving advice, support and guidance

Although the main job of an agent is not to act as an editor or as a literary advisor – and it is certainly *not* to be a shoulder to cry on – many agents are very good at supporting writers on their list with editorial advice and suggestions. An agent may also have an overview of your career, and be able to see directions for you as a writer that you may not have thought of.

Dealing with contracts, legalities and so on

One of the great benefits of having an agent is that he or she can deal with all of the contractual side of things for you. A good agent will be experienced in reading contracts, will know what clauses to take out and what clauses to put in, will know whether the deal that you are being offered is reasonable, will be able to take a clear view of which rights you should grant your publisher, and will be able to negotiate for a higher advance on royalties (see Chapter 23 for more on advances). For these services alone, many writers find that an agent is worth the small percentage of their earnings that they take as a fee.

DISADVANTAGES OF HAVING AN AGENT

There are also potential downsides to having an agent. I know writers who once had agents and who struggled to get published, but who became much more successful once they decided to go it alone. In part, whether you have an agent or not will depend on your temperament and on how suited your agent is to your work. Here are some of the disadvantages.

Loss of control

If you are the kind of writer who likes to keep track of absolutely everything, if you like to have complete control over who is seeing your work and when, and if you find intermediaries frustrating because you never *quite* know what is going on, then perhaps an agent is not for you.

The wrong agent can hold you back

Not all agents are good agents for your work. The best agents have a basic sympathy with the work of the writers that they represent. In other words, the best agents not only represent you because they think that their 15 per cent or whatever is going to be lucrative, but also because *they appreciate your work*. If you have an agent who doesn't like your work, you may find yourself tied into a relationship that ultimately both of you will find frustrating.

Fifteen per cent is more than you can afford

Some people don't have agents simply because they don't want to see 15 per cent of their earnings going to somebody else. This is fine, and if you are happy to do everything yourself, from first contact with publishers to negotiating contracts, then you might as well save the money. But I also think that a *good* agent is almost always worth their relatively modest cut and can often increase, rather than reduce, your earnings.

HOW DO I GET AN AGENT?

Some agents are members of the Association of Authors' Agents (www.agentsassoc. co.uk). There is a list of member agents on the Association's website. Other agents will be listed in the *Writers' & Artists' Yearbook*, a useful annual publication that should be on every writer's shelves. When approaching a literary agent, if they have a website, then have a look to see whether they are taking on new clients and what they are looking for. Do your research, and find an agent who represents the kind of work you do: there is no point in contacting an agent specializing in books for young children if you have written a hard sci-fi novel.

Agents should *never* ask for a reading fee up front. If they are looking for clients, then the effort of reading work from potential new clients should be factored into their costs, not yours.

The agents in the Association of Authors' Agents all follow a code of practice, which is available on the AAA website. If you are signing a contract with an agent, then it might be useful to read through the code of practice to give you a sense of how many agents function.

While some agents can be found through their websites or through lists of literary agents, many people I know have ended up with their agents through personal connections. I initially made a connection with my own agent through one of her other authors, whom I was interviewing about his book for a magazine article. So it pays to make connections with other writers and to ask around.

Where should I place my book?

Margaret Atwood

'Publishing a book is like stuffing a note into a bottle and hurling it into the sea.'

Third-party publishers range from tiny independent operations run by single individuals from their homes, to vast outfits that are branches of huge multinational corporations, with offices in London, New York and Tokyo. Big publishers may have certain advantages: they have publicity departments that can aggressively promote your novel; your book is much more likely to get into the large high-street bookstores; and your advances on royalties are likely to be higher. But they also have disadvantages: they can be more ruthless than smaller publishers that take on a few projects out of love. Often, big publishers will want to see a speedy return on their investment: if your book doesn't sell, then it can very quickly go to remainder. See those piles of books in the remainder bookstores? They mostly come from the big mainstream publishers. Also, if you publish your first book with a big publisher, you may find yourself a very small fish in a very big pond. A smaller publisher may mean slimmer royalties, less chance of getting into the high street, and a smaller publicity budget; but you may find that a smaller publisher nurtures your work much more carefully.

So where you should go to place your book? The answer to this question is this:

The 'slush pile'

You may have heard of the 'slush pile', the rather dismissive term for the pile of unsolicited manuscripts that accumulates on a publisher's desk. In the imagination of writers, the slush pile is a dark and swampy kind of place that exudes the odour of despair and hopelessness. But despair is premature: if you do your work, research publishers carefully and pitch your work to the right place, much of the time you can avoid the slush pile and succeed in getting your work seen by editors.

Researching publishers

If you are pitching your work yourself, you will need to research which publishers to send it to. Some publishers are sent tens or hundreds of manuscripts *every single day*. And one of the reason why *so many* manuscripts are sent out is that their authors are simply not discerning enough to think about where to send their work. This is a terrible waste of time for everyone: it increases pressure on publishers, it wastes trees, it clogs up email inboxes, and it does nobody any good. So, before you send your work out, *do your research*. You will need to look at several things.

THE KIND OF WORK THE PUBLISHER PUBLISHES

Publishers do not publish books at random. Publishers' 'lists' – the books that they publish – tend to be fairly coherent. So one way of drawing up a shortlist of potential publishers is by going through the books that you *like* and the books that are *similar* to your book, and noting who publishes them. Your book may fit into a very clear 'niche' market, or it may have a broader appeal. It doesn't matter either way, but it is good to know what kind of book it is that you have written.

READING SUBMISSIONS GUIDELINES

The next thing you will need to know is what the guidelines are for submission of your work to a publisher. If publishers are actively looking for work, they will publish submissions guidelines on their websites or list them in directories such as the *Writers' & Artists' Yearbook*. If you are going to submit work to a publisher, you *must* read their guidelines. If a publisher asks for a covering letter, a synopsis and three sample chapters, this is what you should send them. If a publisher says that you should submit only by post and not by email, you should not send them an email. If you have *good reason* not to follow the guidelines *to the letter*, you should follow them *in spirit* – and explain why in your covering letter.

For example, if a publisher asks for three sample chapters and your chapters are only two pages long, you might say in your covering letter that you are sending the first 40 pages because this should be a representative sample. Similarly, if your book *only* has three chapters, each 40,000 words long, then send a representative sample – not the whole book – and explain why in your covering letter.

> ## Focus point
>
> Always follow publishers' submissions guidelines.

Publishers will talk about 'unsolicited' submissions. 'Unsolicited' means that the author has not been *asked* to submit work. So, if a publisher says, 'No unsolicited submissions', does that mean you cannot submit to them? Well, no, not exactly. It means that, if you send them your manuscript unannounced, they will simply sigh and hurl it into the recycling bin, without taking a second look. But if you have *good reason* to think that this publisher might be a good home for your book, then you can always find out the name of the editor in question and write them a courteous letter, explaining briefly why you think they might like to see your book. They *may* not get back to you; but, on the other hand, if their curiosity is provoked, they might ask you to send more. Then, when you *do* send them your work, it is no longer unsolicited.

Submitting your work

There are a few obvious pitfalls to avoid when submitting work. In what follows, I'm going to be mainly focusing on submitting your work to publishers. But this advice applies also to submitting your work to agents.

HOW TO PRESENT YOUR MANUSCRIPT

Some publishers will specify exactly how they want you to present your manuscript. If they do so, you should take note. If they do not do so, if you follow the advice below, you shouldn't go too far wrong. You will find different advice in different places, but the following overview should help you avoid most of the common problems.

- Manuscripts should be double-spaced.
- Use either a monospace font like Courier, which is clear and legible, or use a standard, commonly used serif font like Times New Roman. Do not use Arial or other sans-serif fonts.
- Make sure that you have laid out paragraphs and speech according to standard format (new paragraphs need to be indented).
- Do not put extra space between paragraphs.

- Do not use any other fancy fonts (e.g. handwriting or cursive fonts for passages of your novel that are letters, or supposed to be written by hand) unless you absolutely *have* to.

- Font size should be either 11 or 12 point (12 is standard).

- Include a cover-sheet with your name, your agent's name (if you have one), your address, your contact details, the title of the work and the overall word count.

- Do not justify your paragraphs (in other words, the paragraphs should be ragged on the right-hand side).

- Make sure that section and chapter divisions are clearly marked.

- Use a standard format for chapter headings or section headings (for example, a larger font size).

- Make sure that your margins are sufficiently wide – at least 25 mm (1 inch) on each side.

- Use only single spaces between sentences, not double spaces.

- Number all your pages in the header or the footer. It can be useful to have your name and a short version of the title by the page numbers like this: Buckingham / Novel writing.

Snapshot: preparing your manuscript

Look over your manuscript simply from the point of view of *presentation.* How is it presented? How closely does it follow the guidelines above?

If your manuscript diverges significantly from these guidelines, it is time to go through and correct some of the issues. Work through in this order.

1 First, deal with big overall issues like fonts, font size and double line spacing.

2 Next, cut out double spaces between sentences if you have them (you can do this with search and replace).

3 Make sure that your headings are logical, clear and all follow the same format.

4 Check your page numbers.

5 Make sure that you have the right page layout.

6 Deal with formatting of headers or footers.

7 Tidy up the cover page.

HOW TO PRINT YOUR MANUSCRIPT

If you are sending your manuscript by post, you will need to print it.

- Use A4 size in the UK and letter size (8.5 × 11 inches) in the US.

- Print out on white paper. Do not use extra-thick paper or paper that is coloured, embossed or otherwise unnecessarily fancy. Standard copying paper will do.

- Print your manuscript single-sided.

COVERING LETTERS

Publishers will usually ask for a covering letter. This should be relatively brief. This is not the place to give your entire life history. Some publishers will be clear about what they want you to tell them in your covering letter. However, if they don't give you any pointers, a good covering letter should:

• let the publisher know why you are getting in touch

• briefly introduce your work

• briefly introduce you, the author

• let the publisher know why you have chosen to send your work to them (if you think it fits alongside others of their books, you might mention this)

• be factual rather than evaluative: don't gush about your own work

• be written in immaculate prose, without any errors

• be clearly and professionally formatted and laid out.

This should all fit on to a single page. Make sure that your covering letter has no typos, that it is polite and professional (but not overly stuffy), that it is to the point, and that – importantly – everything you say in it is *true*. If you can get the specific name of the editor to whom you are sending it, that is useful. If not, 'Dear editor' will suffice.

Snapshot: a covering letter

It might help to do this exercise with a fellow writer who is also at the same stage as you, so that you can share letters and advice. Failing that, enlist the help of a friend who can read your covering letter for you.

• Write a covering letter for your novel. As this is a test run, you can either choose a publishing house at random, or invent one.

• Make sure that you follow the guidelines above. Be as clear, professional and concise as you can.

• Now give your covering letter to your friend (or exchange letters) and ask them to go through it, using the bullet-points above, looking for any problems or errors.

SYNOPSES

You may be asked to send a synopsis with your manuscript. This is a difficult area because there is no single form that a synopsis can take. 'Synopsis' literally means a brief survey or overview: it comes from the root *syn*, meaning 'together', and *opsis*, meaning 'seeing'.

Key idea

A synopsis is an account of your story that can, more or less, be understood at a single glance.

Keep your synopsis simple. A good synopsis sets out the story as a whole, focusing on the main thread or threads of the plot and the main characters. It is not a sales pitch or a blurb. Instead, it should show the *armature* of your story, the skeleton that lies beneath the skin. The job of a synopsis is to give the reader a sense of the structure of your novel as a whole, and an idea of the mechanics at work in the way you tell your tale. A good synopsis can be both to the point and intriguing.

If you are asked for a synopsis – or if you decide to include one – then avoid embellishment or undue complexity. Again, I would advise making it no longer than a page. If you have to extend to two pages (presented in the same format as your manuscript), then so be it. But if you are extending your synopsis into three or more pages, your reader would probably be better off reading the manuscript itself.

 Write: synoptical

For this exercise, you are going to take 15 minutes to write a synopsis of a novel that you have recently read. So you are writing a synopsis of *somebody else's* novel. Think about how you can convey the shape of the story, and how you can intrigue the reader without embellishment or complexity. Keep the length to a single page.

When you have finished, ask yourself how successful you have been in giving an impression of the book.

HOW TO SEND YOUR MANUSCRIPT

Publishers will ask for manuscripts to be sent either by email or in 'hard copy', as other words, printed. You *must* do as they ask. If they accept only email submissions, they will not take kindly to big wodges of paper coming through their letterboxes. If they accept only hard-copy submissions, they will delete your email.

If sending by post, make sure of the following:

- Do not use staples, paper clips, binders, folders or any other bindings. If you want to keep the pages together, use a simple, plain rubber band, but nothing more.
- Put your covering letter at the front.
- Enclose a stamped, self-addressed envelope if the publisher asks for one, or if you want your work returned.

Remember, professionalism is all here. Do *not* append death threats to your submission. Do not perfume your work (it happens). Do not send photos of yourself (dressed or undressed), your cat or your most recent holiday. Do not plead, because it makes you look ignoble. Do not hand-deliver your submission and insist that you are introduced in person to the editor. Do not add any unnecessary enclosures such as small gifts, nail clippings or locks of your hair.

SENDING VIA EMAIL

If you are emailing your manuscript, make sure you know what format the publisher can deal with. Common formats are .doc, .docx, .rtf and .pdf. If a publisher asks for a .doc file, then that is what you should send them (even if, like me, you harbour a degree of animosity towards Microsoft Word). If you are sending a novel, don't paste it into the body of the email. Send it as an attachment.

Because of the prevalence of spam filters, it can be a good idea to politely ask in the email if the publisher can confirm receipt of your manuscript. This stops you worrying that it might have got lost along the way, and it also establishes some communication between yourself and the publisher.

How many publishers should I submit to?

One common question that is often asked is this: *How many publishers should I contact?* Some publishers say that they disapprove of simultaneous submissions. What they mean by this is that they don't want you sending your work to other people at the same time as you are sending your work to them. This is fine as far as it goes, and if a publisher can guarantee a fairly quick turn-around time – a matter of a few weeks – this request is not unreasonable. If a publisher is nimble, you might want to give them a few weeks' grace before sending your work out elsewhere. But if a publisher is not going to get back to you for six months, then there's no reason why you should be expected to tie up your book for this period. After all, if you try ten such publishers before being successful, it will be five years before your novel is accepted.

In general, publishers *expect* that you will be sending out simultaneous submissions. They know that the publishing world works on glacial timescales. They know that writers are impatient. And it can help quicken their pulse if they know that other publishers are also reading the same brilliant manuscript that they are reading.

However, once a publisher has expressed interest in your work, if you are interested in working with them you should take this seriously. In other words, once a publisher starts to invest time and effort (and hence money) into your book, do them the courtesy of not having any flirtations on the side. You may not be married yet, you may not even be engaged; but there may be a general expectation that you will have a degree of fidelity within this emergent relationship. Publishers don't appreciate you playing the field.

As for how many publishers you should send your work to at any one time, my own advice is that three or four publishers at a time is not unreasonable. Why not fewer? Because publishers are slow, and you might wait for ever. Why not more? Because if publishers *do* get back to you, and if they reject your work, they may at the same time give you some useful feedback.

Sometimes – because they care about what they do – publishers will take the time and trouble to give you feedback. This is advice that comes from professionals in the field, and so it is of potential value to you. If several publishers give you the same advice, you might want to think about correcting some of the problems that they have identified. But you have missed your chance to make good on these problems if you send your manuscript to
20 publishers all at once.

The waiting game

Unlike self-publishing, when you are involved with third-party publishers, your destiny is not entirely in your hands. Once you have bundled up your submission and sent it off, you can do little more than wait. Be warned that most books take a long time to go from final draft to acceptance, and an equally long time to go from there to publication.

If publishers are often slow to respond, it is not that they are sluggish by nature. It is simply that they are often inundated by multiple demands. Manuscripts pile up on their desks, or clog their email inboxes, faster than they can ever read them. And, although your manuscript is the most important thing to you, it is *not* the most important thing to a potential publisher – not, at least, until they have decided to pursue publishing it.

So how long will it be before you hear back from a publisher? Sometimes a matter of days. Sometimes weeks. Sometimes months. Sometimes publishers will *never* get back to you, even if you prod them and poke them. On their websites, some publishers say how long they will take to respond to you. It is not unreasonable, after this period has passed, to send the publisher a letter or an email to see what has happened. If publishers do not tell you how quick their turn-around is, then three months is a reasonable time to wait before sending a query. Usually, protracted silence of more than three or four months is not good news.

All this waiting can be frustrating. But always be friendly and polite. Publishers are not strange, capricious gods who roll dice to decide your destiny. They are people who are struggling to put good books out into the world, often overworked and underpaid. Not only this, but the publishing world is quite a small one. People move around a lot. Getting a reputation as an awkward case does you no favours.

Other routes: competitions

Increasingly, there are other routes to getting publishers' attention, in particular competitions. These competitions often vary wildly. Some are free to enter, while others have an entry fee. Some ask for complete novels, others for sample chapters. Some guarantee publication, others offer cash prizes, mentoring and the 'possibility' of publication. A quick web search for 'novel writing competitions' should bring up some lists.

Entering competitions can be a good way of avoiding the slush pile and getting your work seen; but there is a downside: many competitions cost, and if you enter several, then the costs add up. Competitions make sense for small publishers, because they generate income that can help them keep afloat. There is nothing wrong with this if the competition is well run and if there is a genuine concern with publishing new work; but some competitions are more like cash cows than genuine publishing opportunities.

If you are going to enter a competition as a route to publishing, do your research. Look at how long the competition has been in existence. Research previous winners. Buy their books to see what the quality is like. And, if you want to take this approach, perhaps set yourself a budget for entry, so that you don't find yourself squandering huge sums on entry fees.

Dealing with rejection

Publishing a book is *always* a calculated risk for a publisher. When a publisher decides to publish a book, they are taking a financial gamble on your work, so they have to be sure that the book is one they actively *want* to publish. This is why, more often than not, a book will be rejected several times before it finds a home. There are various reasons why your work might be rejected. What you want to make sure of is that your work is not rejected unnecessarily.

Focus point

You can minimize unnecessary rejections by making sure that:

- you send your book to the right publisher
- your submission is professional
- you have thoroughly read (and followed) the publisher's submissions guidelines.

Publishers might turn down your book for other reasons, too. They may simply have a very full list of forthcoming titles and not be able to take on any more. They may think that the market for your book is too small. The editors may be overruled by the people in sales and marketing.

What rejection looks like

Most rejection letters will be 'form rejections'. What this means is that the publisher will have a standard rejection letter that they will send out, and they will simply add your name to the top. Sometimes you may not even get this: you may just get your manuscript returned with a blank compliments slip.

You can't glean much useful information from a form rejection. Just file the letter and move on. But if the publisher takes the time – and they are by no means obliged to do so – to say *why* they rejected your manuscript, then you should take their advice to heart. Responding individually takes time, and it usually means either: 1) that you have done something so very stupid in your submission that the publisher is irritated into replying individually; or 2) that the publisher takes your work seriously enough to spend a few minutes putting their thoughts in order and giving you a fuller reply.

 Snapshot: what can you learn from rejection?

When you receive your first rejection letters, it can be dispiriting. But if the publisher takes time to comment on your manuscript, then you can learn useful things from their comments. If you have received a personalized rejection, the following approach might help:

- Read through the letter carefully at least twice.
- Now put the letter down and go and do something else. Don't return to it for another 24 hours.
- When you return to the letter, look at it again. Does it offer any useful advice about the following:
  - How the novel might be improved?
  - How you might pitch it more successfully to another publisher?
  - What kind of publisher might be more suited to your book?

Ask yourself whether this advice might lead to strengthening your work. Sometimes you may think a publisher's advice is wide of the mark. But that is perhaps because they are not the right publisher for you. Sometimes the advice may point to a way that you can improve either your novel or your strategy with sending out submissions. So now try this:

- After returning to the letter, try to come up with some *concrete* tasks that might help you improve your next submission.

One thing to remember, if a publisher takes the trouble to write a personalized rejection of your work, is that this is something above and beyond the call of duty. If the feedback is *useful*, even if it is a rejection, then feel free to send a *very* brief note to the publisher thanking them. But remember that a rejection is just that. It is *not* an invitation to dialogue. It is not a chance for you to reply and try to 'talk round' the publisher. Accept a 'no' as a 'no', thank the publisher if you like, and move on.

When the fish start to nibble

Sometimes publishers will not reject your work outright, but instead will get back to you saying that they would like you to rework your book and, were you willing to do this, they would like to see it again. If you get this response, then the first thing to do is ask yourself whether the proposed changes are things that you agree with or not. If you don't agree with them, if you think that the publisher is pushing the book in the wrong direction, then send a polite response saying that you will try your luck elsewhere. It takes courage to do this, but it is not worth being published *at any cost*. When your book is out, you will need to be able to stand behind it.

However, editors read a lot, and so they are often very good at understanding how to turn interesting, but perhaps rather unformed, projects into books that actually work. So if a publisher replies to you to say that they will look at a reworked version, you should take their suggestions seriously. If you do want to make some changes, then get back to them and suggest (if they have not already suggested) a deadline for getting a revised manuscript to them. Then get to work on those revisions!

The big 'yes'

One day, a publisher contacts you and says that they are delighted to say that they are going to publish your book. And you *know* that the delight is real, because they are so excited to find you that they are even willing to take a financial risk on you. Once a publisher has accepted your work (at least informally), you should stop pursuing all other avenues of inquiry, and commit yourself to this one publisher while questions of publishing timescales and contracts and things are all sorted out. Remember that a lot can still go wrong. Publishing houses can fold, the editor who was championing your work can suddenly leave, and so on. So it pays to be circumspect – and perhaps not too celebratory – until you have a signed contract, a legal document that commits both you and the publisher to the publication of your book.

> ## Key idea
>
> Only once you have a signed contract can you be fairly confident that your book will eventually see the light of day.

Do not, however, be *too* hasty to sign a contract. You need to make sure that the contract is reasonable and that you are not committing to anything you do not understand or will later regret. Reading contracts is something of an art: they are forbidding documents, written in dense legalese. Decoding contracts is one reason many writers make use of agents. Whether you have an agent or not, you should *always* read through the contract yourself, as they are ultimately *your* rights that you are assigning. If you are a member, the Society of Authors (www.societyofauthors.org) has a free contract-reading service.

Some publishers may say to you that they are issuing a 'standard contract' and that this is non-negotiable. This is nonsense, and you should feel free to gently point this out to your publisher. A contract *should* be negotiable on both sides, and by both parties: it is not a way of holding one party to ransom. If there are clauses that are problematic, then they should be up for discussion.

 ## Focus point

All contracts are, in principle, negotiable.

Hitting a brick wall

What if you have sent your novel to 40 publishers, you have rewritten it several times, and you have a huge file of rejection letters, none of them saying anything particularly useful? What if you have rewritten and rewritten until you cannot bear to rewrite any more, and you have run out of options for where you might find a good home for your book? What if you wake up one morning, look at your manuscript, and realize that you are sick of the sight of it?

If all this happens, then you have hit a brick wall. It may be that your novel is simply not *good* enough. It may be that it is good, but there is no market for the kind of novel that you are writing. It may be that the novel is somehow *untimely*, that you are trying to publish it at the wrong time. Or it may be that it is timely and good and there is a market, but publishers cannot see any of this. Publishers are not always right. Their notions of the 'market' may be mistaken. It may be that you can find a niche for your book that third-party publishers are unable to access. If this is the case, then go ahead and self-publish. After a bruising series of rejections, it will be bracing to be striking out on your own.

However, if you reach this point, you also need to be brutally honest with yourself, and you need to ask yourself: *Is this novel good enough?* If you are *at all* uneasy with your book, your options are either to go back to editing your book, or else moving on to a new project.

 ## Focus point

Every book worth writing is an experiment; and not all experiments work out.

You can learn a lot from failed experiments. Tucked away in a cardboard box somewhere, I have a nice stack of manuscripts for projects that, whatever their virtues, didn't quite come off. It is painful to put a project to one side; but you should have the discretion as a writer to recognize that sometimes it might be necessary to do so. All of that thinking and planning, all of that *practice*, will not be lost. If you have taken the writing of your novel seriously, you will be a better writer than before, and you will be starting the next novel from a better position. In fact, it could be argued that if, in your novelist's laboratory, you don't have *any* failed experiments, you are simply not taking enough risks.

Anita Shreve

'Don't give up. There are so many obstacles to becoming a writer so it's easy to do. But rejections are tickets to the game.'

Workshop: planning and organizing a publication strategy

Going from your final draft to getting a publication contract can take a long time. The following workshop is a way of getting organized so that you can plan a strategy for getting your novel published. If you have an agent, you may not need to worry about this workshop. But if you are going it alone, it pays to be as organized as you possibly can.

Assume that it will take *at least* a year between finishing your manuscript and getting a publishing deal. It might take longer – you may need to rewrite your novel in response to feedback more than once – but it is unlikely to take less time.

1 Making a list of potential publishers

Either go through the *Writers' & Artists' Yearbook* or do a comprehensive search on the Internet for publishers that publish the kinds of books you are interested in. You are looking for publishers where your novel might *feel at home.* In the first instance, you are aiming to get a substantial list of possible publishers for your book: say around 20–25 publishers.

2 Ranking your list

When you have made a list, look each of them up online. Do some research into this list of publishers. For each of them, visit their website, and find out the following information:

- Is this a small, independent publisher, or part of a large multinational?
- What other novels are on their list?
- Are they currently open to unsolicited submissions? If so, what is their submissions policy? If not, do they indicate when they will be open to submissions?

If any publisher on the list says that they will not accept submissions *or* queries unless they come via an agent, then it is probably worth crossing them off your list. Unless you have an inside connection, this is just going to waste time.

When you have a modified list, you can rank them. Try giving them scores from 1 to 5, with 5 being the highest, taking into account criteria such as the following:

Questions	Publisher 1	Publlisher 2	Publlisher 3	Publlisher 4
How likely is a book deal from this publisher?				
How much do I like its books?				
Are they the kind of publisher with whom I could work?				
How good a deal might they offer?				
How widely will my book be reviewed and promoted?				
Final score (out of 25)				

To answer some of these questions, you may need to do a bit more research. By the time you have done all this, you might end up with four or five publishers scoring 20 or over, four or five publishers scoring 15–20, and so on. Divide the total by five and round up to give each publisher an overall rating from one to five stars.

3 Planning your strategy

Now take a calendar of the coming year – use a diary, or draw out a plan – and decide when you are going to send your book out and to whom. You might want to try a couple of 'five star' publishers first, as well as a 'one star' and a 'three star'. Try to pencil in *all* the publishers some time in the next year, so that you have a strategy for getting your work out there. Remember that this strategy may well change as you get feedback from publishers and so on; but it is good to start with some sort of plan.

4 Putting your plan into action

When you have a rough plan, look up the submissions guidelines for the first small batch of submissions you are going to send out, and make sure that you prepare individual submissions for each of the publishers, according to their guidelines.

Bundle them up (don't put the wrong letters in the wrong envelopes – I've done this once, and it is very embarrassing) and put them in the post.

Keep a note of:

- exactly what you have sent out
- who you have sent it to: both the publisher and, if possible, the name of the individual editor
- the timescale within which you are expecting a response (if the publisher doesn't give a timescale, three months is not unreasonable).

Put dates in your diary to follow up submissions with queries. Now you just have to wait until you get replies. If you get *rejections*, think them through and adjust your plan accordingly. If you need to rewrite, pause sending out your work while you rewrite. Then, with the revised manuscript, pick up again, working through your list. If you get *no response* at all, then send query letters or emails after an appropriate period has elapsed, and try sending your work to another couple of publishers.

Having a clear plan can be useful, because even if you get rejections, there is *always a next step to take.* You just work through your list methodically and carefully, taking on board advice and feedback that comes in. And meanwhile – in the periods while you are waiting for a response from all these publishers – you might as well get started on your second novel.

Where to next?

This brings us to the end of the section on publishing. If you have got this far, and if your book is good enough, there is a decent chance that your life as a published writer will have begun. The final section of this book is about how to promote your book, and how to survive and thrive as a writer.

PART SIX

Now you are published

23

Introduction: surviving and thriving as a writer

You might think that writers are ethereal beings who are concerned above all with their art, that they are superior kinds of individuals who scorn the material things that preoccupy most ordinary humans. If you think this, I can only assume that you have probably not yet spent a great deal of time around other writers – because, if there's one thing that concerns writers almost as much as the writing itself, it is the question of money.

Tracy Chevalier

'Oh, for God's sake, if I were driven by money, I would never have become a writer!'

The reason that writers are interested in money is not because they are unusually grasping or materialistic. It is because writing can be, for many writers at least, a financially precarious activity. In other words, writers are interested in money because, for many writers, it is a fairly limited resource; and, while you might get rich from writing novels, if you are interested in making massive amounts of cash, then there are many more reliable ways of going about this. In fact, if you are interested in making a living from writing, then writing novels may be less reliable as a means to a decent income than, for example, writing feature articles or scriptwriting for TV.

But here, as elsewhere, it is impossible to generalize: different writers have different financial arrangements. So this chapter aims to give a realistic view of what you might stand to make financially out of your writing, and aims to chart some of the financial waters you may need to navigate as a writer.

Royalties and advances

If you are published by a third-party publisher, once they have decided that they want to publish your book, they will offer you a contract. This contract will set out precisely what rights you are offering the publisher, as well as what your mutual obligations are and what you will get in return. One thing that should be stated in your contract is the royalty payment that you will be receiving.

Joyce Carol Oates

'I haven't the faintest idea what my royalties are. I haven't the faintest idea how many copies of books I've sold, or how many books I've written. I could look these things up; I have no interest in them. I don't know how much money I have.'

The quote above from Joyce Carol Oates comes from an interview with the *New Yorker* in 2013; but this indifference is, to some extent, a luxury. Most writers will need to be much more on the ball and will need to keep track.

Key idea

A *royalty* payment is a payment made to you by the publisher for every book that is sold. This will usually be on the basis of either the *cover price* or *net receipts*.

If your book is £10, and if your publisher offers you a 10-per-cent royalty on the cover price, then you will receive £1 per copy sold. Where does the other nine pounds go? You might think it goes to your publisher, so that he or she can buy a gold-plated bowl for the family dog. But you would be wrong. A big chunk goes to the bookseller. Of what remains, some goes to cover warehousing and distribution. Then the publisher has to pay for cover design, for marketing and publicity, for printing costs, for staff salaries, for overheads and so on. Publishers are much like writers: a few may be raking it in; most are not particularly well off.

So, let's say that you earn £1 per book. If you get an advance on royalties for £3,000, this means that the publisher will pay you £3,000 up front, on a non-returnable basis. Often this is paid in chunks: a third on signature of the contract, a third on delivery of the final manuscript, and a third on publication is not uncommon (in this case, £1,000 a time). If your book sells well, then you start getting royalty cheques once you have made back your advance. So once you have sold more than 3,000 books, you will start making £1 per book sold, which will usually be paid every year or (sometimes) every six months.

Not all books make back (or 'earn out') their advances. According to *the New York Times*, back in 2009, seven out of ten books were not earning back their advances; and despite the big headlines that you see from time to time, advances are typically rather modest. A 'five-figure sum' might sound impressive for a three-book deal; but if this translates into £21,000, or £7,000 per book, then, while it is going to be a welcome boost to the bank balance, it is probably not a short cut to a life of luxury.

Key idea

An advance on royalties is an up-front payment of your anticipated future royalties, paid as a lump sum.

Royalties based on *cover price* are straightforward. But royalties based upon *net receipts* are a little more complex. Net receipts (sometimes called 'price received') are what your publisher collects after discounts made to the retailer or to the wholesaler. Say that your publisher sells to the retailer at a discount of 45 per cent. For each copy of your £10 book, the publisher will receive 55 per cent of the cover price, or £5.50. That means that your 10 per cent on net receipts is £0.55.

Focus point

Make sure you know whether your contract specifies royalties as a percentage of *cover price* (sometimes called *list price*) or as a percentage of *net receipts*.

Things can get rapidly even more complex, however. Sometimes publishers will offset other costs against net receipts, so you need to make clear in the contract what net receipts means, and that there are no other costs factored in. You should also avoid any contract that offers you a percentage of *profits*: imaginative accounting could mean that on paper your best-selling book, once all kinds of costs are offset, makes no profit at all, so you receive nothing.

Sometimes there will be a sliding scale of royalties, with higher rates once you have sold, for example, 2,000 copies, and then again 5,000 copies. These are fine, but don't be seduced by the higher rates if the baseline rate is still not good enough.

There is a lot more to be said about royalties. Some of the professional bodies listed in the Resources will be able to help you navigate these complexities; but remember also that, in different parts of the world, approaches to publishing contracts may differ.

A question of rights

Your contract will be divided up according to different rights. You are effectively *licensing* your publisher to publish in particular formats, in particular languages and in particular territories. If you have an agent, you may want to retain as many rights as possible, so that your agent can actively try to sell these. If you do not have an agent and your publisher pushes to handle additional rights – for example, rights to foreign-language editions or to film adaptation – you should make sure that they are actively going to exploit these.

These additional rights matter. Although you may not make it rich out of royalties, you may be able to supplement your income through sale of these other rights. Here are a few areas to think about.

 Focus point

> If you are self-publishing, you will own all the rights to your work, in which case you shouldn't overlook the possibilities of selling subsidiary rights. There are some high-profile cases of self-published authors going on to sell rights to adaptations, translations and so on.

OVERSEAS AND TRANSLATION RIGHTS

Some novels are made to stay at home. Some travel well. You may find that after publication your novel goes down well overseas and goes into overseas editions or into translation. This will lead to some extra income for you, and for no (or very little) extra work. If you sell rights to several countries, this can be a welcome extra boost in terms of income.

Different books do differently in different places. My second novel is set in Bulgaria, and the Bulgarian edition is doing very well. I know of a novelist who writes in English, but who is for some inexplicable reason unloved in her homeland. Her books go straight into translation in French, where they do superbly.

In your contract, your publisher may agree to handle translation rights. If they have a good overseas rights department, this may be sensible. However, there's no point in your publisher sitting on rights that they are not actively going to pursue trying to make use of. If your publisher does not handle these rights, then your agent may have connections, if you have an agent. Handling overseas rights yourself is possible, although it is tricky and complex.

FILM AND TV ADAPTATION RIGHTS

What about the film tie-in? Surely you can retire on *that*? Well, not necessarily. What will usually happen, if there is genuine interest in producing your novel for TV or film, is that a production company will take out an *option*.

Key idea

An 'option' is a payment made by a producer, allowing them to exclusively explore the possibility of securing the rights to an adaptation within a particular period of time.

This is more straightforward than it sounds. If I am a producer, and I like your novel, I may not want anybody else to get to it first. So I pay you an option of £3,000, with a period of 18 months. In this time, I have the *sole* right to explore the possibilities (and financing) for an adaptation. Before the end of the option period, if I decide to proceed, then I can 'exercise' this option by actually buying the rights. If the time period expires and I am still interested, I may decide to renew the option. The option payments may be offset against any earnings you make if the adaptation *is* eventually made.

An option, then, is something short of a full-blown sale of rights. But it is a start. If you do manage to sell the film rights to your book, make sure you are very clear about the contractual agreements involved. I have a writer friend whose book was made into a blockbuster movie with a cast of top Hollywood stars, and who claims that, through the studio's creative accounting, the actual profits he made directly from the film were vanishingly small (although he concedes that he did well on the increased book sales that resulted).

OTHER RIGHTS

There can be all kinds of other subsidiary rights tied in to your novel: for radio and audio adaptations, for ebooks, for Braille editions, for action figures, and so on. An agent can be very useful in advising on these aspects of a contract.

Library lending and other licensing

While we're at it, how *else* can you make money from your work? One way is through library loans and other similar use of your material. There are two schemes, if you are in the UK, that you should sign up to. The first is the PLR, or Public Lending Right, which is currently administered by the British Library (plr.uk.com). This recompenses authors with a small fee when their work is borrowed from libraries. While the sums are often small, they can be a welcome addition to a writer's income. Some books do very well in libraries, even if they do less well in bookshops. In the UK, there is also the Authors' Licensing and Collecting Society, or ALCS (alcs.co.uk), which deals with income from various secondary uses of an author's work, whether through digital reproduction, photocopying, educational recording or repeat use via the Internet.

So... how much will I make?

 Neil Gaiman

'Stories may well be lies, but they are good lies that say true things, and which can sometimes pay the rent.'

Working out how much you might make from book sales, royalties and sale of rights is a complex business. There is simply no straightforward answer to the question of how much you will make. In addition, the book market is changing very fast, particularly thanks to the self-publishing revolution.

In books as elsewhere, it is usually the case that a few writers make a lot of money, some writers make some money, and most writers don't make that much. If you are interested in exploring this question more intensively, there are several places you can look. One is the ALCS, which publishes research every few years into author earnings (www.alcs.co.uk). The other place worth exploring is the Author Earnings site set up by self-published writer Hugh Howey (www.authorearnings.com), which explores the rapidly changing scenes of both self-publishing and third-party publishing.

That stories can *sometimes* pay the rent is remarkable in itself. But they cannot always pay the rent, and you should not be relying upon it. You *may* become rich by writing, but if you care about money – as Tracy Chevalier points out – there may be more reliable ways to make a better living than writing.

This is not meant to put you off: you may find that if you write something popular enough, if you catch the imagination of the public, then you become one of the writers at the higher end of the graph. You may also manage to generate a reasonable income or a supplementary income from writing novels, if you write well, understand the market, have a knack for hitting on what is popular, and are sufficiently canny in your decisions about where and how to publish.

But it is also worth bearing in mind that money is a more transitory and unstable thing than any book. When I look at my bookshelves, I never wonder what the authors earned. I care about what they *said*. Some years I make more from writing than others; but the more I write, the more I find that writing opens up opportunities for new connections, new conversations and new pathways through the world. In other words, I'm sure there would be better ways of making a living; but, for me at least, I cannot think of any better way of making a life.

Making a living as a writer vs. making a living from royalties

It is true that few writers consistently and over a period of years succeed in making their entire living out of royalties from the sale of self-published books. But there is a very useful distinction to be made between making a living out of royalties, and making a living *as a writer*. As a published writer, you can do all kinds of writing-related things that can help you to make a living. These things are the direct result of the fact that you are a writer, even if they are not direct payments from your publisher for your novels.

Here it might be useful to summarize some ways that writers make a living while also sustaining their writing.

FREELANCING

As a writer, you have many possibilities for freelance work open to you: you might like to look at Claire Gillman's *Make Money from Freelance Writing* in this series. But to get you thinking, some of the things you could do include:

- giving lectures, talks and festival events
- writing journalism
- running or participating in residencies
- engaging in freelance teaching, mentoring, etc.
- undertaking commissions and consultancies.

Lectures, talks and festivals

You may be invited to talk at festivals, public events and other venues. This can be a useful financial sideline. Some writers I know do a lot of this kind of work, and it contributes a decent chunk to their income. If you are the kind of person who likes talking in public, then, once your book is out, it may be worth exploring opportunities by contacting festival organizers, local venues, etc. and letting them know what you have to offer. Over the past decade or more, literary festivals have flourished, from the very large to the very small. You can find a list for the UK at www.literaryfestivals. co.uk. Some festivals may be hard to break into without the clout of an established mainstream publisher behind you; smaller festivals might be easier.

Doing events is *work* as a writer, and writers should as far as possible be reimbursed for the work that they do. On the other hand, there may be events that you think are worth doing on a voluntary basis, as a way of promoting your work, helping out friends and so forth. For myself, sometimes I will do some events for free. I do free events for various reasons:

- They are low-budget events run by friends.
- I think they might be fun or interesting.
- The event is in support of a cause or organization I believe in.

If you do free events, at the very least you should be asking whether your expenses can be covered. This will usually mean mileage for travel by car, overnight accommodation if you need to stay overnight, or rail travel. It will usually not mean personal helicopter ride to the venue in question, caviar and champagne.

 Focus point

If you are doing a free event, it is reasonable to ask for travel expenses. If you are doing a paid event, expenses should be on top of your fee.

The best advice here is this: make sure you know what you are agreeing to, and make sure that you are happy with this agreement. If you do charge fees and want advice on what is appropriate, the Society of Authors in the UK has guidelines on rates (see the link here: www.societyofauthors.org/rates-and-guidelines).

Journalism

Many writers I know write journalism pieces for publications both online and offline. This can be a good way of getting more exposure as a writer (although don't assume that everybody who loved your article will go out and buy your book), can help hone your skills, and can be extremely satisfying. It can also, depending on where you pitch your work, pay remarkably well. If you have some track record writing fiction, then you can make the leap to freelancing relatively easily: all it takes is an exploratory email or two, pitching your ideas. If you have a professional online presence, this will help as well.

Residencies

There are all kinds of writing residencies out there. Some residencies are designed to allow you time and space to write, and have competitive application procedures. Some involve more active engagement with the public, for example, residency work in schools and hospitals, in museums and factories and businesses. Sometimes, you may find that unexpected places are interested in having writers working for them, so don't be afraid of approaching people who you think might be interested.

Teaching, mentoring, etc.

Creative writing is a growing interest in the English-speaking world. In every town you can find a creative writing class or two. Some may be for writers who want a serious career in writing, some may be for people who just want to put their thoughts on paper. While some writers are somewhat snooty about this growth of creative writing,

I personally cannot but see it as a good thing. There are many reasons why people might want to explore creative writing, and if you have skills in this area and can help them, then this is a good and noble thing to do.

Commissions and consultancies

Arts development and writing development organizations often commission writers to produce pieces of work, sometimes to tie in with literature festivals, sometimes to tie in with community projects. The things you might end up doing in this line of work could be anything from oral history, to writing for radio and performance, to advising on the development of educational materials for schools.

Snapshot: broadening the net

There are very many opportunities out there for writers, and often they are not very widely advertised. This exercise is about broadening your net to see whether you can find out more about the various professional opportunities that may be open to you. In particular, investigate the following:

- Are there any local book festivals in which you might be able to take part?
- Are there any local information networks for writers that might be useful to be a part of, so that you can develop your networks?
- What organizations locally help with writer development? Can you contact them to tell them about your work?
- Are there any national or international events or organizations that might be interested in your work?

Use the appendices of this book to help you. Once you have a list, if there are any opportunities that you think you could follow up, don't be afraid to write introduction letters and emails, make phone calls and set up meetings.

WRITING AND WORKING

Many writers also work in steady jobs, either in the writing world or in a job that is entirely unconnected to writing. Both have their advantages and disadvantages.

Getting a job

One easy way of solving the problem of income is to find yourself a job that doesn't interfere with your writing, and that allows you time to write. I know of a novelist who is a research chemist by day and a thriller writer (under a pseudonym) by night. I see him as a kind of Dr Jekyll and Mr Hyde character, who every evening glugs down a potion and transforms himself into a writer. I have been told that none of his fellow chemists knows about his strange, nocturnal pursuits. So it is perfectly possible to be a writer on the one hand and to hold down a job on the other. Not only this, but sometimes having a job can help: writing is a solitary pursuit, and some writers would go crazy without the interaction that they have with other people at work.

Work in the writing world

Another way of going about supporting yourself is by finding work in the writing world. There are writers who are editors, writers who run their own publishing houses, writers who teach creative writing in universities, and so on. The literary world is huge, and it seems to need human beings to be able to function. Working in the writing world can not only be a very good way to make contacts (the writing business relies heavily upon contacts), but also working with other writers can be a great way of broadening your outlook.

Snapshot: thinking ahead

Now that your book is published, what do you want to do next? Where do you want to take your career as a writer? Writers develop their careers in different ways. Note down what your main goals are for the coming year. List no more than three.

You may want to focus on promotion and sales; you may want to get going on the second novel and need to support yourself to do that; or you may want to see what other opportunities your recently published book can open up for you.

Now, for each of these three goals, write down some concrete actions that you want to take.

GRANTS

There are some grants available for writers. Many of these are offered on a competitive basis. It may be easier to attract funding for projects that involve the public, or for time to write books that are published by third-party publishers. If you are self-publishing, you may have to work hard to make a strong case. There are some links to potential funding bodies in the Resources section. Writing grant applications is an art in its own right, and it can take time away from writing. But it can be worth doing: research for my second novel was funded thanks to a research and 'time to write' grant from Arts Council England.

Snapshot: exploring grants and funds

Have a look in the Resources section to see whether you can find out the relevant funding bodies for your area (so, if you are in Edinburgh, try the Scottish Arts Council). Visit their websites and see whether you can find what the criteria are for funding.

Have a look further afield. Do a web search for any opportunities that you can find. Make a list of those that you think might be worth applying for.

Managing your money

If you are going to make any income from your writing, you will need to manage your money effectively. There is a lot that could be written about this, and much of it lies beyond the scope of this book. But here are a few thoughts.

KEEP TRACK OF YOUR FINANCES

It is good to know where your money is coming from, and where it is going to. If you are freelancing, you will be issuing invoices for payment, chasing up when the invoices remain unpaid (as, sometimes, they inevitably will), keeping track of the funds going in and out of your bank account and so on.

> ## Focus point
>
>
>
> For tax purposes, you should keep clear records of all of your income and expenditure.

IT'S NOT JUST ABOUT INCOME – IT'S ABOUT CASH FLOW

If you are freelancing, you will soon discover that some people are easy to work with, pay invoices on time, and are generally well behaved. Other people are much trickier: you issue an invoice and the money doesn't turn up for *months*. This can make life very difficult indeed. So it makes sense to plan for some padding so that, when somebody doesn't pay on time, you are not precipitated into a financial crisis.

GET TO KNOW THE TAX SYSTEM

If you are making money from writing, this will be taxable. Tax is good: it pays for useful things like ambulances and infrastructure and care for the elderly (it pays for a few useless things as well, but this doesn't invalidate the principle). Given that your income is taxable, you will want to make sure that you know what you owe.

If you are in the UK and you are set to make any freelance income from writing, you will need to register with the Inland Revenue as self-employed. This will mean that every year you have to fill in a tax return (you can do it online) detailing your income and expenditure, so that you know how much tax you need to pay. You will be taxed on your *profits*. Roughly, this is the difference between your income and your expenditure. So, if in one year you earn £10,000 from writing (lucky you), you may not need to pay tax on all £10,000. Expenses might include:

- heating, electricity and utility bills for your working space
- research expenses
- equipment that you have needed to purchase for your work
- web hosting for your author's website
- telephone bills
- mailing costs of all those heavy manuscripts.

After taking all this into account, you might end up with a profit of, say, £7,500, and a correspondingly smaller tax bill. If this is all too taxing, and the sums in question merit the expense, you can hire an accountant. Otherwise you can do it yourself. If you want a more in-depth view, try reading *Teach Yourself: Run Your Own Business*.

Where to next?

If you are going to make any money at all from your work, you are going to have to let people know about it. Even if you are with a major publishing house with its own publicity department, you may find that you need to do a lot of publicity yourself. This is the subject of the penultimate chapter.

24

Promoting your work

Now that your book is out, you need to let people know about it. There was a time in the distant past when the writer's job was simply to write, and the publisher would deal with everything after that. You could be as reclusive as you liked, safe in the knowledge that your publishers had a phalanx of publicity agents working on your behalf, pushing the book out to reviewers, setting up launch events, letting people know. These days, even large mainstream publishers rely on authors to do a lot of promotion. If you are with a smaller publisher, they simply may not have the budget or the time to push your work as enthusiastically as you would like. After all, a small publisher may be publishing 12 books within a single year, each of which needs attention. And, of course, if you are self-publishing, nobody is going to take charge of your publicity unless you do it yourself.

All authors should give some thought to publicity, to how – once they have actually written and published the book – they are going to go about letting people know about it. When thinking about publicity, it can be useful to think about the *kind* of book it is that you are promoting. Some books are topical or written to tie in with contemporary issues. These books can sell very well for a short while, but when the contemporary landscape changes, their sales can drop rapidly. Other books are more slow-burning. The particular shape of your publicity campaign (did I mention that it was a campaign?) will depend on:

- the topic of the book
- the intended audience
- what you are willing to do to promote the book
- the amount of time you have available
- your own skills and tendencies.

There are many ways in which you can promote your work as a writer, and you need to find an approach that suits you. Some writers love the limelight and delight in the attention of others. Others are more private and can think of nothing worse than standing up on a stage reading their work. So remember that the ideas below are only that: ideas. They are not requirements. As a writer, you need to find your own ways of connecting with your audiences.

Pre-publication buzz

Ideally, you will start letting people know about the book before it is published, to build a bit of 'buzz'. You might blog about the process leading up to publication, write some guest articles on other people's blogs or in magazines, newspapers and journals, or else use social media platforms to generate some initial interest. However: anticipation can only last for so long. If you spend weeks trying to drum up enthusiasm for your forthcoming book, you may find that, by the time the book comes out, the enthusiasm has already waned.

 Focus point

If you are trying to generate pre-publication 'buzz' around your book, don't stretch this out for too long, or your audience will lose interest.

If you are published by a third-party publisher, then your publisher may send out pre-publication review copies (often uncorrected proof copies) to get some early reviews. If you are publishing yourself, you may want to think about trying to get some proof copies sent out – although finding reviewers may be harder.

The trouble with pre-publication buzz is that it doesn't give your audience (or your potential audience, at least) anything to do other than wait and, if you have a date for a launch event, make space in their diaries.

Launches

Key idea

There are several reasons for a book launch: celebration, promotion, sales and networking.

Now that your book is coming out, this deserves a celebration. There was a time when publishers would pay for lavish book launches. Some publishers still do. If your publisher wants to throw some money at launching your book, then you are in luck. If your publisher is less keen, then you could do it yourself. But perhaps the first question is this: *Why should you have a launch?* Here are the most likely answers:

- **Celebration:** a book launch can be fun and satisfying, and can act as a rite of passage to mark your transition from unpublished to published novelist. Invite friends, family and those who have helped you along the way. Throw a good party!

- **Promotion:** invite journalists, other writers and people who work in the writing business. Be realistic. You may want *The Times*, *The New York Times*, the BBC, Al-Jazeera and CNN to be there, as well as several Nobel Prize in Literature winners; but, unless you are very well connected, you'll be lucky if any of them turn up. It might be that you can do better with local press and media, as well as writers from the local community.

- **Sales:** if people like what they hear, they may well buy a copy of your book. Don't expect to sell a copy to everyone who turns up, but make sure that you have copies on hand to sign and sell. Remember: your audience is there to be entertained and they don't want to feel brow-beaten or guilt-tripped into buying your book. They want instead to be enthused, excited and intrigued… and, if they are, their purses and wallets will spring open. If you are organizing and paying for your own book launch, you may be able to offset the costs of the launch against the sales you make, so that you break even or make a small profit.

- **Networking:** a good launch can be a way of widening your connections in the writing world. Bring some business cards along. If you don't have any, get some printed. Go for quality and simplicity (anything too flashy looks desperate; anything too basic looks unprofessional), and if you get into any interesting conversations, offer people your card.

WHERE SHOULD I LAUNCH MY BOOK?

There are various ways you can launch your book. You might want to launch your book in a bar or on a barge, in a bookshop, in a library, in an arts centre, in a zoo or in a museum. Or you may go for a virtual launch and launch your book online. I launched my second novel, *The Descent of the Lyre*, twice: first in an arts venue in my home town, where it was launched alongside several other books written by friends; and then, at the Bulgarian Cultural Institute in London, a fitting place to launch a book about banditry and music in early nineteenth-century Bulgaria. When the book was translated into Bulgarian, I launched the Bulgarian edition in two different

Bulgarian bookshops, as well as getting involved in a number of events and workshops throughout the country. Alongside these physical activities, I blogged about the launch of my books, took part in online interviews, and made a splash virtually for those who could not attend the physical launch.

Wherever you decide to hold your event, don't be overambitious: if you book a thousand-seater theatre to find that only ten people turn up, that will be embarrassing. Find a venue that is appropriate to the book.

 ## David Armstrong, *How Not to Write a Novel*

'*When it comes to book launches, small can be beautiful, a market town a much better bet than a West End venue.*'

WHAT HAPPENS AT A BOOK LAUNCH?

Think about what you want to do at the launch. Whether you have a physical or virtual launch, you will need to think about the kinds of event that might work well for your potential readers.

 ## Snapshot: book launches

If you are thinking of running your own book launch, go to a number of launches in your local area (or get involved in a number of online book launches). Which ones seem to work well and which ones work less well? Note down three factors that you think contribute to a successful launch.

Whether virtual or physical, one thing that often makes a good book launch is variety. Few writers can sustain the audience's interest by just reading for an hour, without anything else happening. If you are one of these few (I once saw Alan Moore reading in precisely this fashion, and he was fascinating and compelling), then good for you! But if you are worried about maintaining your audience's attention, then think about the shape of your event as a whole.

VIRTUAL LAUNCHES

Virtual launches are hard to get right; but, if they succeed, they can be excellent. If you don't yet have a good online presence, and don't have broad connections with an online community, then it is going to be harder to run a web-based launch: these things work best when you can draw upon connections that you already have.

Like all book launches, virtual launches need a degree of imagination. It's a lonely feeling sitting with your glass of champagne in front of your computer screen, looking at your website visitor statistics as they rise from three to four and then fall back to two. You need to persuade your audience why they should get involved, and make them feel welcome rather than just marketed to. You need to give them something to get engaged with. Virtual launches might include:

- live chat

- streaming video of readings

- interviews, inviting questions from potential readers

- social media (find a hashtag and ask people to tweet about one of the themes of your novel)

- competitions and prizes (a book give-away, for example).

You might want to spread your virtual launch over a number of days with a number of related activities. This kind of 'asynchronous' launch can work better online, when you don't expect everybody to be sitting at their machines at the same time. Another thing you can do is produce a trailer video for sharing online, although make sure that you are careful to factor the costs into your overall publicity plan.

PHYSICAL LAUNCHES

If you launch your book at a physical event, have a look round for appropriate venues. Some venues will want you to pay, others will offer you space for free (particularly if they have a bar open and you can guarantee that your literary guests will make good use of it). Aim to at least break even. You are probably not going to make a fortune out of a book launch, so don't break the bank.

When thinking about venues, you may also have to think about questions of hospitality. Do you want to provide free drinks for your guests? Free food? Something to take away with them at the end? All of these things should be factored into the costs.

Nobody should be expected to pay to come to a book launch. You may have a paying bar, you may not provide food and drinks, but you shouldn't expect people who have come to celebrate the birth of your book to pay for the privilege: that would be like going to dinner with friends and being billed afterwards. Nor should you charge for entry and offset this charge against the cover price of the book. Your audience will feel as if they are being coerced into buying the book and will be justifiably annoyed.

A physical launch might involve:

- readings

- interviews

- audience questions and answers

- music

- other entertainment.

Remember that, when giving readings, while people are there to hear your work, they are not there to hear *all* your work. Keep readings relatively short. I have rarely come out of a book launch hearing people complaining that the writer *did not read enough*; but all too often I have come out of book launches hearing people complaining that the writer *wouldn't shut up*.

Focus point

Usually, no more than two (or three at most) ten-minute readings will be sufficient to give the reader a sense of your book and encourage them to queue up to buy it.

Interviews can be a good way of breaking up your event. Get an expert in to interview you about your book. Bribe them with a bottle of wine if necessary. The dynamic between the interviewer and the author can make for an interesting and thought-provoking spectacle for the audience. It is worth talking through the questions and answers before the event, so that you know where you stand.

If you do an interview, you can also open up the floor to questions and answers. This can inject some variety into proceedings, and can help turn a monologue (the author reading) into a series of dialogues.

Think also about other entertainment. Music can make the event more varied. If you have friends who are skilled musicians, this can really set the mood of an evening. As with readings, make sure that the music doesn't go on for too long: you want to give your guests a flavour, not stretch their patience. There may be other things you could integrate into the launch as well. If your novel is about a magician in the nineteenth century, you could have a magic show.

Websites

Launches take place in the first few heady hours, days or weeks of a book's publication. But if you want a more sustained way of promoting yourself and your work over time, then you may want to think, if you haven't already, about setting up an author's website.

WHY HAVE A WEBSITE?

Not all writers have websites: I know writers who have a horror of the Internet, and who just want to be left alone. I know one writer who has a simple one-page website that explains that she doesn't have email, doesn't like writing on a computer, and lives a quiet and relatively lo-tech life, but if you want to contact her, you can do so through her agent. I admire this uncompromising stance. But I also know that my own website has been an important part of my life as a writer. So what use is a website to you? Here are a few things a website can provide:

- **A showcase for your work:** all kinds of people may visit your website, including readers and potential readers, potential publishers, employers, people you meet and your family members to check on what you are up to. Having a website over which you have editorial control allows you to present yourself and your work in precisely the way you want.

- **'Extras' for readers:** if you have readers who are interested in your work, a website can be a way of providing them with 'extras': information about your novels, interviews, video content, special promotions and so on. You can also provide 'teaser' sample chapters and other information that can engage readers and whet their appetites.

- **A blog:** you can use your website as a blog to record ongoing thoughts about your work-in-progress, about the publishing world or about the things you are involved in, building up a community of readers who are interested in your work.
- **A 'hub' for your online (and offline) presence:** I have a lot of feelers out online. I use social media, I write guest blogs, publish stories in online magazines, write interviews, publish articles and so on. This is a pretty disparate range of stuff, so I use my website as a central 'hub' for all this activity: it brings together my Twitter feed, links to new publications, information about what I'm up to and events I'm involved in.
- **A way of selling books:** you can link from your website to online sales outlets so that you can sell copies of your books.
- **A line of communication:** if you have a website, it gives you a point of contact for readers, publishers, other writers and members of the public. If you are a hands-on writer and like responding to reader queries or engaging with readers, then this can be an important part of the job your website does.

WRITING WEBSITES WELL

If your website is scrappy or patchy, if it is badly written or disorganized, then potential readers and publishers will assume – not unreasonably – that your books are scrappy and patchy, badly written and disorganized.

> ## Key idea
>
> If you are a writer, your website needs to reflect this: it must be well written and reflect your professionalism and skill as a writer.

In addition, your website needs to reflect the audience that you anticipate for your work. If you write hard science fiction but your website is in soft pastel tones, then you are giving out decidedly mixed messages. If you work in a number of different genres, think about how to work with these different audiences: a more neutral website can work well, with separate pages for work in different genres.

TECHNICAL DEMANDS

Your website will also need to look technically competent. You should avoid free services. These are simply not up to the task. Ideally, you would set up a website in something like the following fashion:

1 **Set up a domain name.** This is the name that visitors will type into the browser to find your website (for example, my domain name is www.willbuckingham.com). Go for something simple, straightforward and professional-sounding.
2 **Buy some web space.** This is space on a server (essentially a computer connected to the Internet) that will host your website. You can, of course, run your own server; but for most of us, this is overkill.

Together, these shouldn't cost much more than £40 a year or so. Once you are up and running with a domain linked to some web space, you will need to install some software to run your website. Many writers I know use WordPress (www.wordpress. org), which is relatively easy to set up, and – once set up – can allow you to run your website fairly easily. A slightly easier approach is to use the hosted service from WordPress (www.wordpress.com), with a custom domain.

If you are not very tech-savvy, you may want to get somebody to help you set up all of this in the first instance. However, you should own the domain name and all of your content. And you should have all the appropriate login details yourself. I have known too many writers whose web designers have suddenly disappeared to Mongolia, had a nervous breakdown, fallen in love, or all three at once, leaving the writer with a website that they cannot update. A little time working out how to run your own website can save you time, money and frustration later on.

Key idea

If you decide to run your own website, make sure that you own the domain and all the content, and that you have access to all the necessary passwords and login details.

Snapshot: writers' websites

Spend an hour online browsing writers' websites. Find three websites that you think are successful, and three that you think miss the mark.

On the basis of this, see whether you can come up with a list of *five* things that make a writing website work well, and *five* things that are to be avoided.

If you are technically inclined, you can go further and find out what software the websites use (try using the free service at www.builtwith.com). This might give you some indication of how you could set up your own website.

Social media

Social media is here to stay so, if you are going to bother with the online world at all, you should think about your social media presence. There is no law that says that as a writer you *have* to use social media, and however vigorously you tweet or promote yourself on Twitter, Facebook, Google+, or whatever the current flavour of the month is, this may not ultimately translate into identifiable increases in sales.

WHY USE SOCIAL MEDIA?

There are all kinds of reasons why you might want to use social media, including:

- research: social media can be a great way of connecting with people, asking questions and finding out information
- connecting with your readers and fans

- keeping abreast of changes in the publishing world
- building an online presence and reputation
- engaging with a broader community of writers
- distracting you from getting on with writing the next novel.

HOW SHOULD I USE SOCIAL MEDIA?

It can take a while to work out precisely how you want to manage the bewildering array of tools out there to cultivate an audience for your work. But the clue here is in the name: *social* media. Social media is an extension of human social life. When you use social media, you are still subject to laws about what can and can't be said (there have been some high-profile cases of 'joke' tweets landing their authors in trouble or in jail), and you are also subject to more or less the same social understandings as take place in everyday life. As a rule of thumb:

- Be courteous.
- Be friendly.
- Think about engaging rather than simply broadcasting – self-promotion wears thin very quickly.
- Make sure that you write well – you are a writer, after all.
- Be creative and imaginative.

If you take all this advice and dive in with a desire to genuinely connect – to debate, engage, interact and mutually explore – then your social media experience will be much more satisfactory.

DISADVANTAGES OF SOCIAL MEDIA

Of course, there are downsides as well as upsides to the social media revolution. One reason why many writers have found social media to be both a blessing and a curse is that it is notorious for sucking time away from writing. Another disadvantage is that you may *already* use social media, but in ways that are at odds with the image you want to project of yourself as a writer. This problem of the blurring between professional and personal, public and private, is a very real problem for writers in the Internet age. There are two main ways of dealing with this:

1 Make sure that *everything* you put on social media is something that you would in principle be happy to have in the public domain.

2 Alternatively, separate your personal and professional social media presence. Keep the personal stuff for friends and family, and have entirely separate accounts for your public profile.

The first approach is the one I would recommend. Although the second approach has certain advantages, maintaining two sets of parallel accounts can be demanding in terms of time, and you can't always guarantee that there won't be some kind of glitch or human error that causes information to flow from one domain to another.

Snapshot: web audit

Before thinking about what you want your web presence to be, it might be worth having a clear sense of what it is like at the moment. Try the following exercise:

1 Search for your name online and see what results come up. If your name is obscure (for example 'Lupe Varos'), you may be quite easy to track down. In this case, the challenge is making sure that everything that references you, as far as is in your power, reflects the kind of image that you want to project. If your name is less obscure (for example 'Jane Smith'), the issue is different. Here the question is how you can get noticed among all those other Jane Smiths in the world. You might want to use your middle name ('Jane Hypatia Smith') or an initial ('Jane H. Smith') or some other way of distinguishing yourself. You may also want to publish under this more distinctive name.

2 Make as thorough an audit as you can of your web presence, using the following five categories:

   i Things you need to delete / get deleted (photos from your school days of you wearing braces and thick glasses; images from that fancy dress party that might ruin your air of gravitas)

   ii Things you need to set up (new websites, social media accounts, etc.)

   iii Things you need to update (websites, profiles, etc.)

   iv Settings you need to change (for example privacy settings for personal social networking accounts)

   v Things that are working well at the moment.

3 Finally, write an action plan with a list of things that you could do to strengthen your web presence.

Festivals, readings and talks

We have already looked at festivals and talks in the chapter on making a living. Some of these events may contribute to your income, but they are also an opportunity to connect directly with readers and to promote your work.

Media appearances

Another way you can get yourself and your work known is through media appearances. These may be either traditional media such as radio and television, or newer forms of media such as YouTube or podcasts. Local radio stations are often eager to talk to authors (although it is never clear whether this actually sells books – unless your book is of strong local interest). TV is more difficult, but if your novel fits with the theme or format of a TV show, it can be worth contacting the producers.

Some writers hate media appearances, tremble before a microphone, and break into an unseemly sweat when somebody points a TV camera at them. If this is you, then think about other ways of promoting your work. The rule here, as elsewhere, is to only engage in promotional activities that you feel comfortable with or that you enjoy. People will notice if you are not enjoying yourself! But if you are the kind of writer who enjoys being in the public eye, then there are lots of possibilities here.

One thing to remember is that you may be able to promote your book indirectly, by being part of a show that relates only loosely to your book. And if you are not there to talk about your book, you shouldn't go on about it or try to shoehorn it into the conversation, as you will not be invited back. But if you talk engagingly and interestingly, then listeners may well look you up and, if they are so inclined, buy a copy of your novel.

Giveaways

Around the time of publication, you may want to organize a book giveaway or competition, offering one or two free copies of your novel. At the time of writing, Goodreads (www.goodreads.com) is one of the easiest ways of organizing giveaways with a minimum of fuss. Do not give away too many books – between two and five is probably best; but a book giveaway can help put your book on your potential readers' radar.

Reviews

Who you decide to approach for reviews will depend, in large part, upon the way that you are publishing your book. If you are with a third-party publisher, then your publisher should handle the major reviews. They will send your book out to the big newspapers and to trade publications such as *Publishers' Weekly* and *The Bookseller*. As a self-published author, your chances of talking one of the broadsheet newspapers into reviewing your book are minimal to non-existent. But do not let this put you off: there are plenty of other potential places for reviews online. Send out a few copies of your book to people who you think will be interested, or offer to do an author interview for blog sites relating to your book.

When the reviews start rolling in, you will find that some people like your book (all being well), while some are not so enthusiastic. Getting your first really bad review can be difficult. You may be tempted to respond, but there is nothing less dignified than a reviewer and a novelist engaged in a public spat. Bad reviews come with the territory. Read the review once, then file it away and don't look at it again. Or look at it when your anger and hurt have cooled a little, to see whether there is anything you can learn from the review about how to hone your craft. If all else fails, remember Kurt Vonnegut:

Kurt Vonnegut, *Palm Sunday*

'Any reviewer who expresses rage and loathing for a novel is preposterous. He or she is like a person who has put on full armour and attacked a hot fudge sundae.'

If bad reviews can knock you sideways as a writer, so can too many good reviews. If you have too many people telling you that you are a genius, you might start to believe it. And if you start believing that you are a genius, you might start behaving in peculiar and antisocial ways. Reviewers love hyperbole: they love to over-praise just as much as they love to criticize. As the craftsperson you are, when you go back to work on your next project (if there is one), you should put all this praise and blame on one side, and simply get back to writing the best novel of which you are capable.

Focus point

Set up a folder for press clippings, reviews and feedback on your novel. Where your work is well received, keep hold of the contact details of the organizations, publications or individuals in question: these contacts may be useful for further promotion later on.

Literary prizes

Winning the Man Booker Prize won't do your sales figures any harm, of course. If you are published with a third-party publisher, then they may nominate your published novel for literary prizes. Prizes range from very small to very large but, whatever the prize, a shortlisting can give your book a boost. There is also an increasing number of literary prizes for self-published novels.

Here it is useful to distinguish between prizes and competitions for books *prior to publication* (I mentioned these in the chapter on third-party publishing), and those that are for *published* books. Prizes for published books usually ask for books published within a particular period: you can't usually submit a book published two years ago to a literary prize. This means that if you are self-publishing, or if you are with a very small publisher and you are doing some of the legwork yourself in alerting them to what prizes there might be out there, you need to explore what prizes there are and how to submit *well before publication*, so that you can make a plan of action.

Snapshot: researching literary prizes

If possible, before your book has hit the market, explore the possibilities for literary prizes by researching the following questions:

- Are there any prizes for books in my genre?
- Are there *local* prizes for books published in my region?
- What kind of books can be submitted for these prizes? Third-party published, self-published, or both?
- How are books submitted to these prizes? What are the guidelines, rules and deadlines?

When you have explored this, you can start to write a more comprehensive plan of action for submitting (or pushing your publisher to submit) to these prizes.

If you are submitting to prizes, the prize committees may require *multiple* copies of your books, particularly if there are several judges. This means that, if you are responsible for providing the copies (for example, if you are self-published), then you need to make sure that you plan out the costs properly. Sending six copies of an ebook out costs nothing. If your book exists in hardback and ebook, and the prize committee demands copies on paper, then the cost of six hardbacks is going to be considerably more.

A final word: mystery shoppers, or who is buying your books?

Ultimately, there is something mysterious about how the book-buying world works. Word of mouth still matters a good deal, and unless you work for the intelligence services, you probably don't have complete records of everybody's phone calls, emails and conversations that you can pull up to see who is talking about your work behind your back (if you do work for the intelligence services, you probably don't have the records either, because you have accidentally left them on a USB memory stick in the pub).

Focus point

There is an argument that *nobody can really predict which books will become successful:* not you; not your editor; and certainly not the marketing and sales departments. At best, we all make educated guesses.

Sometimes you can mysteriously sell a huge number of books for reasons that are completely and utterly baffling. Perhaps there is an underground secret society which has adopted your novel as a sacred text; perhaps it has been set as required reading on a college course somewhere; or perhaps somebody who you have never met has just been going round and raving to all of their friends about your brilliance until they have all succumbed and bought themselves copies. At other times, you can get a great review somewhere prominent, and sell not a single extra copy.

Of course, sales can be tracked *after the event*: your publisher will do this to calculate your royalties, and self-publishing platforms have mechanisms to track exactly how many copies have been sold. But, *in advance*, it is hard to say how many copies of any book will sell, even if you are a very well-established and well-known writer.

This means that it is difficult to quantify precisely what the benefits of your various promotional activities are. Does tweeting really sell books? If so, how many tweets? Does your Facebook writer's page persuade people to go and read your novel? If so, how many people? And how many of those people who read your website or your blog then go on to purchase the book? There is not necessarily a one-to-one correspondence between a tweet, website, Facebook page or author appearance and the decision to buy a book.

'I have had leisure to think upon the most curious of all the problems that affect the author: Who buys books? Who really does buy books?'

There are books that I've been aware of for a couple of years before I get round to buying them. If you tell people about your book, it may lurk in their minds for a year or two before they suddenly think that the time is right to read it. So if, in the first few months after publication, nobody is picking up on your book, don't despair. It may be being passed around quietly from reader to reader: *you simply don't know.* Keep quietly looking out for opportunities, ways to let people know about the book, and so on. Sometimes books do quietly for a while, and then they explode. Other books sell thousands in the first couple of weeks, and then sales fall away rapidly. The life of every book has a rhythm of its own; and the ways of readers are ultimately mysterious.

Workshop: a publicity plan

If you are going to successfully publicize your book, you need a publicity plan. If you are publishing with a third-party publisher, they *may* do some of the work for you; but they may also rely on you to contribute your time and effort to publicizing your book. If you are self-publishing, you will have to do most of the work yourself.

1 Launches

If you have carried out the snapshot about book launches in this chapter, you will have some experience of what works and what doesn't at a launch. Now you can decide how to launch your own book. First you should ask whether you want an online (virtual) launch, a physical launch, or both. Consider the following questions.

Online launches

- What is your audience for the book launch? How are you going to engage them? Who will you invite to take part? Draw up a guest list.
- What is the timescale for the launch? Will it be asynchronous (over a period of time) or will it be scheduled for a particular time online?
- What kind of activities will you have at the launch? Can you make these *interactive*?
- What platforms are you going to use for your launch? Will it be focused around your website or will you use social media?

Physical launches

- Where will you launch the book? Write a list of three or four potential venues, and go and talk to them to see what they can offer. Get a clear idea of any costs or obligations on either side. Make sure that the venue is appropriate to the book and to the guests you are hoping to invite.
- Who will you invite? Think about i) friends and family; ii) media; iii) local writers and people from the literary world; iv) the general public.

- What will you do? Try to draw up a varied and interesting programme for the evening. Remember that your guests will want to be engaged or entertained.
- How will you publicize the launch? Draw up a timescale, thinking about how you can publicize the launch in good time, send out invites and so on.

Whether you are launching online or physically, you should also think about your budget. If you are organizing your own launch, it may take some investment. Think about offsetting this against a reasonable expectation for profits on book sales so that you can break even.

2 Letting people know about your book

There are all kinds of ways you can let people know about your book. The launch is a good time to generate some initial media interest: try sending a press release to local media. Sometimes targeting your audiences more precisely can help. If your book has a particular focus, then think about where you might generate particular interest among readers. Try the following exercise:

- Write a list of keywords that reflect the content of your book.
- For each of the keywords, explore whether any of the following might be interested in your book:
  - individuals
  - specialist publications
  - specialist websites and online communities
  - organizations and groups.
- Make a list of people to contact.

When you are contacting people, let them know what you are offering, or what you would like from them. So, if you are interested in doing an interview, tell them. If you are willing to send a review copy, tell them this as well. The more precise and clear you can be, the better the response will be.

3 Offering your services

As a writer, you may be surprised how in demand you can be. In this chapter we have looked at festivals, talks and media appearances. Think about places where you might be able to give talks, presentations or signings in the months after your book is published. A few possibilities include:

- bookstores
- conferences (for example, writing and publishing conferences, or conferences related to the subject-matter of your book)
- festivals and literary events
- clubs and societies.

Make a list of people to contact, and a timetable for getting in touch with them.

4 Keeping track of feedback

Finally, remember that enthusiasm gives rise to further enthusiasm; buzz generates buzz. Keep a folder – either hard-copy or electronic – with all your good feedback.

When you get good feedback on your book, or if it attracts favourable reviews, think about blogging or posting links on social media. Update your website to include extracts from the reviews in question.

You can also follow up on feedback. If you get a great review from somebody who runs a small literary festival, drop them a line and ask whether they would like to book you for an event.

5 Keeping track of expenses

Finally, remember to keep track of expenses. Not only can these be claimed as legitimate business expenses, but also it is wise to know what your outgoings are. This will help you see which promotional strategies work better and which do not work so well.

Where to next?

Now that your book is out in the world, your long journey to becoming a published novelist is complete. Congratulations! I hope that the book does well, and may it sell in the hundreds of thousands! The question now is this: What happens next? This is the subject of the next, and final, chapter.

25

Conclusion: what next?

Now that your book is out in the world, now that you have consumed as much champagne as you are able, now that you have gnashed your teeth over the bad reviews and revelled in the good ones, what should you do next? It has probably been a long journey from that initial thought that you might like to write a novel to the final published book being out there in the world. But now, alongside continuing to promote your novel, you need to turn your attention to other things.

The lifespan of a novel

All novels have a natural lifespan. For the average novel, this lifespan is perhaps no more than two or three years. This is not to say that the novel won't continue to exist after this, but sales will probably drop away, and the window of opportunity for promoting the novel will begin to close.

In the first year, you might pick up reviews, prize nominations (or even prizes), and some degree of publicity. It is in this period that your book may take to the skies, or may settle down to become a perfectly respectable part of a publisher's mid-list. In the second year, your book can continue to generate buzz – there may be foreign editions launched, you may be able to give talks and lectures about your book, and if your book goes into new editions, say from hardback to paperback, it may pick up a few more reviews and a bit more coverage. But as you move into the third year, your novel is probably passing its peak in terms of its public impact. If you are lucky, it will establish itself as a modern classic, and you will be guaranteed solid (but probably rather modest) sales in the years to come. If you are very lucky, it will make its way on to the syllabus of some popular courses, ensuring that you have modest sales for the coming years and opening the path to a reissued fortieth-anniversary edition that might ease you through your impoverished retirement.

It may also be that your novel has a long fuse as readers pass on copies among themselves, and in the third year suddenly it bursts into the limelight as that most mysterious of things, a word-of-mouth hit. But, in most cases, after the first three years, you will be ready to think about new books and new possibilities, and so will your readers. There is something a bit disheartening about a novelist still hawking around a 15-year-old novel.

You are a published novelist. So what now…?

Your novel is out there in the world, and you are established as a novelist. Meanwhile, your novel has left home, and headed out into the world to seek its fortune.

The writer Erin Mouré once said, quoting the poet Manuel Rivas, 'Books are emigrants, they belong in the places where they arrive.' Now that your book has gone out into the world, in a sense it is no longer yours. You have done your work; you have contributed one more book to humankind's great chest of stories and myths and dreams and imaginings. And the world is probably a better place, thanks to your novel.

So what should you do now? You can continue to write, of course. If your first novel did well, then you will have the anxiety of writing something half as good as your first. If your first novel did not do so well, you can try to write a better one.

Joseph Heller

'When I read something saying I've not done anything as good as Catch-22, I'm tempted to reply, "…Who has?"'

But you don't have to write another book. Some novelists write a single novel, get it out of their system, and then go off and do other things. Arundhati Roy, after winning the Man Booker Prize in 1998 for her book *The God of Small Things*, turned to activism, politics and writing essays. Still other novelists return again and again to the business of weaving stories, despite the effort it takes, and all of their twitchy anxieties about how they are going to pay the bills and make ends meet.

Writing novels is a good thing, but it is only one of a multitude of good things. Now that your novel is out, my advice would be this: go and do good things, whatever they are. And, if you want to keep on writing, I hope that the advice in this book continues to be of use to you. Good luck!

Resources

RESEARCH

The following places may be useful for researching your novel:

The British Library: The British Library has online resources, and if you are within reasonable distance of London, you can apply for a reader's card and make use of their extensive collections. www.bl.uk

Wikipedia: Not wholly to be trusted, but still often the first port of call for getting an overview of a subject. Use it as the first word, not the last word, in your research. www.wikipedia.org

Snopes: Urban myths run rampant on the Internet. Snopes (www.snopes.com) is a great myth-buster.

The Internet Archive: A massive online library of audio, video and text resources. Something of a ragbag, but full of fascinating bits and pieces. www.archive.org

Google Maps: Google Maps, and the downloadable Google Earth, are not a replacement for actually doing research *in situ*; but they remain a fantastic resource. maps.google.com

Google Books: Full-text search of many books; preview and full-text view of some books. Again, very useful. books.google.com

Google Scholar: Mainly archives of academic research, which is likely to be more reliable than Wikipedia et al. Note that some resources may not be easily accessible. scholar.google.com

JSTOR: Archives of academic journals, books and historical sources. Currently you can read up to three articles online at any one time. If you need more in-depth research, it offers paid options. www.jstor.org

Academia.edu: A social network for academics may sound like a strange idea. But this is a good place to go to find experts in the area you are researching, and even to download research papers (although you will need to register for free to do this). www.academia.edu

Library of Congress Research and Reference Services: A bewildering array of tools and resources to help with your research. www.loc.gov/rr/

FUNDING AND OPPORTUNITIES

The following websites and organizations are a good place to find opportunities and openings for your work.

The Writers' Compass: The National Association of Writers in Education runs this truly excellent resource site (www.nawe.co.uk) with links to jobs, grants, residencies, support and funding opportunities.

A national writing resources website for Ireland: www.writing.ie

Resources for writers in London: www.spreadtheword.org.uk

Arts Councils: Arts Council England (artscouncil.org.uk), the Arts Council of Wales (www.artswales.org.uk), the Arts Council of Northern Ireland (artscouncil-ni. org) and the Scottish Arts Council (scottisharts.org.uk) all offer competitive grant funding for arts projects, including literature.

FundsforWriters: US-based website with updates on funding and other opportunities. www.fundsforwriters.com

Mslexia – for women who write: High-quality and very well-established magazine and organization supporting women writers. They regularly publish opportunities, openings and information about funding. www.mslexia.co.uk

The Writers' Digest: Large US-based website and organization promoting writing and supporting writers. www.writersdigest.com

Duotrope: Mainly, but not exclusively, US site with information about different markets for your writing, with a built-in submissions tracker. Now running on a subscription basis. www.duotrope.com

Poets & Writers: Well-established, highly comprehensive, mainly US website for writers, full of opportunities and information, along with a useful directory of publishers. www.pw.org

PROFESSIONAL ORGANIZATIONS

You may wish to join a professional organization. Often these will charge membership fees; but in return you may get access to professional help, training and resources.

The Society of Authors: If you already have at least one book published by a third-party publisher, or else a book contract, the Society of Authors is worth joining. www.societyofauthors.org.

The Writers' Guild: An alternative to the Society of Authors, offering similar services but with more focus on writing for stage, screen and radio. www.writersguild.org.uk

ALLi: If you are self-publishing, then try ALLi, or the Alliance of Independent Authors. www.allianceindependentauthors.org

NAWE: If you are interested in *teaching* writing, think about joining NAWE, the National Association of Writers in Education. www.nawe.org.uk

Irish Writers' Union: Professional support for writers in the Republic of Ireland. www.ireland-writers.com

The British Science Fiction Association: Offering support and advice for new and established writers. www.bsfa.co.uk

The Crime Writers' Association: A professional association for those who kill for a living. www.thecwa.co.uk

The Historical Novel Society: For readers and writers of historical fiction. www.historicalnovelsociety.org

Lapidus: Professional body for writers interested in writing, well-being and health care. www.lapidus.org.uk

Society of Children's Book Writers and Illustrators: For those writing for children. www.scbwi.org

Romantic Novelists' Association: For those writing romance and related genres. www.rna-uk.org

Horror Writers' Association: A worldwide organization supporting horror writers. www.horror.org

Pen International: An international organization supporting writers and freedom of speech. www.pen-international.org

MONEY, TAX AND LAW

Here are a few resources that are useful when getting to grips with the legal and financial sides of writing.

The Authors' Licensing and Collecting Society (ALCS): If you register with ALCS for a one-off fee (which is taken out of your first earnings, so there are no up-front costs), it will collect money owed to you by those who scan, photocopy or digitally copy your work. www.alcs.co.uk

Public Lending Right (PLR): The PLR scheme is administered by the British Library. PLR is a legal right to payment for borrowing from public libraries. You need to register your books by going to www.plr.uk.com

The UK Copyright Service: A useful website for understanding copyright. See, in particular, its fact sheet P-12 on writers' copyright. www.copyrightservice.co.uk/copyright

Own It: Free advice on copyright and intellectual property. www.own-it.org. Membership is free.

Inland Revenue: You will need to register as self-employed if you are making any income from writing. www.hmrc.gov.uk

WRITERS' GROUPS

There are so many writers' groups that it would be impossible to list them all here. Often, asking in your local library is a good starting point. The following two websites may help point you to groups in your area or online.

The National Association of Writers' Groups: An organization that links writing groups to one another, and provides support. www.nawg.co.uk

Writers Groups Online: Provides a listing of writers' groups across the UK, with contact details. www.writers-online.co.uk

Authonomy: Online writers' community run by HarperCollins. www.authonomy.com

Writers Online: Run by the people behind *Writing Magazine*. A large UK-based online community. www.writers-online.co.uk

WriteWords: A well-established online writing community. www.writewords.org.uk.

AGENTS

Individual agents may or may not have websites, but there are various places online where you can find listings of agents.

Association of Authors' Agents: If you are looking for an agent, your first port of call should be the AAA, which is a professional body for agents. Even if your agent is not a member, their code of practice is considered to be the baseline for good practice within the industry, and so is worth reading before signing a contract with an agent. www.agentsassoc.co.uk

RETREATS AND COURSES

There are all kinds of ways you can spend time writing more intensively, whether with guidance from experienced writers or else on your own. The following list is only a sample. Some of the websites in the 'funding and opportunities' section above list many more.

University courses: University courses in creative writing seem to be booming. Some MA courses specialize in novel-writing, others are more general. You can find out more by doing a search on www.postgraduatesearch.com

The Arvon Foundation: An organization running writers' retreats. Their courses are not cheap but they are consistently highly-rated, and they do offer bursaries. www.arvon.org

The Irish Writers' Centre: Offering courses and guidance to writers in the Republic of Ireland. www.writerscentre.ie

Tŷ Newydd Writers' Centre: Running a variety of excellent courses in West Wales. www.llenyddiaethcymru.org/ty-newydd

The Faber Academy: Billed as an alternative to a creative writing MA, with a price tag to match, the Faber Academy runs intensive courses in creative writing. www.faberacademy.co.uk

Curtis Brown Creative: A new writing school from the Curtis Brown literary agency, running short, intensive courses. www.curtisbrowncreative.co.uk

The Guardian Masterclasses: *The Guardian* newspaper also runs masterclasses in fiction. Find out more on their website www.theguardian.com/guardian-masterclasses/creative-writing-courses

WRITING AGENCIES

There are many agencies and organizations set up to help writers develop their work. Many of these are regional, and work exclusively with writers in their region.

Literature Wales/Llenyddiaeth Cymru: An organization for literature development in Wales. They are connected to Tŷ Newydd Writers' Centre. www.literaturewales.org

Spread the Word: The literature development agency for London. www.spreadtheword.org.uk

Writers' Centre Norwich: A centre for writers in Norwich and in the east of England. www.writerscentrenorwich.org.uk

Free Word Centre: A centre for writing, literacy and free expression in London. www.freewordcentre.com

New Writing North: Help and support for creative writers in the North. www.newwritingnorth.com

New Writing South: Like New Writing North, but in the South. www.newwritingsouth.com

Writing Yorkshire: Exactly what it says it is. They call a spade a spade up there. www.writingyorkshire.org

Writing West Midlands: Supporting writers throughout the West Midlands. www.writingwestmidlands.org

Writing East Midlands: Organization promoting writing and supporting writers in the East Midlands. www.writingeastmidlands.co.uk

Federation of Writers (Scotland): A literature development agency for Scotland. www.writersfederation.org.uk

Literature Works: Based in Exeter, this agency covers the South West of England. www.literatureworks.org.uk

Literature North West: Covering North West England, based in Manchester. www.literaturenorthwest.co.uk

Commonword: Another writing development organization based in Manchester. www.cultureword.org.uk

SOFTWARE AND RESOURCES FOR WRITERS

There is a lot of software out there that you can use to help you with your writing, organization and research. Here are a few suggestions for tools that you might investigate.

Writing software

This is software for actually putting words down on the page. Your options here, more or less, are either to use standard word-processing software (or a text editor) or to make use of specialist tools.

Word processors: Many people are happy with Microsoft Word or with the free alternatives, LibreOffice (www.libreoffice.org) and OpenOffice (www.openoffice.org).

Scrivener and other specialist tools: Other writers swear by Scrivener (www. literatureandlatte.com), which has many features that make it particularly good for writers. Mac users might like to try Ulysses III (www.ulyssesapp.com). For Windows, you might want to try the free tool, yWriter (www.spacejock.com).

Distraction-busters

If you have difficulty with distraction, the following tools might be useful.

SelfControl: For Mac only. Free app to block distracting websites. www.selfcontrolapp. com

Freedom and Anti-Social: Paid (but relatively cheap) apps to banish the Internet, or temporarily block access to social networking sites. These apps work in Windows and Mac, and Anti-Social works on Linux too. www.anti-social.cc

Research software

Keeping track of research can be a complex business. You can have a card-index system; but if you want a more sophisticated electronic database, these options might work for you.

Evernote: This software works on almost all platforms and is good for gathering and processing large amounts of disparate information. You will need to pay a small subscription, however, for their premium ad-free service. www.evernote.com

DevonThink: If you are serious about research, and use a Mac, this might be the tool you need. It comes in different versions according to the level of sophistication you need. www.devontechnologies.com

Zotero: A handy and free tool for keeping track of your various sources during your research. Works with Macs, Windows and on Linux. www.zotero.org

Mendeley: If you gather a lot of research in PDF format, try Mendeley, a free tool for organizing your research materials. www.mendeley.com

Bookends: Another reference manager. It does cost, and is only available on a Mac, but I use it all the time, and it is a worthwhile investment if you work in PDFs and need to keep track of more scholarly references. www.sonnysoftware.com

Aeon Timeline: For Mac and Windows, a sophisticated timeline tool. May be more complex than you need, but undeniably powerful. www.scribblecode.com

Backup services

Backing up is essential. The following services may be useful as they will all back up your files and folders automatically. All of them are fairly similar, so have a look around and see what suits you.

Crashplan: www.code42.com/crashplan

Backblaze: www.backblaze.com

Spideroak: www.spideroak.com

Carbonite: www.carbonite.com

Amazon Glacier: aws.amazon.com/glacier Perhaps the cheapest option, but also more difficult to set up. You may need a separate tool to use this, such as FastGlacier for windows (www.fastglacier.com – free), and Arq for Mac (www.haystacksoftware. com/arq – one off payment)

Dropbox: If you want a free option, for limited storage, try Dropbox (www.dropbox.com)

USEFUL SOFTWARE AND RESOURCES FOR EBOOK AUTHORS

If you are producing ebooks, then you *can* export ebook files direct from .doc files and hope for the best; but if you care about proper formatting, you should go back to basics and get your hands dirty. Some of the following tools and resources might help.

Calibre: Not beautiful to look at, but Calibre is a powerful cross-platform toolkit for working with ebooks and for converting between ebook formats. Good for Windows, Mac and Linux. www.calibre-ebook.com

Sigil: A free, open-source and multi-platform editor for .epub files. code.google.com/p/sigil. Like Calibre, will run on almost anything – Windows, Mac, Linux, the lot.

jEdit: A nice, free, cross-platform programmers' text editor, which may be useful for ebook formatting. www.jedit.org

notepad++: For many Windows users, this is their favoured free text editor. www.notepad-plus-plus.org

Guido Henkel's Guide to Formatting: Already several years old, but extremely thorough. This is absolutely worth reading. www.guidohenkel.com/2010/12/take-pride-in-your-ebook-formatting/

AUTHORS' WEBSITES

There are various tools you can use to run your website. Here are a few options. Remember that free services will almost always be inadequate.

WordPress (hosted): Perhaps one of the easiest ways to a professional website. You will need to pay for your own domain name, but this is easy to set up. www.wordpress.com

WordPress (self-hosted): You have a bit more flexibility (and it may be a bit cheaper) if you host your own WordPress site, rather than using their hosting. You can download the software for free from www.wordpress.org

Ghost: A relatively new, simple and elegant blogging platform. Download and self-host for free, or use their hosting services. www.ghost.org

Joomla: If you are running a site with more community interaction, Joomla may do the trick. www.joomla.org

ROYALTY-FREE, PUBLIC DOMAIN AND OTHER IMAGES

If you are self-publishing and need images, then the following places may be useful. Make sure you check the licences for every image you use. Can also be useful for materials for producing promotional materials, etc.

iStockPhoto: Stock images and photographs. www.istockphoto.com

MorgueFile: Don't be scared of the forbidding name: this is a good site for free-to-use images. Check their licence terms before use. www.morguefile.com

Deviant Art: A community of artists and designers. Often a good place to source images: you can contact their creators to negotiate permissions for use. www. deviantart.com

Wikimedia Commons: In theory, all public domain images, although check the precise licence terms, and use with caution. http://commons.wikimedia.org

OTHER SERVICES

The Literary Consultancy: One of the best-known and best-established literary consultancies, offering mentoring, manuscript appraisal services and support. www.literaryconsultancy.co.uk

The Society for Editors and Proofreaders: SfEP is the place to go to find professional copy-editing and proofreading help. www.sfep.org.uk

The Oxford Literacy Consultancy: Manuscript appraisal services as well as editing, proofreading and more. www.oxfordwriters.com

The Writers' Workshop: Critique and appraisal service. www.writersworkshop.co.uk

Contact an Author: Offers listings for writers interested in working in schools and the community. The website feels dated, but it works well for some writers. www. contactanauthor.co.uk

FESTIVALS AND CONFERENCES

Finally, here are a few places to go to find out about conferences, festivals and other events.

LiteraryFestivals.co.uk: The best place to go for the low-down on literary festivals across the UK. www.literaryfestivals.co.uk

Great Writing: Annual international creative writing conference held in the UK. www.greatwriting.org.uk

NAWE Conference: The National Association of Writers in Education runs conferences once or twice a year. www.nawe.co.uk

Further reading

This is a non-exhaustive list of books that may be useful to you. Some are referenced in the text of this book; others are books that I have found useful, or that I often recommend to students.

Aristotle, *Poetics* (Penguin Classics, 2006). The classic book on how stories work. Still highly influential.

Armstrong, David, *How Not to Write a Novel: Confessions of a Midlist Author* (Allison & Busby, 2003). An enjoyable and engaging read.

Austin, James H., *Chase, Chance, and Creativity: The Lucky Art of Novelty* (MIT Press, 1978). One of the most interesting books I know on creativity and the art of getting lucky.

Baker, Barbara, *The Way We Write: Interviews with Award-winning Writers* (Continuum, 2007). Excellent interviews with a variety of award-winning writers.

Baverstock, Alison, *The Naked Author: A Guide to Self-publishing* (A & C Black, 2011). A good, well-written overview of what it means to take your own words into print.

Bayard, Pierre, *How to Talk about Books You Haven't Read* (Granta Books, 2009). A fun and intriguing exploration of our different relationships with books.

Bell, Julia, and Andrew Motion, *The Creative Writing Coursebook: Forty Authors Share Advice and Exercises for Fiction and Poetry* (Macmillan, 2001). Varied and engaging advice about all stages of the writing process, from start to finish.

Bernays, Anne, and Pamela Painter, *What If?: Writing Exercises for Fiction Writers* (HarperCollins Publishers, 2005). A good book of advice, full of excellent exercises to kick-start your writing.

Brady, Catherine, *Story Logic and the Craft of Fiction* (Palgrave Macmillan, 2010). A little self-consciously literary in its tastes, but a very interesting technical exploration of the craft of writing stories.

Brande, Dorothea, *Becoming a Writer* (Macmillan, 1996). One of the earliest and most influential of books about creative writing. Still worth reading.

Bringhurst, Richard, *The Elements of Typographic Style: Version 4.0* (Hartley & Marks Publishers, 2013). If you are serious about self-publishing and typography, this is a fascinating – if technical – guide.

Browne, Renni, *Self-editing for Fiction Writers, Second Edition: How to Edit Yourself into Print* (William Morrow & Company, 2006). A detailed and rigorous book on self-editing.

Corbett, David, *The Art of Character: Creating Memorable Characters for Fiction, Film, and TV* (Penguin Books, 2013). One of the best books I know on character, managing to be both practical and also to pack a philosophical punch.

Cowan, Andrews, *The Art of Writing Fiction* (Routledge, 2011). An excellent book, packed with exercises, on the art of writing fiction.

Currey, Mason, *Daily Rituals: How Artists Work* (Picador, 2013). If you are curious about how different artists and writers have worked and set up routines, this is a fun survey.

Doughty, Louise, *A Novel in a Year: A Novelist's Guide to Being a Novelist* (Simon & Schuster, 2008). A week-by-week guide to writing a novel in a year. Down to earth and enjoyable.

Eco, Umberto, *Reflections on the Name of the Rose*. (Secker & Warburg, 1985). A beautiful little book full of advice about how to build convincing fictional worlds. Worth returning to again and again.

Forster, E.M., *Aspects of the Novel* (Penguin Classics, 2005). You may not agree with everything Forster says about character, but this is a classic nonetheless.

Gardner, John, *The Art of Fiction: Notes on Craft for Young Writers* (Vintage Books, 2001). Cantankerous, opinionated and enjoyable, with some fiendish exercises at the end.

Gardner, John, *On Becoming a Novelist* (W. W. Norton & Co., 2000). Not as enjoyable as *The Art of Fiction*, but fun to argue with.

Garfield, Simon, *Just My Type: A Book about Fonts* (Profile Books, 2011). A breezy, journalistic exploration of type and typefaces. If you are self-publishing and want to start thinking seriously about typography, this is an easy way to start.

Gaughran, David, *Let's Get Digital: How to Self-publish, And Why You Should* (CreateSpace, 2012). A very good overview of what you need to do to self-publish well.

Goldberg, Natalie, *Wild Mind: Living the Writer's Life* (Rider, 2009). A good book to kick-start your writing. Lively, engaging and fun.

Hendel, Richard, *On Book Design* (Yale University Press, 1999). Not a how-to book, but instead a guide to the principles of book design. Well worth reading.

Howard, Catherine Ryan, *Self-printed: The Sane Person's Guide to Self-publishing* (CreateSpace, 2012). An extremely chatty and friendly introduction to what you need to know to publish yourself.

Kawasaki, Guy, and Shawn Welch, *APE: Author, Publisher, Entrepreneur – How to Publish a Book* (Nononina Press, 2012). An encyclopaedic guide to the art of self-publishing, although geared a bit more towards non-fiction.

King, Stephen, *On Writing* (Hodder Paperbacks, 2012). Veers into weirdness towards the end, but a lot of good solid advice.

Leder, Meg, and Jack Heffron, *The Complete Handbook of Novel Writing* (Writer's Digest Books, 2002). Advice on writing, and some interesting interviews with top-notch writers.

Lodge, David, *The Art of Fiction* (Vintage, 2011). A series of articles on what makes fiction work.

Manguel, Alberto, *A History of Reading* (Flamingo, 1999). An interesting history of readers and reading.

McKee, Robert, *Story: Substance, Structure, Style and the Principles of Screenwriting* (Methuen, 1999). Written for screenwriters, but widely referenced, and useful if you do not follow the advice too slavishly.

Mittelmark, Howard, and Sandra Newman, *How NOT to Write a Novel: 200 Mistakes to Avoid at All Costs If You Ever Want to Get Published* (Penguin, 2009). Jokey, a bit scattergun, but a good breezy read that might help you avoid committing some of the worst fictional crimes.

Moore, Steven, *The Novel: An Alternative History: Beginnings to 1600* (Continuum, 2010). An excellent overview of the early history of extended prose fiction.

Morley, David, *The Cambridge Introduction to Creative Writing* (Cambridge University Press, 2007). A very thoughtful introduction to creative writing.

Mullan, John, *How Novels Work* (Oxford University Press, 2008). A series of bite-sized essays and reflections on different aspects of fiction.

Pennac, Daniel, *The Rights of the Reader* (Walker Books, 2006). Not about writing so much as about the pleasures of reading. Worth reading!

Prose, Francine, *Reading Like a Writer: A Guide for People Who Love Books and for Those Who Want to Write Them* (Union Books, 2012). About creative reading and creative writing.

Saller, Carol Fisher, *The Subversive Copy Editor: Advice from Chicago* (University of Chicago Press, 2009). Sensible, clear-headed, and perhaps the best book in existence on what copy editing is.

Smiley, Jane, *13 Ways of Looking at the Novel* (Anchor Books, 2006). Novelist Jane Smiley's huge, idiosyncratic exploration of novels, what they are, and how they do what they do.

Stevens, Karen, *Writing a First Novel: Reflections on the Journey* (Palgrave Macmillan, 2013). Novelists write about writing first novels. Varied and enjoyable.

Wood, James, *How Fiction Works* (Vintage, 2009). A fascinating exploration of the mechanics of fiction.

Yorke, John, *Into the Woods: How Stories Work and Why We Tell Them* (Penguin, 2014). A well-known book on story structure, with a focus largely on screenwriting. Worth reading, although there's more than one kind of story in the world...

Finally, the following reference books are both useful and reliable:

Butcher's Copy-editing: The Cambridge Handbook for Editors, Copy-editors and Proofreaders (Cambridge University Press, 2006). A superb companion to the business of copy-editing. Should be on every writer's shelf.

New Oxford Style Manual (Oxford University Press, 2012). A comprehensive style manual for both US and UK usage. Far better as a handbook than the somewhat dubious but much-loved *The Elements of Style* by Strunk and White (Macmillan, 1979).

Writers' & Artists' Yearbook (A & C Black). Published annually, with listings of agents, publishers and writers' services, as well as plenty of advice for writers. Essential.

Index

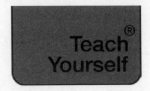